KT-199-470

access to religion and philosophy

a
t
r
p

ɔks are to be returned on or before
the last date below.

Issues of Life and Death

Second edition

052903

THE HENLEY COLLEGE LIBRARY

access to religion and philosophy

a
t
r
p

Issues of Life and Death

Second edition

Michael Wilcockson

I am very grateful to Julian Dobson, Vicky Bunting and Clare Wilcockson for their comments and advice on many parts of this book. But I am especially indebted to Alison Wilcockson for her close critical reading of the whole book.

The Publishers would like to thank the following for permission to reproduce copyright material:

Photo credits
Cover © akg-images; **p.24** © Bettman/Corbis; **p.37** © Joe McBride/Corbis; **p.46** The foetal developmental stages © Visuals Unlimited/Corbis with the exception of (top left) © Anatomical Travelogue/Science Photo Library and (bottom middle) © Mediscan/Corbis; **p.67** © Larry Mulvehill/Corbis; **p.84** © Hulton-Deutsch Collection/Corbis; **p.85** © Getty Images; **p.127** © Bettman/Corbis; **p.128** © Durand-Hudson-Langevin-Orban/Sygma/Corbis; **p.152** (left) © Ron Howard/Corbis; **p.152** (bottom right) © Corbis

Acknowledgements
p.16 'Jim and the Indians' case study from *Utilitarianism: For and Against*, Smart, J.J.C. and Williams, B., 1973, Cambridge University Press; **pp.25–26** Extract from 1961 Suicide Act © Crown copyright 2002–2008; **p.42** The *Daily Telegraph* for the quote on the abortion debate, 17 March 2005; **p.42** *The Times* for the quote from 'Abortions soar as careers come first', by Ann Furedi, 28 July 2005; **p.49** Extract from Grounds for Abortion, 1967 Abortion Act, amended under Section 37 of the Human Fertilisation and Embyology Act 1990 © Crown copyright 2002–2008; **pp.50** The Office of Public Sector Information (OPSI) for the abortion statistics published by the Department of Health, Bulletin 2007/01. Reproduced under the terms of the OPSI Licence; **p.67** Extract from 1961 Suicide Act © Crown copyright 2002–2008; **p.68** Extract from Assisted Dying for the Terminally Ill Bill, 2004. Reproduced under the terms of the Parliamentary Licence, P2008000106; **pp.70–71** *The Times* for the quote from 'Cheers as GP is cleared of murdering patient', by Paul Wilkinson, 12 May 1999; **p.76** *The Times* for the quote by Daniel Johnson, October 1991; **pp.85–86** Amnesty International for the death penalty statistics published by www.amnesty.org; **pp.92–93** Random House Inc. for the quote from *Dead Man Walking* by Helen Prejean; **p.96** The Death Penalty Information Center for the murder rates in death penalty states and non-death penalty states statistics published by www.deathpenaltyinfo.org; **p.154** Church House Publishing for the fission nuclear weapon explosion statistics published in *The Church and the Bomb*

Every effort has been made to trace all copyright holders, but if any have been inadvertently overlooked the Publishers will be pleased to make the necessary arrangements at the first opportunity.

Although every effort has been made to ensure that website addresses are correct at time of going to press, Hodder Education cannot be held responsible for the content of any website mentioned in this book. It is sometimes possible to find a relocated web page by typing in the address of the home page for a website in the URL window of your browser.

Hachette's policy is to use papers that are natural, renewable and recyclable products and made from wood grown in sustainable forests. The logging and manufacturing processes are expected to conform to the environmental regulations of the country of origin.

Orders: please contact Bookpoint Ltd, 130 Milton Park, Abingdon, Oxon OX14 4SB. Telephone: +44 (0)1235 827720. Fax: +44 (0)1235 400454. Lines are open 9.00a.m.–5.00p.m., Monday to Saturday, with a 24-hour message answering service. Visit our website at www.hoddereducation.co.uk

© Michael Wilcockson 1999, 2009

First edition published 1999
This second edition first published in 2009
by Hodder Education,
An Hachette UK Company
338 Euston Road
London NW1 3BH

Impression number   5 4 3 2 1

Year   2013 2012 2011 2010 2009

All rights reserved. Apart from any use permitted under UK copyright law, no part of this publication may be reproduced or transmitted in any form or by any means, electronic or mechanical, including photocopying and recording, or held within any information storage and retrieval system, without permission in writing from the publisher or under licence from the Copyright Licensing Agency Limited. Further details of such licences (for reprographic reproduction) may be obtained from the Copyright Licensing Agency Limited, Saffron House, 6–10 Kirby Street, London EC1N 8TS.

Illustrations by Alex Machin and GreenGate Publishing Services
Typeset in Bembo by GreenGate Publishing Services, Tonbridge, Kent
Printed in Great Britain by Martins The Printers Ltd, Berwick-Upon-Tweed

A catalogue record for this title is available from the British Library

ISBN 978 0 340 95775 2

CONTENTS

Preface   vii

1   **Value of life**   1
     1. What makes a life valuable?   1
     2. Human beings and human persons   4
     3. Sanctity of life arguments   8
     4. Quality of life arguments   13

2   **Suicide**   24
     1. Suicide and society   24
     2. The psychology of suicide   26
     3. Arguments against suicide   28
     4. Arguments for suicide   32
     5. Paternalism   36

3   **Abortion and infanticide**   41
     1. Women's autonomy and rights   41
     2. The personhood problem   45
     3. The law and abortion   48
     4. Hard cases   50
     5. Normative ethical responses to abortion   56

4   **Euthanasia and doctors' ethics**   65
     1. A problem of definition   65
     2. The law and euthanasia   66
     3. Allowing to die and cutting short a life   70
     4. Non-voluntary euthanasia   73
     5. Normative ethical responses to euthanasia   74

5   **Killing as punishment**   **83**

    1. Capital punishment   83

    2. Aims and justification of punishment   86

    3. Retribution   88

    4. Deterrence   93

    5. Reform   100

    6. Normative ethical responses to killing as punishment   102

6   **War and peace**   **114**

    1. Why war?   114

    2. Public and private values and the use of lethal violence   115

    3. Pacifism   116

    4. War realism   121

    5. Militarism   125

    6. Just war   128

    7. Normative ethical responses to war and peace   134

7   **Nuclear war and deterrence**   **147**

    1. The moral paradox of nuclear deterrence   147

    2. Why use nuclear weapons?   151

    3. The morality of nuclear war   154

    4. The morality of nuclear deterrence   158

    5. Normative ethical responses to nuclear war and deterrence   161

Glossary   **175**

Further reading   **177**

Index   **179**

PREFACE

To the student

Access books are written mainly for students studying for examinations at higher level, particularly GCE Advanced Subsidiary (AS) level and Advanced (A) level. A number of features have been included to assist students, such as the study guides at the end of chapters.

To use these books most effectively, you should be aware of the following features:

- At the beginning of each chapter there is a checklist, which is a brief introduction about the key elements that the chapter covers.
- Key questions, words, people, thoughts and quotes in the margin highlight specific points from the main text.
- Profiles of key individuals give information on a philosopher's background and work.
- There are summary diagrams throughout the chapters to aid revision.
- The revision checklist at the end of each chapter summarises the main points.

General advice on answering essay questions

Structured questions will tell you what to include. The following advice is for those questions which leave it to you to work out.

- The most important thing is to read the question carefully and work out what it really means. Make sure you understand all the words in the question (you may need to check some of them in the dictionary or look up technical terms in the glossary at the back of this book).
- Gather the relevant information for answering the question. You will probably not need everything you know on the topic. Keep to what the question is asking.
- Organise your material by drawing up a plan of paragraphs. Make sure that each paragraph is relevant to the question. Include different views within your answer (most questions require arguments for and against).

- Start with an introduction that explains in your own words what the question is asking and defines any technical words. Work through your answer in carefully planned paragraphs. Write a brief conclusion in which you sum up your answer to the question (without repeating everything in the essay).

1 VALUE OF LIFE

Chapter checklist ✓

This chapter considers whether a life is valuable only when it has some use or whether it is always valuable regardless of circumstance. This problem depends on what it means to call a human being a person. Some consider a person as someone who has consciousness, memory and rationality. Others argue for an enduring self or soul which is given at conception or is potential from conception or develops later. Being a person determines how life is treated morally. Two views of the value of human life are compared: the sanctity of life and the quality of life.

1 What makes a life valuable?

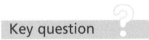

Key question

Is killing people always wrong?

Why is it wrong to kill people? Is it *always* wrong to kill people? Are some lives more worthwhile than others?

These questions about human life, its worth and its value, pose some very basic and difficult moral problems. The questions are not just deceptively simple; they are intriguing because often our intuitive reactions give equally opposite answers. For instance we might feel that it is outrageous for a terrorist to blow up a shop full of people, but we would have no hesitation shooting a violent intruder in our house.

a) Killing

Consider, for example, what the following cold-blooded killing from André Gide's novel *The Vatican Cellars* illustrates about our attitudes to people and the value of life.

Case study
A killing without motive

Lafcadio is sitting in a train opposite a complete stranger called Fleurissoire. The thought enters his mind that he could, as a completely unprovoked and free act, kill him. The 'game', as he calls it, is not so much about the morality of killing, but seeing if he can get away with it.

In order to make the act even more arbitrary Lafcadio decides that if by the time he has counted to twelve he has not seen a light from a house outside then he will not kill Fleurissoire. He begins to count and at nine he spots a light in a house and without further thought pushes the hapless man out of the carriage to his certain death. The incident ends later on that day:

> When the evening paper came he bought the Corriere *from a newspaper-seller in the Corso; then he went into a restaurant, but he laid the paper all folded on the table beside him and forced himself to finish his dinner without looking at it — out of a kind of bravado, and as though he thought in this way to put an edge on his desire; then he went out, and once in the Corso again, he stopped in the light of a shop window, unfolded the paper and on the second page saw the following head-line: CRIME, SUICIDE OR … ACCIDENT.*

(André Gide, *The Vatican Cellars*, page 190)

The story raises a number of important issues concerning the ethics of life and death:

- Is killing human life always wrong? Can we say that killing Fleurissoire was self-evidently wrong because all innocent life must be protected?
- Is it only external factors which make killing wrong (i.e. being caught, fear of reprisals, anger of others, they happen to be your friend or family or member of the community)?
- What constitutes a worthwhile life? For Lafcadio it seems to be a mixture of freedom, bravado and fulfilment of pleasure or desire.
- Are some lives more valuable than others? Lafcadio regards Fleurissoire as an arbitrary and worthless object of his game. Do we do the same in real life? For instance how can we justify spending thousands of pounds rescuing a child stuck down a well but allow thousands to die of starvation in a third world country? Do we think it more or less tragic when a young person dies rather than an old person?
- How should Lafcadio be punished? Would the death penalty be the only appropriate form of punishment for a cold-blooded murder?

b) The sanctity of life v. quality of life debate

Until recently western morality has explained our special regard for human life through what is termed the **sanctity of life** argument. The term sanctity of life literally means a 'life set aside' because it is created specially and uniquely by God. In other words it argues that human life is **intrinsically** (i.e. in itself) worthwhile; there is no other justification for its value but the fact that it is alive. The Judaeo-Christian basis for the sanctity of life further suggests that humans have a duty to preserve life (a view shared equally by Islamic theology).

But in recent years two factors have challenged the traditional sanctity of life position. Western society has become more critical of religious claims and advanced medical technology has blurred the boundaries between life and death. As a result many philosophers have proposed a rival viewpoint to the sanctity of life. The proponents of the **quality of life** argument have argued that the sanctity of life view does not account adequately for the strongly intuitive feelings about the preservation and value of life and the equally important sense that humans have of the freedom to dispose of their own lives as they wish. Unlike the sanctity of life position, with its premise based on intrinsic values (perhaps natural or God-given), the quality of life view suggests that the value of life is to do with external or **extrinsic** factors such as the desire to live and the right to die. The chief feature of the quality of life view is that it removes the *absoluteness* of life and argues that people also have a right to die when they wish.

Key quote

'Every legislator, every doctor, and every citizen needs to recognize that the real issue is whether to affirm and protect the sanctity of all human life, or to embrace a social ethic where some human lives are valued and others are not. As a nation, we must choose between the sanctity of life ethic and the quality of life ethic.'

PRESIDENT RONALD REAGAN, 1983 (QUOTED IN PETER SINGER, *RETHINKING LIFE AND DEATH*, PAGE 106)

Cross-reference

Read pages 13–20 for quality of life arguments.

2 Human beings and human persons

Key question

Is a human being always a human person?

Key people

Ronald Dworkin (b. 1931) is an American legal philosopher and professor of law at Oxford, London, Yale and New York universities. He is critical of utilitarianism and argues that human rights should 'trump' anything which does not take human dignity seriously. *Life's Dominion* (1993) supports a liberal sanctity of life position in the debate on abortion and euthanasia.

Ethics of life and death depend to a large extent on an important distinction between the biological description of a human being as a member of the species *homo sapiens* and a human being as person. **Ronald Dworkin** usefully employs the two Greek terms for life to clarify this distinction: 'zoë' – life as an animal – and 'bios' – life as an account of a person's actions and history. Whereas there is no philosophical problem determining when a human may be described as *homo sapiens* (i.e. as soon as the process of biological life begins), his or her bios as person presents us with answers that are far less cut and dried. For example we quite often distinguish degrees of person-hood. For example when **Aristotle** (384–322BC) discussed what constitutes a person (*Ethics* I:1098a27) he concluded with the proverb 'one swallow does not make a summer'. What he meant was that being fully a person is a whole life's project. Being a person is a whole series of actions and thoughts in which we learn to realise our potentials.

Case study
The ship of Theseus

Over a period of years, in the course of maintenance a ship has its planks replaced one by one – call this ship A. However, the old planks are retained and themselves reconstituted into a ship – call this ship B. At the end of this process there are two ships. Which one is the original ship of Theseus?

(Michael Clarke, *Paradoxes A–Z* [2002], page 184)

In the same way, over a life-time the body replaces its cells many times over. Therefore, am I the same person as I was at seven, fourteen, twenty-eight, etc. years of age? And if, as in the ship of Theseus, those discarded cells could be used to reconstruct another replica body, would it also be me?

Finally it might be argued that not all human beings are human persons and equally not all persons are human beings. Other life forms may satisfy the conditions of being considered persons. Given that we often give higher value to persons than merely living beings it is important to establish exactly what we mean by 'person' and therefore who is entitled to personhood.

a) Necessary and sufficient conditions

Let us suppose that each one of us knows that we are a person. What characteristics would this include? We might start by saying that I have to exist physically and this means being a member of *homo sapiens*. We might go on to say that I have to have emotions, show response to external stimuli, be able to communicate, have plans and be able to form a view of the world.

We might agree that each of these is a necessary element of being a person but that without consciousness personhood cannot be guaranteed. This might be expressed in the following way:

> *An entity is only a person if and only if it is conscious.*

This is known as a **biconditional** because not only is consciousness a necessary condition in itself but without it all other conditions would not be possible.

b) Consciousness

An influential thinker on modern debates about personhood is **John Locke**. Here is Locke's famous definition of a person:

> *... we must remember what a person stands for; which I think, is a thinking intelligent being, that has reason and reflection, and can consider itself, the same thinking thing, in different times and places; which it does only by that consciousness which is inseparable from thinking and seems to me essential to it; it being impossible for any one to perceive without perceiving that he does perceive.*
>
> (*An Essay Concerning Human Understanding,* Book II, Chapter 27)

A person is therefore someone who is not only able to have conscious and rational thought, but also able to *remember* himself doing so 'in different times and places'.

c) Change and continuity

The major criticism of Locke's proposal is the problem of **continuity**. Locke argued that just as the body changes and its cells are replaced or not replaced many times over in a life-time, so consciousness may also change. The question is whether these changes mean that we are still talking about the same person. For example, consider another paradox similar to the ship of Theseus given at the start of this chapter. If the members of a string quartet gradually change over ten years so that at the end of ten years none of the members are the same as the original four, could they still be regarded as the same quartet? We might argue that as each member was changed, the others carried on the memory

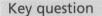

Key thought

Necessary and **sufficient** **conditions** makes a distinction between what is needed and what will guarantee a condition. A necessary condition is where in order for x to exist y is needed but cannot guarantee it; a sufficient condition is where y guarantees x.

Key quote

A human being is *'an individual substance with a rational nature'*.
BOETHIUS (C. 512), *CONTRA EUTYCHEN* 5, IN *THEOLOGICAL TRACTATES*, 101–2

Key people

John Locke (1632–1704) was one of the great English philosophers. His philosophy was influenced by his practical study of medicine and chemistry. He was influenced by Descartes but critical of his views. His book *An Essay Concerning Human Understanding* (1690) investigates the origins and limits of reason.

Key question

If a person forgets his earlier life is he now a different person?

of the previous members so that although change takes place the string quartet still produces its characteristic sound (possibly improved or worsened by each new player). So Locke argues:

- Even if consciousness changes, a person retains their identity through a set of historical circumstances which are unique to that body.
- Even if consciousness changes, it could not be transferred to anything else (another body such as a cat or another human being).

So Locke allows that in some extreme circumstances we might agree that a person is not the person that they were, but in general memory is sufficiently good enough to allow for continuity.

d) Enduring self

Key question

Do humans have souls?

For many, however, Locke's notion of personhood fails to give sufficient account of the uniqueness of each individual. For example, if shortly after I rob a bank I suddenly lose my memory, could I claim that the person who committed the crime was not me but someone else? Or if I look at a picture that my parents tell me is of me aged four but have no recollection of that time, do I regard the child as a different person from me? The alternative to Locke's argument is to propose an enduring self or soul. The characteristic of the soul is that it is a **single substance** and, unlike bodies which are composite, it cannot change.

There are many theories about the nature of an enduring self. **Dualists**, such as **Plato** (427–347BC) and **Descartes** (1597–1650), believe that as the soul is quite distinct from the body a person remains a person whether they have a body or not. This view supports the **vitalist** position. But not everyone who believes in an enduring self is necessarily a dualist. **Aristotle** (384–322BC), for example, argued that the soul is the primary dynamic 'animating' principle of the body, which enables it to fulfil its **potential**. In philosophical terms he said that the soul is the form of the body, but without the body the soul is not able to exist. When one dies, one's soul ceases to exist.

Key words

Mind–body dualists believe that souls and bodies are made of quite different substances.

Vitalism is the view that for the human body to be alive it must also possess a soul.

e) Potential and actual persons

Key words

Cartesian is the adjective describing those who follow Descartes' view of the soul.

Epistemology means the study of knowledge.

One of the problems faced by **Cartesian** dualists is an **epistemological** one. The question is how we can know whether a fully functioning body does or does not possess a soul. For example, an android built to function fully as a human being and possessing all the necessary characteristics outlined above (see page 5) need not have a soul. I might argue that because it behaves just like me, and I know I have a soul, then it *must* have one also. But arguing from the particular to the general does not confirm the truth; it merely sets up a supposition which cannot be tested.

Key quote

'Therefore this principle by which
we primarily understand, whether
it be called the intellect or the
intellectual soul, is the form of
the body.'

AQUINAS, SUMMA THEOLOGICA 1
Q. 76

Key people

Thomas Aquinas (1225–74) was
born in Roccasecca, Italy, where he
went to a Benedictine school and
then completed his studies in
Naples. Against his family's wishes
he joined the Dominican Order in
1244. Further studies in Paris
introduced him to Aristotle's work.
He taught theology and philosophy
in Naples, Cologne and Paris.
During this time he wrote his
Summa Theologica. His ideas
continue to exert great influence
on the Catholic Church.

A problem faced by Aristotelians is **ensoulment**; that is, the moment when the human being receives its soul. **Aquinas** (*Summa Theologica* 1, Q. 76), for example, follows Aristotle's notion that the characteristic of soul is rationality but it only functions as such when attached to the body. For like Aristotle he agrees that as the soul is the first principle of the body, as form is to matter, then a body without a rational soul is not fully a human person. Unlike Aristotle, though, he argued that the soul can exist separately from the body but as an incomplete person; only at the resurrection is the soul re-united with the body.

Aquinas follows Aristotle's notion that the generative force is transmitted from the soul of the father through his sperm which then develops in the womb. As the foetus develops the soul animates it at the vegetative and animal levels until it is fully formed, at which stage it gains its intellectual or rational soul. For boys this is at 40 days and girls 90 days. Aquinas argues that the intellectual soul is given by God, whereas for Aristotle it is part of the natural process. Either way the foetus does not become an actual human person until some time after conception. This notion of **delayed ensoulment** is significant for many ethical debates today.

In the modern Roman Catholic tradition ensoulment is given at the moment of conception. The embryo is not at this stage a 'person' in its fullest sense, because although it has the potential to be so, the process is a long one. In Aristotelian terms the actualisation process is a journey from embryo to foetus to baby to child to adulthood. Each stage seamlessly gives rise to the next. A few cells does not constitute an actual person, but has the potential to become so. In the official instruction *Donum Vitae* (1987), the Pope comments that observation of the physical state of the embryo is not sufficient to determine whether it is or is not a person:

> *No experiment datum can be in itself sufficient to bring us to the recognition of a spiritual soul.*

(*Donum Vitae*, Chapter 1, paragraph 1)

f) Critique

- **Rationality and competency.** Locke's notion of personhood has been adopted by radical liberal Christian thinkers such as Joseph Fletcher as well as secular thinkers such as Peter Singer. But its problem is that it leads logically to contradictory ethical views about the treatment of people. For example if a person is defined as being a conscious rational being then infanticide (the killing of children) and non-voluntary euthanasia of senile and non-communicative humans is justified. But this is contrary to the Christian teaching on the protection of the weak and the ancient prohibition of infanticide. Furthermore it defines rationality in a very narrow sense, when in Aquinas' terms having a 'rational nature' is not the same as being rational. In other words competency and rationality are too particular and open to misuse when defining human persons and how to treat them.

- **Monozygotic twins.** The criticism of any form of vitalist position is posed by the problem that it is possible for an embryo to split within the first 14 days of its development and become another human being (as an identical or monozygotic twin). This suggests that the embryo up to this stage is either a human being (being genetically a member of *homo sapiens*) but not a human person, or neither a human being nor person. Once it is accepted that personhood and being a member of *homo sapiens* are not necessarily the same, then our moral judgements will vary depending on the physical development of the human being.

3 Sanctity of life arguments

Key question

Is all human life intrinsically worthwhile even from conception?

Key people

Immanuel Kant (1724–1804) was a German philosopher who lived all his life in Königsberg and taught at the university, becoming professor of logic in 1770. He developed his own distinctive rational theory of knowledge based on the mind's innate capacity and experience. From this basis he developed his moral philosophy in a number of books. The arguments here are taken from his book *The Grounding for the Metaphysics of Morals* (translated by James W. Ellington).

We often give special status to persons over and above the value of other animals and plant life. But how is the value of a person's life to be decided? The traditional position is referred to as the sanctity of life. Sanctity of life appears in various versions both religious and non-religious or humanist. The religious version is that exemplified in the West by Christianity as a 'revealed law' and 'natural law' and the non-religious position is that of the philosopher Kant.

Within Christian traditions there are many versions of the sanctity of life argument because although the basic proposition is that life is sacred and given to humans by God, modern medical advances have made it increasingly more difficult to determine whether a person has reached a stage where 'life' is still worth living. Some suggest that this **weak sanctity of life** view is really just another version of the quality of life argument; there is fierce discussion whether this is so, and whether it matters. Those who hold to a **strong sanctity of life** view strongly defend the sanctity of life against all humanistic or utilitarian effects, which dilute or attempt to dilute or modify it. A number of terms are used to define their position. One popular phrase to describe those who hold a strong sanctity of life position is **pro-life group**. A better, more philosophical term is **vitalism**; this is the view that as ensoulment takes place at conception then there are no **ordinary or extraordinary** means that justify the deliberate termination of a human life at any stage.

a) Kant's sanctity of life argument

Kant's argument for the sanctity of life may owe its outlook to his Christian upbringing but his argument is based neither on revealed or natural law but on what he calls **moral law**. Moral law is derived by our powers of reason from the **good will**. The good will cannot

Key word

The **categorical imperative** is Kant's notion that morality is based on universal, rational, absolute and consistent duties which treat all people in a dignified manner. The categorical imperative is to: 'Act as if the maxim of your action were to become through your will a universal law of nature.'

IMMANUEL KANT, *GROUNDING FOR THE METAPHYSICS OF MORALS*, PARAGRAPH 421

Key quote

'Act in such a way that you treat humanity, whether in your own person or in the person of another, always at the same time as an end never simply as a means.'

IMMANUEL KANT, *GROUNDING FOR THE METAPHYSICS OF MORALS*, PARAGRAPH 429

Key quote

'Act in accordance with the maxims of a member legislating universal laws for a merely possible kingdom of ends.'

IMMANUEL KANT, *GROUNDING FOR THE METAPHYSICS OF MORALS* PARAGRAPH 438

Cross-reference

See pages 30–31 below for a fuller discussion on Kant and suicide.

Key word

Maxim. Kant defines maxim as a 'subjective principle of acting' that is a general rule or principle governing the action of all rational people.

be proved because it is just something we have and which defines us as human beings. This notion is the bedrock to Kant's subsequent ethical theory. As the good will is an intrinsic property of being human, it follows that all our moral decisions must assume that whatever is good for me must consistently and universally be good for all. The **categorical imperative** is, therefore, the exercise of the good will universally. Kant stated the categorical imperative in many different ways but two are particularly important in expressing his idea of the sanctity of life:

- The **practical imperative** expresses what Kant considered to be very important, and that is that people should never be treated as a means to an end but as an end in themselves.

  In other words, when we will our neighbour's good we do so for no other reason than that they are a fellow human being. Obedience to the categorical imperative, Kant argues, ensures that we treat all humans with equal dignity. No law or action may treat a person as less than a person or as an instrument to some other purpose. Kant entirely rejects the utilitarian view that in some cases a life may be worth less if it cannot yield more benefit than another.

- The **kingdom of ends** expresses Kant's view that every rational being is capable of being a law-maker whose autonomous decision takes into account the desire of being a member of the kingdom of ends. Kant defines the kingdom as 'a systematic union of different rational beings through common laws' (*Grounding*, paragraph 433). The kingdom of ends is the idea that all rational beings (humans) have equal dignity as law-makers and law-doers.

The practical imperative and kingdom of ends therefore strongly support the notion that our lives are not ours to dispose of when we wish. This is why he rejects suicide. In Kant's example the person feels that he has the right to shorten his life if continuing to live would only lead to more misery. But on reflection he realises that if this **maxim** were to become a universal law then he would be willing a principle which would both promote future life and also a law which would cut it short. This is a rational contradiction and he resolves it in favour of preserving life. And so Kant concludes, 'such a maxim cannot possibly hold as a universal law of nature and is, consequently, wholly opposed to the supreme principle of all duty' (*Grounding*, paragraph 422).

i) Critique of Kant

- **Reason or people**: Kant places such emphasis on reason and duty keeping that he appears to contradict the practical imperative. For example: do I always tell the truth even if this leads to innocent people being harmed or killed? If truth telling

Cross-reference

For a more detailed account of natural law read Mel Thompson, *Ethical Theory*, Chapter 7.

Key quote

Cicero's widely accepted definition of natural law is: *'True law is right reason in agreement with nature. It is applied universally and is unchanging and everlasting.'*

CICERO, *DE RE PUBLICA* (54–51BC)

Key thought

Secondary principles are derived from the general or primary principle. For example, the general principle might be that children need two parents to be brought up and the secondary principle is that marriage is therefore necessary to do this properly.

Key quote

'Nevertheless, the slaying of a sinner becomes lawful in relation to the common good, which is corrupted by sin.'

AQUINAS, *SUMMA THEOLOGICA* 2.2, Q. 64, ART. 6

Cross-reference

Vitoria's notion of intention and proportionality is important for the just war argument. See pages 128–34.

is to be preferred, then human life is not as intrinsically worthwhile as Kant suggests.

- **Clashing duties**: As Kant gives no clear way of deciding how to obey two equally demanding duties then we may prefer to adopt W.D. Ross's system of *prima facie* duties. Ross's system simply states that in some circumstances it will be clear that some duties are more appropriate than others. But as Kant views this as undermining the absoluteness of the categorical imperative, it has to be assumed that for Kant a life may have to be sacrificed for principle and this appears to contradict the essence of his moral theory.

b) Natural law sanctity of life arguments

Aristotle argued that all things are created with a distinctive purpose. The purpose or 'final cause' (the *telos*) marks a stage when a thing or person is most fully functioning as it is intended (by the efficient cause). For **Aquinas**, God is the efficient cause of nature, so the world is purposeful and designed. Everything has a *telos* which it aims to fulfil. The primary purposes of human life are:

- self-preservation, progress and reproduction
- self-perfection (the pursuit of justice)
- to learn and live by reason
- to live in an ordered society
- to worship God.

He further argues that although there are **primary principles** that always remain the same, there are many **secondary principles** which are derived from first order laws and are not always as binding.

- He allows for **situation** to alter secondary precepts.
- He also allows that some things may be right **in proportion** to a given end.

Natural law, though, does not think that all human life should be preserved at all costs. For example, if the aim is to establish peace and restore justice, then life may be taken if it discriminates in favour of those who are innocent over those who are not and is proportionate to these ends.

This establishes an important natural law principle that **innocent** human life must be preserved. However, there is much debate about what constitutes an innocent life. Augustine argued that self-defence was not sufficient reason to kill an aggressor, but **Francisco de Vitoria** (1486–1546) defined a non-innocent life in terms of someone who intentionally intends harm. The principle of proportionality crucially ensures that the **intention** of the person protecting an innocent life is that and no more (for example, revenge). Natural law ethicists argue, therefore, that the aggressor loses the right to the protection of his life.

Cross-references

Read pages 71–73 below on how the doctrine of double effect makes an important contribution to the euthanasia debate.

Read page 54 for more detailed discussion of ectopic pregnancies

More problematic is whether killing of innocent life is ever justified. Aquinas developed what has been termed the **doctrine of double effect**, which permits the killing of an innocent life if it is not the primary intention and it is not disproportionate to the good ends. For example, a woman whose life is threatened by an ectopic pregnancy may remove the foetus even though this will almost certainly kill the baby. Every attempt should be made to save the life of the baby but the primary intention to save the mother's life by giving her treatment is not disproportionate to the unwilled death of the foetus.

i) Critique of natural law

- **Naturalistic fallacy**: For many ethicists, natural law suffers from the category mistake of deriving an 'ought from an is' (sometimes referred to as the naturalistic fallacy). This is particularly the case now that most biologists do not think that every aspect of nature is designed to have a particular purpose.
- **Casuistry**: Casuistry means law making, but it is often used negatively to mean the use of clever arguments to get round a legal problem. The doctrine of double effect is in effect a utilitarian argument, even though it tries to maintain the sanctity of life principle.

c) Revealed ethics: strong sanctity of life arguments

Within Christianity there are many versions of the sanctity of life argument because although the basic proposition is that life is **sacred** and given to humans by God, modern medical advances have made it increasingly more difficult to determine whether a person has reached a stage where 'life', in any proper sense of the word, is still a life. Those who hold to a **strong sanctity of life** view fiercely defend the sanctity of life against all humanistic or utilitarian arguments which attempt to dilute or modify it. A number of terms are used to define their position. Sometimes, especially in political circles, this is called the **pro-life** position and in philosophical terms such a view corresponds to **vitalism**. Vitalists argue that a human life is always sacred because it possesses a soul and that there are no **ordinary or extraordinary** means that justify the termination of a human life – even from the moment of conception.

Sanctity of life is defined according to **revealed ethics** by the following biblical texts:

- **Set apart**: In Christian thought every human being is created in the image and likeness of God. To be created in God's image implies that humans are set apart and different from all other creatures and that every human being possesses a 'spark' of

Key thought

Revealed ethics is the aspect of religious ethics that is derived primarily from the Bible (in Christian ethics).

Key quotes

'So God created man in his own image, in the image of God he created man.'

GENESIS 1:27

'Be fruitful and multiply, and fill the earth and subdue it; and have dominion over ... every living thing that moves upon the earth.'

GENESIS 1:28

'And the Word became flesh and dwelt amongst us, full of grace and truth.'

JOHN 1:14

Key words
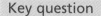

The **incarnation** is the Christian notion that God became human in the form of Jesus Christ.

Holiness means 'set apart' or sanctified. It is this word which gives rise to the phrase 'sanctity of life'.

Key quotes

'Naked I came from my mother's womb, and naked shall I return; the Lord gave and the Lord has taken away; blessed be the name of the Lord.'

JOB 1:21

'You shall not murder'

EXODUS 20:13

'I call heaven to earth to witness against you this day, that I have set before you life and death, blessing and curse; therefore, choose life ... '

DEUTERONOMY 30:19

'For God so loved the world that he gave his only Son, that whoever believes in him should not perish but have eternal life.'

JOHN 3:16;

'Love bears all things, believes all things, hopes all things, endures all things.'

1 CORINTHIANS 13:6

'A person who, because of illness, handicap or, more simply, just by existing, compromises the well-being or life-style of those who are more favoured tends to be looked upon as an enemy to be resisted or eliminated. In this way a kind of "conspiracy against life" is unleashed.'

EVANGELIUM VITAE,
CHAPTER 1, PARA. 12

Key question

Why might it be better to replace the word 'sanctity' in the phrase 'sanctity of life', with 'respect for' or 'dignity'?

divinity (Genesis 1:27) within them which sets them apart from other creatures (Genesis 1:28). The **incarnation** of the Word of God as man in the person of Jesus (John 1:14) reaffirms the sanctity, **holiness** and **intrinsic value** of every human life **unconditionally** in its relationship with God.

- **Loan and destiny**: If God is the author of life then it follows that he is the one who determines when it should end (Job 1:21). It is not up to the individual whether he or she might add or subtract from his or her life or anyone else's because life is a gift, or a loan, from God. God is a providential God who through nature or other means is the only being who may directly terminate a person's life.

- **Respect and honour**: Taking a life is broader than simply killing and the prohibition in the Ten Commandments (Exodus 20:13) not to murder is part of the social glue that equally shows respect for parents, property, marriage, husband and neighbour. The command in Deuteronomy 30:19–20 to 'choose life' is the believer's response to honour God and respect life.

- **Love and protection**: Love requires the Christian to respect and protect all humans regardless of status, gender and age. This is famously illustrated in Jesus' parable of the Good Samaritan (Luke 10:29–37). The Greek term often used by the New Testament is *agape* and in its Christian usage suggests that love is active and requires a person to sacrifice his own greatest happiness for others (1 John 3:17–18). Jesus' life is an explicit reminder that life is God's gift of love (John 3:16).

But for many Christians sanctity of life in addition to revealed law is also supported by natural law. This is the **Roman Catholic** view as set out by Pope John Paul II in *Evangelium Vitae* (1995). *Evangelium Vitae* considers how contemporary society has undermined the sanctity of life and by developing a 'culture of death' has devalued the dignity of human life. In particular it has marginalised the weak, the ill and the handicapped or disabed.

d) Revealed ethics: weak sanctity of life arguments

The main problems of sanctity of life lie not so much in the principles but in the applications to situations which become more and more complicated as medical science blurs the boundaries between life and death. Some supporters of sanctity of life appeal to **extraordinary means** as a justification for killing when someone is no longer able to live a worthwhile life. This might be due to extreme suffering or irreversible brain damage.

Key word

Weak sanctity of life. By using the term 'weak' the principle is modified to allow for exceptions, i.e. in this case that human life should not always be preserved at all costs.

Key people

Stanley Hauerwas (b. 1940) is the Gilbert T. Rowe Professor of Theological Ethics at Duke University, USA. He is a Protestant theologian whose aim is to rediscover the Christian virtues in the context of ongoing life of the Church as a living community.

In these cases those who support a **weak sanctity of life** argue that agape should be the primary determining principle. The weak sanctity of life view argues that being alive, in a Christian sense, means being able to live life in body and soul as a 'living sacrifice' (Romans 12:1). Being 'alive' is not sufficient unless a person can express himself physically *and* spiritually.

Some warn against making life so absolute that it turns it into an idol worthy of worship. As **Stanley Hauerwas** has argued, since the Church has allowed martyrdom on occasions it follows that the sanctity of life principle is not so absolute and it permits taking life when it is for the well-being of others. He concludes:

Appeals to the sanctity of life as an ideology make it appear that Christians are committed to the proposition that there is nothing in life worth dying for.

(Stanley Hauerwas, *Suffering Presence* [1986], page 92)

i) Critique of revealed ethics

- If shortening life is against sanctity of life, then is prolonging it also bad?
- If life is a gift then isn't it mine to do with as I wish?
- People don't actually believe in the sanctity of life because they frequently find reasons to make it less absolute. The weak sanctity of life is a good example of this. Peter Singer argues that the next logical step should be to replace it with a non-religious rational quality of life principle.

4 Quality of life arguments

Key question

Should the quality of life argument replace the sanctity of life argument in discussions about life and death?

Quality of life arguments take an **instrumentalist** view of human life. In other words a life is only worthwhile if it can fulfil those things which make life worth living. There is nothing intrinsically good about being alive except as a means of enabling us to experience those things which are desired.

Peter Singer is a prominent philosopher who has strongly argued that it is time now to abandon the sanctity of life principle in favour of the non-religious quality of life argument. Singer's arguments develop Locke's notion that the value of life depends on a person's ability to have desires and preferences and not on some mystical 'enduring self' which automatically gives priority to humans above all other animals. In *Rethinking Life and Death* (1995) Singer sets out his five new rational quality of life commandments to replace those of the traditional sanctity of life position:

Key people

Peter Singer (b. 1946) is an Australian philosopher specialising in medical ethics and animal rights and liberation. He was director of the Centre for Human Bioethics, Monash University, Australia, for many years and is now a professor at Princeton University in the USA. As a consequentialist he has developed his form of preference utilitarianism.

- Recognise that the worth of human life varies.
- Take responsibility for the consequences of your decision.
- Respect a person's desire to live or die.
- Bring children into the world only if they are wanted.
- Do not discriminate on the basis of species.

(from Peter Singer, *Rethinking Life and Death*, pages 190–202)

In 1983 Singer caused controversy with the following comment on the Baby Doe abortion case in the USA:

If we compare a severely defective human infant with a nonhuman animal, a dog or a pig, for example, we will often find the nonhuman to have superior capacities, both actual and potential, for rationality, self-consciousness, communication, and anything else that can plausibly be considered morally significant.

(quoted also in Peter Singer, *Rethinking Life and Death*, page 201)

However, if the quality of life principle is adopted there is still the difficult task of determining the primary principle that permits or restrains a person taking a life (their own or someone else's). Set out below are various versions of the quality of life arguments, each of which offers a rational basis for determining what constitutes a worthwhile life.

a) Utilitarianism as the basis of quality of life

What 'goods' make life worthwhile? Utilitarianism is a modern non-religious ethic which offers a clear maxim that what makes life worthwhile is when the greatest happiness is achieved for the greatest number of people. This appears to offer a rational means by which to judge the quality of an individual's life within the context of society and is frequently used in the context of medical ethics.

However, despite its seemingly simple aims, utilitarian philosophers offer several different versions of the maxim which reinterpret what is meant by happiness as the basis of what makes a life worthwhile.

Key question

Is happiness the major factor which determines whether life is worthwhile?

Cross-reference

For a more detailed account of utilitarianism read Mel Thompson, *Ethical Theory*, Chapter 9.

Key people

Jeremy Bentham (1748–1832) was a British philosopher. He used utilitarianism as a rational means of reforming the law.

- **Hedonic utilitarians** such as **Jeremy Bentham** argue that the quality of life is judged when the amount of pleasure achieved is greater than any experience of pain. Judging a worthwhile life therefore is highly subjective both from the individual's point of view and from the perspective of others. Bentham suggested that pain and pleasure could in some sense be calculated in terms of duration, intensity and those affected. But even if this could be done, many utilitarians argue that there is more to life than pleasure and absence of pain.

Key people

G.E. Moore (1873–1958) was a British philosopher. In his most influential book *Principia Ethica* (1903) he argued that goodness is a special non-natural quality which can only be known through intuition and especially in the experience of beauty and friendship.

Robert Goodin is professor of both social and political theory and philosophy at the Research School of Social Sciences, Australian National University. His argument for welfare utilitarianism may be found in Peter Singer's *A Companion to Ethics* (1993).

- **Preference satisfaction utilitarians** such as Peter Singer argue that the quality of life is to be judged against whatever people consider to be the most desirable – and that might equally be wanting to live as wanting to die. Preferences might also include other feelings such as generosity and altruism. For example being tortured in war for one's country would not usually be considered pleasurable but as a duty to others it is a preference which significantly makes a valuable contribution to society.

- **Ideal utilitarians** such as **G.E. Moore** argued that the problem with preference utilitarianism is that there is no means by which to judge the usefulness of one preference over another. There are some goods such as justice and beauty which are generally regarded to be of higher quality than the lower qualities such as pleasure.

- **Welfare utilitarians** such as **Robert Goodin** argue that although the ideal utilitarians are right to say that there are some goods which are more valuable than others, they have made these qualities too abstract. For utilitarianism to work we need to be able to deal with qualities that can be demonstrated to enhance human society. These, he suggests, are general welfare preferences such as health, money, shelter and food. An important feature of welfare utilitarianism is that it gives a concrete **duty** to all in society to provide for all its members. So, for example, a welfare utilitarian doctor might choose to overrule a patient's preference to refuse medication and die in favour of medicines which he knows will have long-term good effects.

i) Critique of utilitarianism

There are many criticisms of utilitarianism but those which are the most important in terms of the quality of life argument are:

- The principle of utility **dehumanises** others by making them a means to an end. Kant influentially dismissed utilitarianism on the grounds that it fails to treat people as an end in themselves and to treat humans with equal dignity.

- The maxim is **too subjective** and gives no clear account of what is meant by a valuable life. This can be seen by the fact that there is no agreement amongst utilitarians about as to what constitutes the most basic human quality or good which should be maximised.

- Utilitarianism could lead to a **slippery slope** whereby killing humans initially for good reasons (i.e. where a life has ceased to be worthwhile) inevitably results in less good reasons being adopted in other cases.

- Utilitarianism fails adequately to take into account other moral values and plans which are part of a person's identity. **Bernard Williams** argued that for utilitarianism to work it has therefore

Key thought

The **slippery slope** is not so much an argument as an observation that people often weaken a principle or rule which then creates a generally undesirable state of affairs.

Key people

Sir Bernard Williams (1929–2003) was one of Britain's most influential philosophers and wrote on the philosophy of personal identity and ethics. In *Utilitarianism: For and Against* (1973) he argues against J.C.C. Smart that utilitarianism offers the best form of ethics.

to take these other moral raines into account. If it doesn't then it **denies personal integrity**; in other words utilitarianism may work in theory but not in practice. As he says, 'it cannot coherently describe the relations between a man's projects and his actions' (*Utilitarianism: For and Against*, page 100). Williams' thought exercise 'Jim and the Indians' illustrates the problem of taking one life to save many even if this makes sense from a utilitarian's perspective.

Case study
Jim and the Indians

Consider the following thought exercise Bernard Williams uses to criticise utilitarian thinking on issues of life and death:

Jim finds himself in the central square of a small South American town. Tied up against the wall are a row of twenty Indians, most terrified, a few defiant, in front of them several armed men in uniform. A heavy man in a sweat-stained khaki shirt turns out to be the captain in charge and, after a good deal of questioning of Jim which establishes that he got there by accident while on a botanical expedition, explains that the Indians are a random group of the inhabitants who, after recent acts of protest against the government, are just about to be killed to remind other possible protestors of the advantages of not protesting. However, since Jim is an honoured visitor from another land, the captain is happy to offer him a guest's privilege of killing one of the Indians himself. If Jim accepts, then as a special mark of the occasion, the other Indians will be let off. Of course, if Jim refuses, then there is no special occasion, and Pedro here will do what he was about to do when Jim arrived, and kill them all. Jim, with some desperate recollection of schoolboy fiction, wonders whether if he got hold of a gun, he could hold the captain, Pedro and the rest of the soldiers to threat, but it is quite clear from the set-up that nothing of that kind is going to work: any attempt at that sort of thing will mean that all the Indians will be killed, and himself. The men against the wall, and the other villagers, understand the situation, and are obviously begging him to accept. What should he do?

To these dilemmas, it seems to me that utilitarianism replies that Jim should kill the Indian ... A feature of utilitarianism is that it cuts out a kind of consideration which for some others makes a difference to what they feel about such cases: a consideration involving the idea, as we might first and very simply put it, that each of us is specially responsible for what he does, rather than for what other people do. This is an idea closely connected with the value of integrity.

(J.C.C. Smart and Bernard Williams, *Utilitarianism: For and Against*, pages 98–99)

Key question

Do you agree with Williams' conclusion that utilitarianism is too detached and fails to take into account our own sense of moral identity?

b) Autonomy as the basis of quality of life

Many argue that the arguments above could be more coherently expressed without necessarily referring to utilitarianism. The value of life comes from the ability to determine one's future, that is, 'self-rule' or autonomy. So, although utilitarianism may value autonomy as the means by which preferences can be made, it is not valuable *in itself*. The value of autonomy as an expression of being a human person has a long history but is particularly significant from the period of the Enlightenment (eighteenth century) to the present day.

In the nineteenth century **J.S. Mill** developed what has become the basis of **liberalism** in his famous *On Liberty* (1859). Liberty is the chief means by which a person determines his morality and values. A liberal society avoids 'tyrannising' (Mill's phrase) the minority by the majority and aims to maximise personal freedoms wherever possible. Mill's form of liberalism suggests that taking one's own life is a matter of personal autonomy; the only reason for interference would be if doing so would cause **harm to others**. But, as Mill argues, causing self-harm is not in itself a reason for interference:

He cannot rightfully be compelled to do or forbear because it will be better for him to do so, because it will make him happier, because, in the opinions of others, to do so would be wise or even right.

(J.S. Mill, *On Liberty*, Chapter 1)

Key question

Is the ability to govern one's own life the most important quality humans possess?

Key people

John Stuart Mill (1806–73). As a child he met many radical thinkers and politicians including Jeremy Bentham. His marriage to Harriet Taylor greatly influenced his thinking on social policies. His basic philosophical position is that all knowledge is based on experience and that our desires and beliefs are products of psychological laws. Ethics, for example, is based on the psychological law that all humans desire to be happy (although he famously differed from Bentham in that he considered that intellectual pleasures are higher than other forms of happiness).

Key quote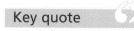

'Over himself, over his own body and mind, the individual is sovereign.'

J.S. MILL, *ON LIBERTY* (1859)

Key word

Paternalism means literally to 'act in a fatherly way' and justifies overriding a person's autonomy if it is for their own good.

Mill's argument raises many problems. For example, how is harm to be defined – physically or mentally? Is interference justified if the person is not acting rationally, either because they are too young or because they are temporarily mentally disturbed? Mill's liberalism can allow for **paternalism** if it is in a person's **best interests** to over-rule their autonomy. But to do so implies that there is either a standard greater than autonomy which justifies interference or that an individual may not know themselves what is good for them. In many cases the liberal may just have to leave it to the individual to make their own decisions regardless of whether it causes them harm. It is a matter of dispute whether self-harm which leads to death justifies paternalism or not. This is why the issue of suicide is particularly important.

i) Critique of autonomy

Quality of life arguments that prioritise autonomy as the essential quality of being human might be criticised for the following reasons:

- Personal autonomy is **over-valued** at the expense of obligations to the community.
- Autonomy can undermine the **collective morality** of society.
- Autonomy might permit very **anti-social behaviour** from those who hold extreme views, which are in themselves anti-liberal.
- Autonomy is **meaningless** unless it is coupled with other qualities such as self-control and obedience (to God or society).

c) Rights as the basis for quality of life

Key question

What are human rights and how do we know what they are?

Key people

Thomas Hobbes (1588–1679) came from a lowly family but was educated at Oxford and then became a tutor to the Earl of Devonshire's son. During this time he began writing political pieces. His major work *Leviathan* (1651) developed his political thought.

Key quote

'Every man has a right to every thing; even to one another's body.'

THOMAS HOBBES, *LEVIATHAN*

PART 1, 14:4

Another way of considering quality of life arguments is in terms of rights as social contract. Social contract theories have many different starting points, all of which offer widely divergent accounts of taking and preserving life.

Thomas Hobbes in his book *Leviathan* argued that humans are essentially no different from animals whose primary aim is to survive. Survival is prior to pain/pleasure or concern for others. He argues that survival is the *right* to preserve one's own life at all costs – killing, stealing, adultery are all legitimate means.

But Hobbes realises that the anarchy which would inevitably follow is not in his best interests. He therefore sacrifices 'his right to all things' in exchange for protection and for peace so as to exercise as much liberty as possible. The role of the state is to ensure that the exchange of rights for contract is maintained. There is, therefore, no intrinsic reason why the taking of life is wrong; for life is protected only insofar as it is in society's best interest to do so. **David Hume** (1711–76), who shared some of Hobbes' observations, argued that a person who 'withdraws' from the social contract and takes his own

Cross-reference

Hume's argument is presented in more detail in his essay on suicide on pages 33–35 below.

Key question

Does a right to life also imply a right to die?

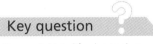

Key people

Jonathan Glover (b. 1941) is professor of applied ethics at King's College London and chaired a European commission working party on assisted reproduction.

life 'does no harm' to society. It follows then that he has a right to take his own life whenever he considers that he has no part to play in society and expects nothing from it in return.

i) Critique of rights and contract

The problem with a social contract view of rights is that it questions what is meant by a right. Most rights theories include ideas that affirm the value of being human in terms of:

- worth due to persons
- basic human needs
- freedom and autonomy
- self-ownership.

Rights then appear to be more than merely a contract established between the individual and society. Human rights must also be universal entitlements which, as **John Locke** (1632–1704) argued, are intended to protect the individual against governments. If this is so rights are intrinsic to nature and cannot be removed. **Natural rights** are placed by God in nature to ensure that all human beings do not harm each other's lives, health, liberty and possessions. Equally therefore everyone has a *duty* not to harm the lives, liberty and possessions of others.

d) Consciousness as the basis for quality of life

Jonathan Glover in *Causing Death and Saving Lives* (1977), argues against the indirect utilitarians who claim that the extrinsic side-effects make killing unacceptable (hurt felt by others, loss of hope, etc.) because they fail to credit the intuitive value we place on life itself. Instead he adopts Locke's standpoint and suggests that life is always valuable providing it is a conscious life. Killing is not, therefore, an intrinsic wrong, but wrong because of its 'direct' and detrimental effect on consciousness. A 'life' is not defined simply as a body which is alive in biological terms, but which is conscious. Glover takes an **instrumentalist** view of the body; the body is important only in so far as it enables conscious experiences to be possible.

> *I have no way of refuting someone who holds that being alive, even though unconscious, is intrinsically valuable. But it is a view that will seem unattractive to those of us who, in our own case, see a life of permanent coma as in no way preferable to death. From a subjective point of view, there is nothing to choose between the two.*
> (Jonathan Glover, *Causing Death and Saving Lives*, page 45)

Length of life is mostly irrelevant to the *value* of a life, so whilst it is true that a longer life enables a person to fulfil their preferences and desires, for others the length of life might be the very factor that makes their life unbearable. It follows, therefore, that a conscious life is a valuable life and should be protected.

i) Critique of consciousness

Consciousness then is considered the basis for a valuable life. Without it the other qualities such as the ability to feel happiness or have preferences or have rights would be considerably reduced in their significance. In terms of how we treat life consciousness is an important factor; we appear to value conscious life more than we do non-conscious life, as can be seen in the debates on abortion and euthanasia. However, the criticisms of this position are:

- Consciousness is **elusive**. Some would argue that there are various levels of consciousness (for example different sleep states, to ordinary waking life, to deliberate acts of self-reflection). It is unclear whether these are all to be considered equally valuable or whether some states are more valuable than others.
- Consciousness may be less basic than **sentience**. Many argue that the ability to feel pain is a better basis for deciding on the quality of a life. In debates about abortion a human foetus may not become fully conscious until several months after birth, yet few would justify infanticide on the grounds that lack of consciousness makes it a less valuable life.
- We are assuming that consciousness is the same for non-humans as it is for humans and therefore the valuable life criteria are necessarily the same. But this need not be so. Non-human consciousness might reveal a very different kind of existence in which quality of life as we understand it could be meaningless.

Key word

Sentience means being able to have sense perceptions.

John Harris concludes his discussion of quality of life arguments:

> *Even if we felt confident that we could find a very general account of what makes life valuable for human beings, perhaps by singling out the most important or most frequently occurring features from the lists of what they value of a large cross-section of people, we would have no reason to suppose we had arrived at a satisfactory account. For one thing, people's reasons for valuing life might well change over time; but more importantly, there would be no reason to suppose that our list bore any relation at all to the account that might be given of the value of life by non-human people, people in other worlds.*
>
> (John Harris, *The Value of Life*, pages 15–16)

Summary diagram

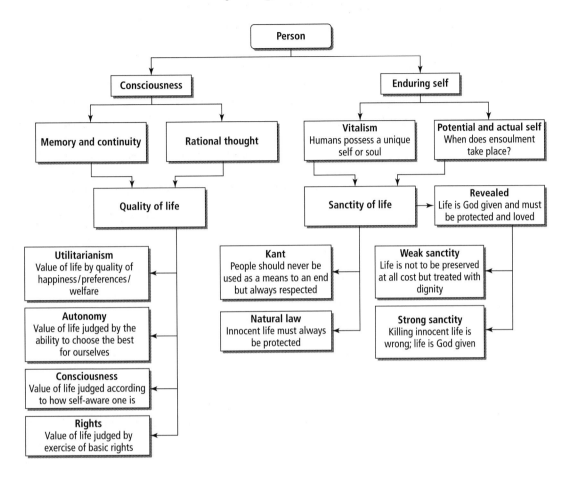

Study guide

By the end of this chapter you should have considered various reasons why people have adopted a sanctity of life argument either based on revealed ethics, universal duty (Kant) or natural law. You should also understand why the sanctity of life argument has been rejected by many in favour of a quality of life view based on the view that life is worthwhile because it is conscious or capable of pleasure or able to be autonomous. Both arguments depend on what it means to exist as a person; whether humans have a soul or enduring self which makes them intrinsically worthwhile or whether we are a bundle of qualities, none of which make us uniquely human.

Revision checklist

Can you define:

- necessary and sufficient conditions
- vitalism
- autonomy
- weak sanctity of life.

Can you explain:

- Locke's definition of person
- Aquinas' natural law principle and the absolute protection of innocent life
- the difference between actual and potential person arguments
- Peter Singer's quality of life argument.

Can you explain:

- why bodily change is a problem for Locke's theory of personhood
- Aristotle's notion of the soul as an animating first principle of the body
- why Aquinas' idea of soul is slightly different from Aristotle's idea of soul.

Can you give arguments for and against:

- using the double effect to justify unintended negative side-effects
- Kant's sanctity of life argument and the universal good will
- having a strong sanctity of life argument
- having a quality of life argument.

Essay question

1 a) Explain what is meant by a 'quality of life' argument.

1 b) 'Quality of life arguments fail to treat people with respect.' Discuss.

The essay might begin by stating that quality of life arguments argue that what makes a life worthwhile is due to extrinsic factors; quality of life arguments reject the sanctity of life view that life is intrinsically worthwhile regardless of status or situation. Quality of life views are therefore non-religious but there are a variety of views as to what constitutes a worthwhile life. Peter Singer's preference utilitarian position might be explained perhaps by illustrating his views (as in the Baby Doe case) that animals as well as humans are part of moral decision making because they also have preferences. Other utilitarian views hold that happiness and freedom from pain or maximising welfare needs are the basis for quality of life decisions. Mill's emphasis on autonomy might be used to illustrate what many consider to be the most important factor in bringing about a worthwhile life.

The evaluative part of this essay might argue that as it is very hard to know what is meant by 'quality of life', then the basic state of nature could be one where we might all treat each other as a means for our own ends (as Hobbes argued). This contrasts considerably from Kant's view that we all have a 'good will' or the Christian sanctity of life position which treats all human life as intrinsically valuable being made in the image of God. On the other hand Mill's liberal view suggests that we are our own best judges and the burden of treating all human life as inviolable can lead to cruel decisions to keep people alive at all costs rather than respect their decisions to determine their own future.

Further essay questions

2a   Explain the difference between being an actual and potential person.

2b   'At the moment of conception the human embryo is a person.' Discuss.

3   Assess the practical implications of natural law ethics when dealing with issues of life and death.

4   'As a nation, we must choose between the sanctity of life ethic and the quality of life ethic' (Ronald Reagan). Discuss.

Chapter checklist ✓

Although suicide is often regarded as a tragic act, to dispose of one's life is also regarded by many as an important expression of human freedom. This chapter considers the view that suicide is ultimately selfish, a failure to obey God, blasphemous, existential moral failure and socially polluting of society's values. Psychological reasons for suicide have helped modify some of these views. However, altruistic suicide is often commended as an example of selflessness. The final part of the chapter considers to what extent we should interfere with someone's autonomy if they are doing something which is 'suicidal' such as dangerous sports.

1 Suicide and society

Key question ?

Does a person have a right to die whenever they choose?

Case study
Maximilian Kolbe

Maximilian Kolbe (1894–1941), a Polish Franciscan priest, was a prisoner in Auschwitz concentration camp when in late July 1941 a prisoner from Cell Block 14 escaped. The authorities ordered a search and when he could not be found ten other prisoners were rounded up and told that if the missing man were not found they would die by starvation. The man could not be found so Commandant Fritzsch selected the ten men. One of the men selected burst into tears, saying he had a wife and children and that he was not prepared to die. Then Father Kolbe stepped forward and asked to speak to the commandant. He explained that he wanted to die in place of the man. Hearing that he was a priest the commandant told him to join the others selected to die. He did so. Despite starvation he lived on to be killed three weeks later by lethal injection.

Many people would regard Kolbe's action as a morally virtuous act. But if he deliberately acted so that he would die, did he throw away a worthwhile life? Many consider any form of self-killing, such as suicide, to be morally very wrong.

On the other hand, the right to end one's life as one wishes is an important aspect of living in a **liberal society**. What we value is to be able to choose what is best for us and if this means choosing suicide then society should not interfere.

However, even in liberal societies the debate is not nearly as clear cut as it at first seems. Many of those who have experience of a friend or family member who has committed or attempted suicide do not regard it as an expression of a right, but rather a selfish and degrading act and a sign that society has failed in its care of the individual.

a) Changing attitudes to suicide

The term 'suicide' was coined in the seventeenth century; other terms include 'self-murder', 'self-destruction' and 'self-slaughter'. But when using the term 'suicide', moral judgements can vary depending on what kind of suicide is being discussed. For the purposes of this topic we shall limit suicide to mean the taking of one's own life without the involvement of a third party. The question of **assisted suicide** has its own legal and moral problems, which will be considered under **euthanasia** in Chapter 4.

The history of social attitudes to suicide also give us an insight into shifting attitudes in the Church, the law and class structures. For instance in the sixteenth century someone who commited suicide was buried at the crossroads with a stake through his heart, and in many European countries suicide meant automatic loss of property. In France, for instance, during the late seventeenth century a nobleman who had committed suicide was reduced to the rank of a commoner, his castles demolished and his estate passed to the crown. But with the **Enlightenment**'s emphasis on reason, philosophers considered that suicide was morally wrong only as an act of defiance against the state rather than nature or God. In France, by the time of the French Revolution (1789), the suicide laws had been repealed.

b) Law and suicide

Until 1961 suicide in the UK was a criminal offence. Although the **1961 Suicide Act** decriminalised suicide, it *did not* make it morally licit or permissible.

1 *The rule of law whereby it is a crime for a person to commit suicide is hereby abrogated.*

Cross-reference

Read pages 17–18 above for J.S. Mill's description of liberalism.

Key thought

The **Enlightenment** refers primarily to the eighteenth-century thinkers such as Hume and Kant who argued that knowledge could only be obtained through human reason and observation and not through divine revelation or other authorities.

*2 (1) A person who aids, abets, counsels or procures the suicide of another
or an attempt by another to commit suicide shall be liable for a term
not exceeding fourteen years.*

*(2) If on the trial of an indictment for murder or manslaughter
it is proved that the accused aided, abetted, counselled or procured the
suicide of the person in question, the jury may find him guilty of
that offence.*

(Office of Public Sector Information)

Many think that the law now supports the principle of autonomy.
But, in fact, the act reinforces the principle of the sanctity of life by
criminalising any form of assisted suicide. On the other hand the act
does not hold the vitalist position that all life is equally valuable and
should be preserved at all costs because there are cases when
allowing a person to die is the better course of action.

c) Egoistical and altruistic suicide

As we have seen in the Kolbe case, not all forms of self-killing are
the same. It is important to distinguish between two kinds of
suicide: **egoistical suicide** and **altruistic suicide**. This distinction is
important in the present complex debate about euthanasia.
Egoistical suicide leaves the choice entirely to the individual and in
many philosophical and religious traditions this is considered to be
selfish and wrong. The aim of altruistic suicide, on the other hand, is
only indirectly to take one's own life and is primarily for some
greater cause that necessitates death as a side-effect. The question of
volition or what is willed or intended is an important ethical
principle (especially for natural law and virtue ethics). Altruistic
suicide is often more acceptable than egoistical suicide, but the
distinction is less clear when applied to voluntary euthanasia.

Key thoughts

Egoistical suicide is often seen as
a selfish act of rebellion or escape.

Altruistic suicide is when a
person voluntarily gives up their
life for another.

Cross-reference

See Chapter 4 for discussion on
euthanasia.

2 The psychology of suicide

a) Suicide due to unsound mind

The social taboo against suicide held fast in many societies. It wasn't
until 1961 that the last anti-suicide laws were removed in Britain
(following the strong recommendation of the Church of England's
Christie Committee in 1960). The law had effectively, and for some
time, been circumvented by lawyers using the phrase that a person
who committed suicide had died whilst 'the balance of his mind
was unsound'. The phrase indicates another influence in moral
reasoning. For almost a century advances in psychology had helped
us to understand what drives someone to suicide. In most cases the
phrase 'unsound mind' was to safeguard an attempted suicide victim
from the punishment that would logically follow a murder or

attempted murder. The shift in the law recognised that a major moral taboo had finally come to an end after 1500 years of discrimination. Even so, as late as 1969, a boy was birched in the Isle of Man for attempted suicide.

An example from nineteenth-century England illustrates how increasingly people found punishment for attempted suicide absurd and ridiculous. In 1860 Nicholas Ogarev wrote to his mistress, Mary Sutherland, on the following news from the London newspapers. The papers had merely commented on the slightly bizarre occurrence, not the suicide itself. But for Ogarev the event said a great deal about society:

> *A man was hanged who had cut his throat, but who had been brought back to life. They hanged him for suicide. The doctor had warned them that it was impossible to hang him as the throat would burst open and he would breathe through the aperture. They did not listen to his advice and hanged their man. The wound in the neck immediately opened and the man came back to life again though he was hanged. It took time to convoke the aldermen to decide the question of what was to be done. At length aldermen assembled and bound up the neck below the wound* until he died. *Oh my Mary, what a crazy society and what a stupid civilisation.*
>
> (quoted in A. Alvarez, *The Savage God*, page 63)

If David Hume and other philosophers liberated suicide from the religious and philosophical restrictions, the work of psychologists has given the moral philosopher important data by which to assess the motives of the suicide. For the past hundred years suicide has been regarded not as a deliberate act against society or God but the act of a desperate or confused person. Ironically the conclusions from psychology do not necessarily confirm the conclusions of liberal philosophers. If anything, psychologists suggest that suicide is the result of a distorted society. Philosophers treat suicide in terms of 'rights', 'liberties', 'justice' and so on. A. Alvarez, who attempted suicide himself, reminds us that suicide is not just a philosophical exercise:

> *The act is removed from the realm of damnation only at the price of being transformed into an interesting but purely intellectual problem beyond tragedy and morality.*
>
> (A. Alvarez, *The Savage God*, page 92)

b) Sigmund Freud

Alvarez finds in the writings of **Sigmund Freud** a genuine attempt to understand the deeper and complex motivations behind suicide. Freud's initial thesis on human psychological motivation had been based on the pleasure principle: the basic instinctive drives for survival and sex (libido). But he also observed that humans are equally driven by a destructive **death instinct** (thanatos). Holding

Key people

Sigmund Freud (1856–1939), considered to be the father of psychoanalysis, taught, practised and developed his ideas of the mind (in particular the place of the unconscious) in Vienna before moving to London in 1938. Amongst his influential books are *The Interpretation of Dreams* (1900) and *The Ego and the Id* (1923).

these two forces in check is the **ego**, the conscious of self. Most of the time the ego is able to divert the death instinct outward in terms of competitive and aggressive human behaviour. But there are times when traumatic events in a person's life make the ego unable to control the death instinct and it reverts to initial state of self-destruction. One of they key reasons for this, Freud suggests, is loss.

- Loss might occur literally when a person loses someone close to them. In the process of bereavement the ego initially tries to restore that person, but slowly it comes to realise that the dead person no longer exists in the external world but is now valued internally.
- However for those suffering from **melancholia** (i.e. severe depressive illness) the person feels guilty and responsible for the person's death and tries to restore the situation by taking their own death.
- Loss need not be an actual death of a person, but the loss of childhood security (e.g. moving home, divorce). In adult life a traumatic event can cause a person to revert to the childhood state but lack the psychological resources to overcome the powerful drive of the death instinct.

Key word

Melancholia is severe depressive illness.

Freud's analysis suggests that egoistic suicide is not really so much an act of free will as a delusion caused by the complexity of the human psyche. Most humans feel that suicide is a wasted life and make every attempt to dissuade someone from taking their own life.

3 Arguments against suicide

Traditionally Christianity has taught that suicide is an abrogation of one's duty to God to preserve life.

a) Suicide as an abrogation of duty to God

i) Suicide rejects God's redemption

Key question

What are the moral and religious objections to suicide?

Some Christians consider suicide to be a great sin because it rejects God's promise of life after death. In traditional Christian thought death is regarded as a punishment for sin and so to deliberately choose death rather than life is to turn down God's promise of salvation which is expressed through Jesus' resurrection and triumph over death (1 Corinthians 15:54).

Key word

Abrogation means to defy a rule, duty or law and therefore to abolish it.

Though not commented on explicitly, egoistic suicide is often seen as the result of **God's judgement**. King Saul dies by falling on his own sword (1 Samuel 31:4) having disobeyed God's laws (1 Samuel 13:8–15) and Jeremiah 8:3 sees suicide of the people as a consequence of having failed to keep to God's covenant (the special agreement between God and his people).

Key quote

'When the perishable puts on the imperishable, and the mortal puts on immortality, then shall come to pass the saying that is written, "Death is swallowed up in victory."'

ST PAUL'S LETTER,
1 CORINTHIANS 15:54

Key people

Augustine of Hippo (354–430) was born in Thagaste, North Africa, and studied at Carthage University. He taught rhetoric and philosophy in Rome and Milan and was much influenced by neo-Platonism. He converted to Christianity in 386, was ordained a priest in 391 and consecrated Bishop of Hippo in 395. His two great influential works are *The Confessions* (387) and *The City of God* (413–26).

Key word

A **mortal sin** in Catholic teaching is a deliberate and conscious rejection of God's grace and results in eternal damnation.

ii) Suicide is blasphemy

Augustine developed his argument against suicide because of his objections to men such as Tertullian who were actively encouraging martyrdom as a sign of faith in imitation of Christ's sacrificial death. Augustine uses Plato's argument against suicide to re-interpret Biblical texts. His argument from *The City of God* (1:17–27) is that:

> *For it is clear that if no one has the private right to kill even a guilty man (for no law allows this) then certainly anyone who kills himself is a murderer, and is the more guilty in killing himself the more innocent he is of the charge on which he has condemned himself to death.*
>
> (Augustine, *The City of God*, 1:17)

- Killing is condemned in the sixth of the Ten Commandments (Exodus 20:13): 'You shall not murder.'
- Self-killing is murder and doubly wrong because only executions may be carried out under the authority of the state/Church and suicide is a private act.
- Natural law states that a guilty man cannot condemn a guilty man or, if he is innocent, he cannot condemn an innocent man to death.
- An untimely death allows no time for repentance for the act of killing. Judas' suicide (Matthew 27:3–5) confirms that Judas was indeed a despicable person (having betrayed Christ).

> *We rightly abominate the act of Judas, and the judgement of truth is that when he hanged himself he did not atone for the guilt of his detestable betrayal but rather increased it, since he despaired of God's mercy and in a fit of self-destructive remorse left himself no chance of repentance.*
>
> (Augustine, *The City of God*, 1:17)

- Self-killing indicates a rejection of God's providence and love.
- Suicide is not a sign of bravery (as the Stoics claimed) or strength of spirit but weakness. This life is preparation for the next (as Plato argues in the *Phaedo*) and real strength of character comes when hardships have been endured.
- Suicide is a **mortal sin** because it rejects the grace of God.

By using Judas' example as the epitome of evil, suicide was equated with all those who had been instrumental in the death of Christ. Later church law followed Augustine's conclusion: a victim of suicide was treated as a heretic and could therefore not have Christian burial rites – even attempted suicides were excommunicated (Council of Toledo, 693). St Bruno called suicides or martyrs, 'martyrs for Satan'.

Augustine's argument still forms the heart of the official teaching of the Roman Catholic Church today but the condemnation of the suicide to eternal punishment is modified because of our better understanding of the psychological reasons that cause someone to take their own life.

> *Grave psychological disturbance, anguish or grave fear of hardship, suffering or torture can diminish the responsibility of the one committing suicide. We should not despair of the eternal salvation of persons who have taken their own lives. By ways known to him alone, God can provide the opportunity for salutary repentance. The Church prays for persons who have taken their own lives.*
>
> (*Catechism of the Catholic Church*, page 492)

Key quote

'By ways known to him alone, God can provide the opportunity for salutary repentance. The Church prays for persons who have taken their own lives.'

CATECHISM OF THE CATHOLIC CHURCH, PAGE 492

b) Suicide as a sign of human failure

The **existentialist** writer **Albert Camus** (1913–60) set out to consider whether killing oneself could be considered the greatest expression of human freedom and the fundamental question for all philosophers. His essay, *The Myth of Sisyphus* (1946), was written shortly after the end of the Second World War when many felt that the war had achieved freedom but at a huge cost in terms of human life. So many had died, so was life worth living? Camus re-tells the classical story of Sisyphus who is condemned to an eternity of hauling his stone in the underworld to the top of the mountain, where for a brief moment it hovers before rolling back to the bottom. The story considers that if life is essentially meaningless or **absurd**, then maybe the only option is suicide. But, Camus argues, it is in grappling with absurdity (i.e. the stone) that Sisyphus learns to enjoy and appreciate his predicament. It is by mastering the absurd that a person comes to appreciate true happiness by grasping **despair** and turning it into his *own* goal or fate. Suicide denies the creative freedom to master absurdity and be happy. Despair, rather than faith, reduces man to an unthinking thing, which he is not.

Key thoughts

Existentialism begins with the view that to live an authentic human existence we must act consciously and freely without imagining that our lives are predetermined in any way.

> *There is no sun without shadow, and it is essential to know the night. The absurd man says yes and his effort will henceforth be unceasing … For the rest, he knows himself to be the master of his days.*
>
> (Albert Camus, *Myth of Sisyphus*, page 110)

Camus' justification for rejecting suicide is a poetic humanism. His argument is mystical and depends on the poet's licence to personify absurdity as something almost objective and real. Camus' absurd world is without God but their acceptance of life and rejection of suicide in the end comes very close to traditional Christian theological thinking.

c) Suicide as defiance against moral law

Kant's secular version of the sanctity of life argued that suicide was wrong because it would be contrary to the universal duty (or **moral law**) to preserve life. Kant sets out his argument as follows:

A man reduced to despair by a series of misfortunes feels sick of life but is still so far in possession of his reason that he can ask himself whether taking his own life would not be contrary to his duty to himself. Now he asks whether the maxim of his action could become a universal law of nature. But the maxim is this:

from self-love I make as my principle to shorten my life when its continued duration threatens more evil than it promises satisfaction.

There only remains the question as to whether this principle of self-love can become a universal law of nature. One sees at once a contradiction in a system of nature whose law would destroy life by means of the very same feeling that acts so as to stimulate the furtherance of life, and hence there could be no existence as a system of nature. Therefore, such a maxim cannot possibly hold as a universal law of nature and is, consequently, wholly opposed to the supreme principle of all duty.

(Immanuel Kant, *Grounding for the Metaphysics of Morals*, l. 422 translation James W. Ellington, pages 30–31)

- Kant assumes *a priori* that a stable society in which members can be happy self-evidently depends on the duty to preserve life. A duty to kill oneself would therefore undermine the stability of society on which the duty to protect life depends.
- Rationally we know a law seeks to be consistent and universal (the **categorical imperative**). A selfish 'law' is neither consistent nor universal and so cannot be a law.
- Kant sets out the argument for suicide as a logical impossibility: from self-love I wish to abolish myself. If I love myself it is not possible to destroy the object of my love.
- Suicide is also contrary to the **practical imperative** never to treat people as a means to an end. If suicide treats oneself as a means of escape, it would clearly not be respecting self.

Despite the problems inherent in the categorical imperative, there is something psychologically persuasive in Kant's observation that suicide *does* undermine the stability of society (for example the effects on family and friends).

d) Suicide as moral pollution of society

Many philosophers have argued that suicide undermines the moral stability of society. In **virtue ethical** terms, suicide is not only cowardly but represents a breakdown in relationship between citizen and society.

- **Plato** (c.428–c.348BC) continued the line of thinking that he inherited from the Pythagorians and incorporated it into his notion of the soul. The soul has its origins with the gods and at birth dwells in the body until death, at which stage it is deemed

Key quote

'We must not put an end to ourselves until God sends us some compulsion like the one we are facing now.'

PLATO, *PHAEDO*, 61C–62D

pure enough to enter into oblivion or if, insufficiently worthy, is reborn into a new body. Suicide, therefore, is regarded as an act of defiance against the gods and the moral order. The analogy that is often repeated is that suicide is like a soldier who abandons his duty and deserts the battlefield.

- **Aristotle** (384–322BC) considered suicide in the context of the city or 'polis'. The individual exists not to perfect his soul for the after-life, as in Plato's philosophy, but to promote the common good. The primary end of man is to be happy in communion with others. Suicide therefore breaks two important aspects of civilised life. First, suicide pollutes the state not only as an act against the gods but also as a rejection of the laws of that city. Second, a city loses an economically valuable member of that society. The Aristotelian model of society may sound unduly cold and contractual, but it suggests an important principle in that the individual does not act alone in his moral decision making but must constantly consider the obligations he has to society and society to him.

e) Suicide as violation of the principle to protect innocent life

Aquinas' arguments in the *Summa Theologica* reinforce Augustine's position; however, in the context of justice and **natural law** Aquinas, in the natural law tradition, argued that suicide is wrong because it undermines the principle that it is intrinsically wrong to kill an innocent life. This position reinforces many of the arguments made above and forms an important aspect of current debates. Whereas we may argue for the right to life it does not follow that we also have a right to end our life. An innocent life is no threat to society and must therefore be protected.

Aquinas develops the argument by christianising Aristotle's observation that man's existence is to be part of a community. Suicide is not only breaking God's law but a tacit rejection of the natural justice of society.

- Suicide is wrong because it is against natural law. Natural law suggests that our natural will is 'to love and cherish oneself'. It is therefore a 'fatal sin against nature' to commit suicide.
- Suicide is injurious to society as a whole.
- Suicide wrongs God. Life is a gift from God who ultimately has control of life and death and we as the stewards of life have a duty to protect innocent life.

Key quote

'Because life is God's gift to man, and is subject to His power, who kills and makes to live. Hence whoever takes his own life, sins against God, even as he who kills another's slave, sins against that slave's master, and as he who usurps to himself judgment of a matter not entrusted to him.'

AQUINAS, SUMMA
THEOLOGICA 2.2,
Q. 64, ART. 5

4 Arguments for suicide

There are many arguments which support suicide because to condemn it would be assume that society has the right to judge a person's sinful intentions, or to impose unnecessary suffering or to limit autonomy.

a) Suicide is not a sin

The poet and theologian **John Donne** was one of the first to criticise traditional Christian teaching against suicide as a mortal sin. His argument in *Biathanatos* (1607–8) is based on the principle of **voluntarism** that as each person is responsible for his or her own decisions about their life they are equally responsible for decisions about their death. And so, if neither the state nor Church is able to judge all the motives which lead a person to make the decisions which make up their life, then there is no way in which they can condemn suicide to be a crime (against the state) or a mortal sin (in the judgement of the Church).

Donne is particularly sensitive to the state of mind which leads people to take their own lives.

- Not everyone who commits suicide has despaired of God's mercy; in fact it is because they trust in God's love and forgiveness that death is not a blasphemous act of defiance.
- Not all desperate acts are necessarily so sinful that they cannot be forgiven. Desperation is often caused by weakness and lack of control which God, who understands our motives better than the Church, is able to forgive.

b) Suicide as avoidance of unnecessary pain

For hedonic and welfare utilitarians suicide might be justified if pain becomes so acute that it outweighs any other pleasures. There may be other considerations to take into account such as the effects on family and friends but utilitarians consider that there is nothing intrinsically good or bad with suicide as such. Preference utilitarians might argue that suicide does not simply have to be justified on grounds of physical pain or welfare. A person might have other preferences such as the desire not to grow old or that life does not hold any interest for them any more.

c) Suicide as exercise of autonomy

David Hume's essay 'Of Suicide' (1784) reinforces the view that if I am the owner of my life then I have the right and autonomy to dispose of it as I wish. Hume's argument provides the basis for the liberal view expressed by J.S. Mill that 'over himself, over his own body and mind the individual is sovereign'.

Hume's moral philosophy is likewise motivated in the most general terms by a sense of **general benevolence** (or what he called 'sympathy') and a tolerance of traditions and customs providing these do not impinge unduly on the freedom of the individual.

Key question

How can suicide be morally and religiously defended?

Key people

John Donne (1572–1631) was brought up a Roman Catholic but later converted to Anglicanism, was ordained a priest and was later appointed Dean of St Paul's Cathedral, London.

Key quote

'Self-homicide is not so naturally sin, that it may never be otherwise.'

JOHN DONNE, *BIATHANATOS*

Key people

David Hume (1711–76) was one of the most important philosophers of the eighteenth century. He was born in Edinburgh and educated at a time when Isaac Newton's natural science and John Locke's philosophy were influential in Scottish universities. He was sceptical of religion but was also aware of the limits of reason. His essay 'Of Suicide' was published after his death.

Cross-references

Hume's essay 'Of Suicide' may be found in Peter Singer, *Applied Ethics*, Chapter II.

Read pages 17–18 above for a fuller discussion of Mill's liberalism.

Key quote

'Has not every one of consequence, the free disposal of his own life?'

DAVID HUME,
'OF SUICIDE' (1784)

'But the life of a man is of no greater importance to the universe than that of an oyster.'

DAVID HUME, 'OF SUICIDE'

Key quote

'A man who retires from life, does no harm to society: He only ceases to do good ... Why may I not cut short these miseries at once by an action which is no more prejudicial to society?'

DAVID HUME, 'OF SUICIDE'

Hume's precise logic and powerful prose cut away the arguments to the basics so that wherever he saw excess moral restriction he sought to reduce its influence.

His essay argues:

- The argument against suicide based on **natural law** is false. **Nature gives** a number of conflicting imperatives, which humans mistakenly take to indicate what is the right way of behaving. Besides often giving contradictory commands there is also a philosophical error. Those who do so commit a **category mistake**, that is, of confusing **first order** observations of fact (nature) with **second order** judgements of value (morals). As morality cannot be derived from nature, then there is no intrinsic reason to value a human life over any other part of nature. As Hume provocatively put it: 'But the life of a man is of no greater importance to the universe than that of an oyster.'

- The argument from **revealed law** or religion is of very little help. God's will cannot be known by reason. If God acts in the world then everything that happens is God's will, in which case morally we are no better off (because nature is contradictory). Alternatively God does not act in the world, in which case his existence is of little concern to us. So, as Hume argues: 'When I fall upon my sword, therefore, I receive my death equally from the hands of the Deity as if it had proceeded from a lion, a precipice, or a fever.'

- The argument that suicide corrupts society is false. Morality is mostly a question of **social contract**. Hume noted that most social customs evolved from the complex relations surrounding ownership of property. Morality is therefore essentially a process of negotiation. So, if a person chooses to end their life, he does not corrupt society, he merely fails to contribute to it.

Here we have an antithesis to Aristotle's social obligation of the individual to the state, a denial of Plato's rejection of egoist suicide and a repudiation of the Christian teaching of suicide as a mortal sin. Hume was quite conscious that his essay was a response to all these traditions and an echo of another equally fluent advocate of suicide, **Seneca** (4BC–AD65). The significance of suicide for Hume and Seneca is that, more than anything else, it is the one act where the individual can decisively exercise his autonomy.

Hume concludes his essay:

Why may I not cut short these miseries at once by an action which is no more prejudicial to society? That suicide may often be consistent with interest and with our duty to ourselves, no one can question, who allows that age, sickness, or misfortune may render life a burden, and make it worse even than annihilation. I believe that no man ever threw away life, while it was worth keeping. For such is our natural horror of death that small motives will never be able to reconcile us to it … If suicide be a supposed crime, 'tis only cowardice can impel us to it.

(David Hume, 'Of Suicide')

d) Altruistic suicide as virtue

Altruistic suicide in particular illustrates that not all forms of suicide are the same. Although in general the Greek philosophers condemned suicide because it was regarded as a treacherous act against the state and equated with the same moral outrage as killing a member of the family, other forms of suicide were commended as being acts of virtue. Homer included it as an act of heroism. Maximilian Kolbe's gesture in the concentration camp was an example of Christian agape or generous love.

In the New Testament Jesus commends the person who lays down his life for his friends as the greatest act of love. Likewise in war we may commend the soldier who defends his comrades knowing he himself will be killed as a result.

- **Plato**'s view was greatly modified by the death of **Socrates**, his philosophy master and teacher. Socrates had been condemned to death by the state for corrupting the morals of young Athenians. He was allowed by way of mitigation to take his own life. Socrates' death therefore was not an act of defiance against the gods but on the contrary the death of a man who died *because* of his moral integrity and his belief in the truth. So, without actually calling it altruistic suicide, Plato permitted self-death in cases where the individual had displayed a selfless act of moral virtue and not as an easy means to escape a difficult situation.
- In the **Bible**, altruistic death, a death out of love or **agape** for others, is, on the other hand, commended as the supreme act of faith for others. The writer of Hebrews (11:32–38) cites the death of Samson in the Old Testament (Judges 16:23ff) as a great act of faith. Samson had used his great strength to pull down the building he was chained to, killing himself and his enemy, the Philistines. His action was in response to God's will over Dagon, the pagan god of the Philistines.
- **Augustine** does not condemn *all* suicide. In the cases cited so far what he rejects is martyrdom for self-glory, or escape from persecution, i.e. egoistic suicide. At the end of his discussion on suicide in *The City of God* he writes that some like Samson may have 'acted on divine instruction and not through human mistake – not in error, but obedience'. In other words Augustine, like Plato, accepts that in some cases self-killing *is* the mark of a very great person because of their altruism and obedience to God.

Key quote

'Greater love has no man than this, that a man lay down his life for his friends.'

GOSPEL OF JOHN 15:13

Key word

Agape is the Greek word sometimes used in the New Testament to mean generous, sacrificial love.

5 Paternalism

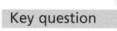

Key question

Is it right to stop someone
attempting suicide?

Because all forms of suicide are irreversible then many feel that there
are good reasons why we should interfere with a person's decision to
kill themselves and at least make them consider again the
consequences of their actions. But to what extent may we interfere in
a person's autonomy for their own best interests? Those who support
a quality of life view and rate autonomy highly might nevertheless
want to make sure that a person is fully informed and rational in their
decision, whilst those who consider that human dignity is based on
the sanctity of life might have to decide whether in some cases it
would be wrong to interfere with a person's decision.

Paternalism is often used in two senses. In its positive usage
paternalism justifies overriding or interfering with someone's
autonomy for their best interests. But in its negative use opponents
of paternalism argue that interfering in a person's rational decision is
disrespecting their autonomy and dignity.

There are two major considerations which paternalism raises:

- How does one decide what is in a person's best interests?
- How does one decide whether a person (who wishes to die or is
  willing to risk their life) is acting rationally?

This issue is particularly important when it comes to consider
whether a very sick child should be allowed to die or whether a
sick adult who wants to die should be allowed to do so. These cases
are discussed further in Chapter 4 on euthanasia.

However, supposing the situation was less obviously extreme but
still potentially very dangerous to personal welfare; what reasons
would there be to interfere? For example Nigel Warburton argues
that even though boxing is very dangerous this is not sufficient
reason to ban the sport. To do so would be to act in an
unnecessarily officious paternalistic manner.

The British Medical Association (BMA) argue that boxing should
be banned because:

- boxing causes chronic damage to the brain leading eventually to
  dementia or 'punch drunk syndrome'
- boxers intend to cause injury; causing deliberate harm is morally
  offensive and dehumanising
- it is in people's best interests not be placed in situations of great
  risk to health and life
- paternalism is justified.

Cross-reference

Nigel Warburton, 'The Freedom to
Box', in *Journal of Medical Ethics*,
volume 24; also in Nigel
Warburton, *Philosophy: Basic
Readings*, pages 192–201.

Case study
The case for and against boxing

Nigel Warburton makes a case for allowing adults to take part in risky and potentially lethal activities on the grounds that on balance it is better to let adults make up their own minds what they want to do than to act paternalistically. He argues against the British Medical Association that boxing should not be made a criminal offence.

Key quote

'If the BMA is principally concerned to minimise harmful injuries, then it must at least address the possibility that the proposed ban on sport, if implemented, could make matters considerably worse than they are now.'

NIGEL WARBURTON,
'THE FREEDOM TO
BOX', IN *PHILOSOPHY:
BASIC READINGS*, PAGE 200

Key thought

The **companions in guilt** move is intended to show the weakness of someone's argument by demonstrating that if they wish to be consistent their argument would logically condemn other cases which they wish to defend.

Warburton argues that boxing should not be banned because:

- provided that an adult boxer gives informed consent and knows the risks, then a liberal society should allow adults to choose – even if they choose badly
- causing deliberate harm to one's self may be offensive but it is not clear why it should follow that this is dehumanising. As intentions are very difficult to measure it is better to consider the consequences of action
- if the BMA's argument is accepted then they would have to accept other **companions in guilt** (e.g. motor sports, rugby, horse riding) in which many people are harmed or killed each year but yet are not banned from participating in these activities. To be consistent the BMA would also have to make smoking and heavy drinking (for example) a criminal offence and to do so would make society worse off
- paternalism is not justified.

Summary diagram

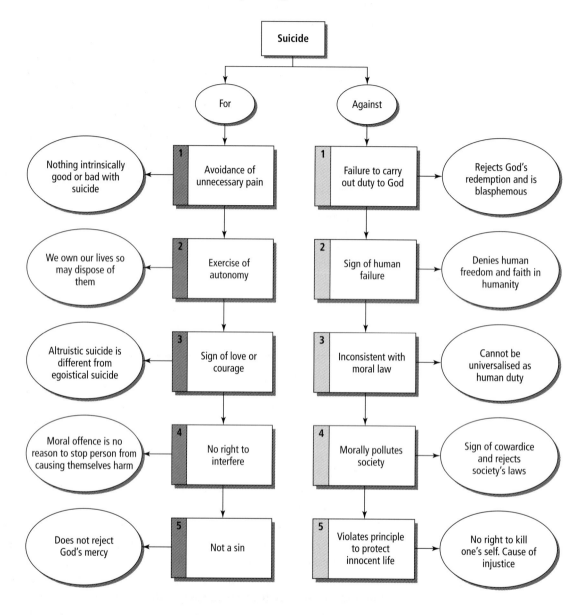

Study guide

By the end of this chapter you should have considered why both religious and non-religious thinkers consider that suicide is morally wrong. You should know Augustine's argument that suicide is a mortal sin and Plato and Aristotle's view that suicide is a cowardly corrupting of society's values. You should be able to contrast these views with David Hume's detailed reasoning why suicide is not against natural law or the will of God, nor does it break a person's obligation to society. Finally, you should be able to discuss Mill's liberal principle and consider whether the principle of autonomy permits someone to risk harming their own life without interference from others.

Revision checklist ✓

Can you explain what the following argue for and against suicide:

- Plato
- Augustine
- Aquinas
- Kant
- Freud
- Camus
- Hume
- Donne.

Can you define:

- paternalism
- mortal sin
- category mistake
- altruistic suicide.

Can you give arguments for and against the view that suicide:

- is a matter of personal autonomy
- is always blasphemous
- is a sign that society has failed in its duties to its members.

Essay question

1) Assess the view that there is intrinsically nothing wrong with suicide.

The essay could begin by considering those who would support this view. It could outline the argument of David Hume and the reasons why suicide is neither defiance of God's will (his example of the falling stone), or against nature (his example of a flooding river) or pollution of society (our relationship with society is a human contract). As he considers that our lives are intrinsically worth no more or less than an oyster, value is gained by what we do, not what we are. Mill's autonomy view could then be used to justify suicide on the grounds that the exercising of autonomy enables us to live worthwhile lives, even if that means choosing to die.

The evaluative aspect of the essay might begin with an analysis of Hume. His argument against natural law treats all nature as 'natural', whereas natural law distinguishes between human purpose or *telos* and the rest of nature. Living well as a human means living according to reason and, according to Aquinas, as the natural will is 'to love and cherish oneself' and enable society to flourish, suicide is an intrinsic wrong. Furthermore, Camus' existential approach suggests that Hume is wrong; suicide is wrong because it always is cowardly. Augustine's argument might be used to question Hume's misrepresentation of God. Augustine might be contrasted with John Donne's teaching on sin and God's mercy.

Further essay questions

2a   Explain the Christian teaching on suicide.
2b   'Christian teaching on suicide is too harsh.' Discuss.

3a   Explain David Hume's argument for suicide.
3b   Assess the view that participating in very dangerous sports is entirely a matter of personal choice.

4   'Suicide is either the greatest heroic act a person can perform or the most miserable and selfish.' Discuss.

Chapter checklist ✓

This chapter considers whether having a child is a right or a gift. However, if it is a mother's right to have a child is it equally her right to terminate a pregnancy if she wishes? Abortion is discussed with reference to a woman's right to privacy, autonomy, the abortion pill and the problem of when a foetus becomes a person with rights. The problem of 'hard cases' such as rape, pregnancy as a threat to a mother's life and handicap or disability are discussed. Several normative ethical systems and their views on abortion are considered.

1 Women's autonomy and rights

Case study
Two cases of abortion

In 1962 a patient in a state mental hospital raped a fellow patient, an unmarried girl ill with a radical schizophrenic psychosis. The victim's father, learning what had happened, charged the hospital with culpable negligence and requested that an abortion to end an unwanted pregnancy be performed at once, in an early stage of the embryo. The staff and administrators of the hospital refused to do so, on the ground that the criminal law forbids all abortion except 'therapeutic' ones when the mother's life is at stake – because the moral law, it is supposed, holds that any interference with an embryo after fertilisation is murder, i.e. the taking of an innocent human being's life ...

Even self-defence legalism would have allowed the girl to kill her attacker, no matter that he was innocent in the forum of conscience because of his madness. The embryo is no more innocent, no less an aggressor or unwelcome invader! Is not the most loving thing possible (the right thing) in this case a responsible decision to terminate the pregnancy?

(Joseph Fletcher, *Situation Ethics*, pages 37–39)

> *The abortion debate intensified yesterday when the Rev. Joanna Jepson failed in her attempt to bring criminal charges against two doctors involved in a 'late' abortion on an unborn child with a cleft lip and palate.*
>
> *The Crown Prosecution Service said it was satisfied that the doctors involved in the abortion on a woman more than 24 weeks pregnant had acted in good faith and there would be no prosecution. The CPS inquiry into the case in Herefordshire reopened after a judicial review sought by Miss Jepson, 28, who had a successful operation on a jaw deformity and whose brother has Down's syndrome.*
>
> (*Daily Telegraph*, 17 March 2005)

In both of these cases abortion could be seen as a solution to a social problem. But are the moral reasons equally weighted and equally persuasive? What, if anything, does it say about a society that allows abortion for a cleft lip and another society that refuses abortion even though a schizophrenic girl was raped?

Key quote

'We should stop seeing abortion as a problem and start seeing it as a legitimate and sensible solution to the problem of unwanted pregnancy.'

ANN FUREDI, BRITISH PREGNANCY ADVISORY SERVICE

In 2006 the abortion rate rose 3.9 per cent to 18.3 per 1000 women aged 15 to 44, the highest recorded in England and Wales. In other words 193,700 women resident in England and Wales had an abortion in 2006, compared to 185,415 in 2004. Ann Furedi's response, recorded in *The Times*, is typical of those who see the issue primarily in terms of a woman's right to choose whether she wishes to have a baby or not.

> *'Women today want to plan their families and, when contraception fails, they are prepared to use abortion to get back in control of their lives,' Ms Furedi (British Pregnancy Advisory Service) said. 'Motherhood is just one among many options open to women and it is not surprising that younger women want to prioritise other things. We should stop seeing abortion as a problem and start seeing it as a legitimate and sensible solution to the problem of unwanted pregnancy.'*
>
> ('Abortions soar as careers come first', *The Times*, 28 July 2005)

Key question

Consider the feminist philosopher Ellen Willis' key question: '*Can it be moral, under any circumstances, to make a woman bear a child against her will?*'

VILLAGE VOICE (16 JULY 1985, PAGE 15)

For many women abortion is more than just a debate about the status of the foetus but rather about the place of women in society and their ability to determine the kinds of lives they wish to live. Ellen Willis' answer to her question is that until women have the same autonomy as men the answer is that it is always wrong to make a woman have a baby against her will. Nevertheless, not all feminists think the same and many have to grapple with the view that the unborn child may also have rights as well. The question, therefore, is how to balance these against the rights of women.

a) Foetus' right to life v. woman's right to bodily integrity

THE HENLEY COLLEGE LIBRARY

Key people

Judith Jarvis Thomson (b. 1929) is an American philosopher who taught at the Massachusetts Institute of Technology (MIT).

One of the most influential arguments is by the philosopher **Judith Jarvis Thomson**'s 'A Defence of Abortion' (1971). Her argument focuses primarily on rape cases or faulty contraception where a woman finds herself pregnant against her will. In her famous thought exercise of the unconscious violinist Thomson sets herself the harder task of assuming that the foetus is a person, even if he or she is unconscious.

Case study

But now let me ask you to imagine this. You wake up in the morning and find yourself back to back in bed with an unconscious violinist. He has been found to have a fatal kidney ailment, and the Society of Music Lovers has canvassed all the available medical records and found that you alone have the right blood type to help. They have therefore kidnapped you, and last night the violinist's circulatory system was plugged into yours, so that your kidneys can be used to extract poisons from his blood as well as your own. The director of the hospital now tells you, 'Look, we're sorry, the Society of Music Lovers did this to you — we would never have permitted it if we had known. But still, they did it, and the violinist now is plugged into you. To unplug him would be to kill him. But never mind, it's only for nine months. By then he will have recovered from

> *his ailment, and can safely be unplugged from you.' Is it*
> *morally incumbent on you to accede the situation?*
> (Judith Jarvis Thomson, 'A Defence of Abortion',
> reprinted in Peter Singer [editor], *Applied Ethics*, pages 38–39)

Thomson argues that:

- A woman **owns** her body, in the same way that we might say she owns her own house or owns her own life. Therefore, as a woman has a *prior* claim to her body before pregnancy, she may remove the foetus any time she wants.
- An unwanted pregnancy poses an enormous strain on a woman's body. She is entitled to some form of **self-defence** even if this means the 'direct killing' of an innocent party.
- Foetal rights and the mother's rights **are not equal**. The foetus does have rights but they cannot be equivalent to the mother, even though the foetus is innocent. The mother and foetus are not two tenants in the same house rented by both. The foetus is using the mother's body and therefore has tenant's rights, not ownership rights. She may choose to acknowledge the rights of the foetus but she is not compelled to do so. Having a right to life does not give one a right to use someone else's body.
- There is no law or **prima facie duty** that **compels the woman to be a good Samaritan**, especially at her own expense. It may of course be *prima facie* wrong for a woman to abort having had voluntary intercourse, but not necessarily a breach of her rights.

Key word

Prima facie duties were developed as an idea by W.D. Ross (1877–1971) to mean that some duties can be overridden by a stronger moral duty according to situation. *Prima facie* means literally 'on first appearance'.

b) A woman's *prima facie* right to privacy

The problem with Thomson's argument is that, although it may justify foetal *extractions*, it does not necessarily justify foetal *extinctions*. Other feminists argue therefore that the issue is not so much about body integrity but a woman's *prima facie* right to privacy to decide on her own and her unborn foetus' best interests; that will usually mean the death of the foetus.

Christine Overall (*Human Reproduction: Principles, Practices and Policies*, 1993) argues that it is morally wrong not to respect the private wishes of the mother even if she wishes to kill the foetus. Her argument is:

- keeping the foetus alive against the mother's wish violates the **reproductive autonomy** of the mother; she has a right to break her genetic obligations to the foetus as well as her social duties
- the mother's genetic relationship to the foetus makes her the most appropriate person to decide on its best interests – and that will usually result in death

- making her keep the foetus would be like compelling her to give up one of her organs against her will; there is nothing to justify an intrusion into her privacy of this kind
- removing her right to decide on the fate of the foetus is another example of a patriarchal society which treats women as being incapable of deciding on their own reproductive status.

c) Early abortions and RU-486

Many of the arguments above apply to later abortions where the status of the foetus is more contentious. So the prospect of using the 'abortion pill' **RU-486** for early abortions is attractive.

Its chief advantages are that it:

- is less traumatic than surgery
- is available to more women; women don't have to travel so far to a clinic
- is less expensive than other forms of abortion
- leaves women more in control of the process
- is private and out of the gaze of anti-abortionists.

But it has not met with complete favour. Some argue that in fact by making abortion too easily available that it actually reduces women's autonomy. Many women feel that the pressure from pro-choice groups is to have an abortion rather than to be a mother. Real choice would mean providing the support of having a child without feeling that this has betrayed other women who want an abortion.

Finally some consider that the relative privacy of RU-486 hides the problem of unwanted pregnancy from men. As the process is hidden from them it trivialises the significance and possible trauma which an abortion entails, leaving a woman more isolated and less able to ask for help.

2 The personhood problem

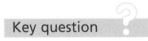

Key question

To what extent do you agree with this headline: 'This foetus is 20 weeks old and can be legally aborted ... some scientists say she should have a painkiller first.'

DAILY TELEGRAPH,
OCTOBER 2000

For many people the abortion issue hinges on one important issue and that is establishing whether or not the foetus is a person. Once it can be established that the foetus is a person then it becomes entitled to the same **basic rights** of protection as any other person. If the foetus is not a person the abortion issue focuses on other contingent factors such as the psychological effects on the mother (and others) rather than on the foetus itself.

As we have seen in Chapter 2, the personhood problem also **begs the question**: what is a person? For those who argue for an **enduring self** the question is at what stage the foetus acquires a

1–4 weeks

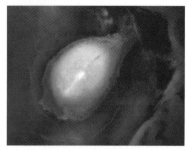

Embryo approximately 3–4 mm long. Basic heart. Spinal column beginning to develop.

5–8 weeks

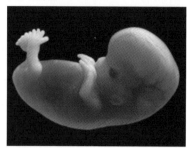

Embryo approximately 10 mm long. Limb buds grow into hands and feet.

9–12 weeks

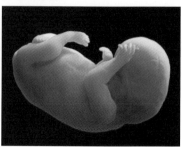

Arms close to reaching final proportion. External sex organs clearly developed.

13–16 weeks

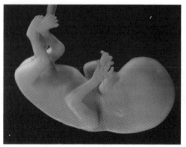

Foetus approximately 14 cm long. Muscles and bones strengthen. Unique fingerprints form.

17–20 weeks

Foetus weighs up to 240 g. Rapid growth of brain functions. Mother may feel foetus' movements.

21–24 weeks

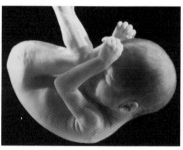

Foetus weighs more than 500 g. As bones and ears develop the foetus can recognise maternal sounds.

The foetal developmental stages from conception to full term.

Key word

Begging the question is when the conclusion is implied in one of the premises of the question. Often an argument which begs the question has failed to give a convincing case for the conclusion.

Key quote

'Human life must be respected and protected absolutely from the moment of conception. From the first moment of his existence a human being must be recognised as having the rights of a person – among which is the inviolable right of every innocent being to life.'

CATECHISM OF THE CATHOLIC CHURCH (1994), PAGE 489

soul, and for those such as Locke and others who consider that the term 'person' refers to a **bundle** of characteristics, the question focuses on when the foetus has acquired sufficient of these characteristics to be treated as a person.

a) Ensoulment at conception

Ensoulment at conception is supported by those who take a vitalist view of life. The attractiveness of this position is that, as soon as conception takes place, what is created genetically could only be a member of *homo sapiens* and nothing else. For those, such as the Roman Catholic Church, who hold a natural law moral position, the life now formed is **innocent** and must be protected absolutely from the moment of conception. Conservative Christians also argue for ensoulment at conception based on biblical texts such as Psalm 139:13–16 and Jeremiah 20:16–18 where the writers speak of the special status of the foetus in the womb as created by God.

b) Delayed ensoulment

Key quote

*'For you created my inmost being:
you knit me together in my
mother's womb. I praise you
because I am fearfully and
wonderfully made.'*

PSALM 139:13–14

Delayed ensoulment (or progressive ensoulment) is supported by
those who may still hold a vitalist position but who do not consider
conception to be the moment of ensoulment. Aquinas' argument
developed Aristotle's view that the foetus only acquires an
intellectual soul once the vegetative and animal aspects of soul are
fully developed, that is, at 40 days for boys and 90 days for girls.
Although Aristotle and Aquinas were guessing as to when
biologically the foetus acquired a soul, the notion of a delayed
ensoulment is attractive to those who consider that there has to be
more to a person than a few cells to support the functioning of the
self (or soul). But the problem with this view (as much as it is for
those who hold the 'bundle' view of self) in modern terms is to
determine when, in biological terms, a 'soul' could emerge or be
supported.

Cross-reference

Read pages 4–7 above on
Aquinas' and Aristotle's view of
personhood.

c) Primitive streak

Up to 14 days it is possible for **monozygotic twins** to develop and
the **primitive streak** is then discernible. After this stage the foetus or
foetuses develop **individually**. Some have referred to the foetus before
this stage as the **pre-embryo** and in law experimentations are
permitted to take place up to the fourteenth day.

However, some argue that although one or more persons emerge
after 14 days this doesn't mean to say that before this stage there is
no person. The Society for the Protection of Unborn Children
concludes:

Key thought

The **primitive streak** later forms
the spinal cord.

Monozygotic twins are twins
who are genetically *almost
identical* as they have developed
from the same egg and sperm.

> *…if one body can become two, we should therefore have no difficulty in
> accepting that one soul can become two.*
>
> (SPUC, *Love Your Unborn Neighbour*, page 98)

d) Brain activity

Key people

**The Society for the Protection
of Unborn Children** (SPUC) is a
pro-life and anti-abortion
organisation and pressure group.
Their aim is 'To affirm, defend and
promote the existence and value
of human life from the moment of
conception, and to defend and
protect human life generally'.

Brain activity is important both for those who support delayed
ensoulment and those such as Locke who consider consciousness as
the essential characteristic of persons. The attractiveness of selecting
brain activity as the start of life is that it not only uses the **cognitive
criterion** as the start of life but that it can also be used as the
criterion to determine the end of life. The problem here is whether
brain activity has to be continuous or whether life begins at the first
spasmodic moment. Spasmodic brain activity occurs at 54 days,
continuous brain function at 32 weeks. Less certain is whether brain
activity is in any sense conscious and whether or not the foetus can
feel pain. Some argue for a minimal case that it marks the first phase
in consciousness, in the same way that a person could later fall into a
coma and then recover.

e) Viability and birth

Viability refers to the ability of the foetus or baby to become self-sufficient outside the womb. The older term 'quickening' was used to refer to the movement of the baby in the womb as a person but today the issue of viability has become a crucial one to determine the upper limit of abortion in legislation. At present UK law sets the upper limit for abortion at 24 weeks. The problem is that if modern neo-natal medicine is good enough to treat a baby of twenty weeks and enable it to survive then how is its status any different from a baby whose life is to be terminated? But viability is an elastic term: it could also refer to any stage after birth, when the baby is not directly dependent on its mother, or to a stage when it could make decisions for itself.

Michael Tooley and **Peter Singer** both follow Locke's position of personhood and argue that the developmental process of the child is still so limited at this stage by any reasonable definition of what a person is that many animals such as chimpanzees display *more* developed characteristics of being a person than the new-born human. On these grounds infanticide will of course be wrong to those who would *prefer* the child not to die. But as the child itself displays no particular preferences whether to live or die (especially in severely handicapped cases) then direct and intentional killing of babies is not an intrinsic wrong.

Finally viability might be expressed in terms of a child being able to have a reasonable **quality of life**. So a baby which is severely handicapped or severely diseased might be considered not to have a viable life, in which case abortion would be a reasonable decision.

Cross-reference

Read page 5 above on Locke's view of personhood.

Key quote

'An organism possesses a serious right to life only if it possesses the concept of a self as a continuing subject of experiences and other mental states, and believes that it is itself such a continuing entity.'

MICHAEL TOOLEY,
'ABORTION AND INFANTICIDE',
IN PETER SINGER (EDITOR) ,
APPLIED ETHICS, PAGE 82

3 The law and abortion

Key question

Should all abortions be available on demand? Is there a need to regulate abortion by law?

Key thought

Therapeutic abortion refers to abortion on health grounds and not for some other reason.

According to J.S. Mill's liberal principle, the law and the state should not interfere with private morality. As we have seen, many argue that abortion is essentially a private affair but, contrary to what many people may think, abortion is not available on demand in the UK. The law as it has evolved implicitly recognises the need to protect the life of the foetus but equally tries to balance this against harm done to the mother and existing children.

The **1967 Abortion Act** remains the foundation of the law but an important modification in 1990 resulted in two changes. First, the upper limit was reduced from 28 to 24 weeks (on the basis that many foetuses were being aborted alive at 28 weeks) for most **therapeutic abortions** and, second the implied sanctity of the baby's life was undermined by the change which permitted abortion of any handicapped child up to the moment of birth.

The law in the USA was established by the landmark **Roe v. Wade** case in 1973. From 1965 the Supreme Court had already agreed to personal liberty in the use of contraception and the same principle was upheld in the case of abortion. However, the right of the woman had to be weighed against the rights of the foetus that increased as the foetus developed, having a 'gradient view of personhood'. For legal reasons viability (when the foetus is 'potentially able to live outside the womb', i.e. between 24 and 28 weeks) was drawn as a line after which individual states could if they wished make abortion illegal. The law was modified by the Supreme Court in 1992 (after the *Planned Parenthood* v. *Casey* case) to allow greater freedom for a woman to decide whether to terminate her pregnancy before viability (which a doctor has to assess in each individual case).

a) Abortion law in the UK

Grounds for Abortion 1967 Abortion Act and amended under section 37 of the Human Fertilisation and Embryology Act 1990

A   The continuance of the pregnancy would involve risk to the life of the pregnant woman greater than if the pregnancy were terminated;

B   The termination is necessary to prevent grave permanent injury to the physical or mental health of the pregnant woman;

*C The continuation of the pregnancy would involve risk greater than if the pregnancy were terminated, of injury to the physical or mental health of the pregnant woman;

*D The continuance of the pregnancy would involve risk, greater than if the pregnancy were terminated, of injury to the physical or mental health of any existing child(ren) of the family of the pregnant woman;

E   There is substantial risk that if the child were born it would suffer from such physical or mental abnormalities as to be seriously handicapped; or in an emergency:

F   To save the life of the pregnant woman; or

G   To prevent grave permanent injury to the physical or mental health of the pregnant woman.

- *Grounds C and D may take place up to 24 weeks. All other grounds are without time limit.
- Two doctors must give their assent to permit a doctor to carry out the abortion.
- A conscience clause permits a doctor to refuse to be involved with an abortion.

b) Abortion statistics

Abortion Statistics, England and Wales: 2006

- the total number of abortions was 193,700, compared with 186,400 in 2005, a rise of 3.9%
- the age-standardised abortion rate was 18.3 per 1,000 resident women aged 15-44, compared with 17.8 in 2005
- the abortion rate was highest at 35 per 1,000, for women aged 19
- the under-16 abortion rate was 3.9 and the under-18 rate was 18.2 per 1,000 women, both higher than in 2005
- 87% of abortions were funded by the NHS; of these, just over half (55%) took place in the independent sector under NHS contract
- 89% of abortions were carried out at under 13 weeks gestation; 68% were at under 10 weeks
- medical abortions accounted for 30% of the total compared with 24% in 2005
- 2,000 abortions (1%) were on Grounds E, i.e. risk that the child would be born handicapped.

(Source: Department of Health (issued 19 June 2007), Bulletin 2007/01, www.dh.gov.uk/en/Publicationsandstatistics/Publications/PublicationsStatistics/DH_075697)

4 Hard cases

Both the pro-choice and the pro-life groups have a common premise that 'every child is a wanted child'. Both agree that there is nothing worse than bringing a child into the world who is unwanted, unloved or rejected. But after that initial agreement the extremes of each viewpoint diverge. The strong sanctity of life *a priori* is that as all life is wanted no direct abortion is possible, whereas supporters of the quality of life position tend to favour the autonomy of the woman in making the best decision.

However, both pro-life and pro-choice are faced by a number of hard cases which test the limit of each position. Some of these cases suggest to the supporters of the sanctity of life viewpoint that there might have to be exceptions to the rule; and for those who advocate a quality of life position hard cases test the degree to which autonomy is the only major factor.

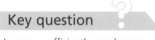

Key question

Is rape a sufficiently good reason for abortion?

a) Rape

It was the rape by British soldiers of a young girl in 1938 which justified Dr Aleck Bourne in carrying out an illegal abortion in order to safeguard her mental health. At the trial he was acquitted.

The precedent established grounds for abortion as an exception and eventually became the basis of the UK 1967 Abortion Act. In the famous case of *Roe* v. *Wade* (USA, 1973), 'Roe' (whose real name was Norma McCorvey) claimed she had been gang raped and, suffering from suicidal feelings, requested an abortion. The decision of the Supreme Court of the USA to allow the abortion effectively liberalised all US federal abortion laws.

i) Arguments for abortion due to rape

- A very common argument from those who take a broadly **utilitarian/consequentialist** line is that continuing with a pregnancy due to rape will not only continue the trauma for the mother but the quality of life for her existing family. Furthermore it might also be argued that any child of rape might also suffer the trauma of learning of his violent origins. Dealing with a rape in its early days where it is believed that the development of the foetus is not yet an actual person presents fewer problems. Even a late abortion might be justified because the complex emotions caused by rape may take time to resolve.

- Those who hold a **weak sanctity of life** position often argue that although abortion is undesirable, existing life has sometimes to take priority over early human life. The Church of England's report (*Abortion: An Ethical Discussion*, 1965) sees rape in the context of the existing family. The Christian principle of love cannot insist that a woman must have a child at all costs; love also judges the context of the situation. Abortion is not without its own pain and those who pursue it consider it as an act of sacrificial love.

- **Judith Jarvis Thomson**'s ('A Defence of Abortion', 1971) argument justifies a woman who is pregnant through rape (or unplanned pregnancy) having an abortion primarily on the grounds of ownership **rights** over her body. Thomson argues that a woman has a right to **self-defence** on the grounds that the strain on the woman's body warrants 'direct killing' of an innocent party. As the **owner** of her body she has a *prior* claim to her 'property' and can remove the foetus at any time. Even though the foetus may have rights, the woman has **priority of rights**; the possible rights of the foetus are always less than hers because he is *using* her. Any rights the foetus has are only possible if she chooses to acknowledge them. She may on the other hand choose to ignore them. The foetus can have no right to claim her unless she has **consented fully**. Finally there is no law which compels us or her to be a good Samaritan, especially at our own expense. The woman might wish to help

Key word

Consequentialists argue that an action is right if it has good results regardless of motive.

Cross-reference

Read pages 43–44 for Thomson's example of the violinist and the kidnapped man.

the foetus but if the sacrifice is too much then abortion is a justified option.

ii) Arguments against abortion due to rape

But in all these justifications that consider the foetus as a person the objection is that the foetus is still being killed directly or indirectly. The objections to rape as a legitimate ground for abortion include:

- In almost every consideration above, abortion was justified in terms of the mental health of the mother. In other words, it was no more than her preference not to continue with the pregnancy. For many this is the **slippery slope** where all exceptions lead, and will result in **abortion on demand**.
- Consequential arguments often fail to take into account the psychological damage that abortion can cause to the mother. Some argue that although the short-term consequences of an abortion may help, the ensuing guilt caused by killing the baby adds to the initial trauma of the rape. The evidence here is difficult to assess on both sides – there are those who claim that abortion reduces the pain of rape. SPUC, for instance, argues from the Christian strong sanctity of life perspective that by having the child good may come out of bad through a woman's 'courageous and generous commitment to life' (*Love Your Unborn Neighbour*, page 58).
- It is very difficult to imagine a case where one would be justified expelling an innocent person from one's **property** if this resulted in death. Furthermore the argument is distasteful to some feminist writers who object to the de-personalising of the woman's body as 'property'.
- Abortion as a form of **self-defence** assumes that the foetus has evil intentions. Rape *may* result in a life-threatening situation, but the foetus itself does not have malevolent intentions. If anyone is to blame it is the rapist not the foetus.
- Whilst it may be acknowledged that the foetus cannot have the same **rights** as a fully grown and responsible adult and also that a woman cannot be expected to rear the child unless she wishes to, her rights do not include the right to kill an innocent child. She may have to carry the child for some time but it can then be passed on for adoption at birth or earlier through extraction.

b) Handicap

Many pregnant women undergo as a matter of course amniocentesis tests, which show if the foetus has a chromosome abnormality (e.g. in the cases of spina bifida or Down's syndrome). In almost every

Key thought

Although the term handicap is used in law, the preferred term by many is disabled.

Key question

Is it right to allow an abortion even for full-term babies if they are handicapped?

Key quote

'When we do that [i.e. assume animals have rights], however, we will not be able to avoid noticing that, if we set the standard anywhere above the bare possession of life itself, some human beings will fail to meet it. Then it will become very difficult to continue to maintain that these humans have a right to life, while simultaneously denying the same right to animals with equal or superior characteristics and capacities.'

PETER SINGER, *RETHINKING LIFE AND DEATH*, PAGE 183

Key word

Speciesism means to discriminate against animals in favour of human beings.

Cross-reference

Read pages 48–49 for the law on abortion.

Key people

Joanna Jepson is a Church of England priest. Her complaint was not upheld by the court, the verdict being that the doctors had acted in good faith.

case abortion is recommended as standard practice. The **Human Fertilisation and Embryology Act** (1990) for instance permits abortion at any stage on grounds of foetal abnormality. In other words there is already an accepted implicit view that some human beings are of less value than others.

i) Arguments for abortion because of handicap

Handicap or foetal abnormality covers a wide range of conditions but the central issue is whether the quality of life of the abnormal foetus will be sufficiently low to justify abortion.

- One aspect of Peter Singer's quality of life argument points out how inconsistent, **speciesist** and irrational we are when we give priority to a very handicapped human baby but ignore the rights of a healthy primate. Being alive, Singer argues, is not sufficient reason to a **right** to life.
- **Preference utilitarians** also argue that no parent should necessarily be made to bring up a child with severe disabilities if that is the prognosis of the doctors. It is far better to minimise the suffering of the parents by terminating the pregnancy and allow them to have another healthy baby.

ii) Arguments against abortion because of handicap

A crucial issue in this debate is what is meant by handicap. In the much publicised case of **Joanna Jepson** in 2004, Mrs Jepson won her case to prosecute the doctors for carrying out a late abortion, at 28 weeks, for a baby with a cleft palate. Her argument was that a cleft palate does not constitute an abnormality 'as to be seriously handicapped' according to the law. As Jepson herself had suffered from a major jaw defect which later surgery was able to correct, she felt that the law had become too loosely interpreted. Many who supported her argued that the doctors' actions indicated the UK's increasingly 'eugenic' attitude to life which only values perfect babies.

Advocates for the strong sanctity of life view argue that a handicapped child should be given the same nursing care as any other child, even though by not using **extraordinary means** the chances of the child living for long are greatly reduced. Peter Singer's view is strongly rejected on the grounds that human life is intrinsically worthwhile whatever the degree of handicap.

Others argue that the foetus or baby is not solely owned by the mother. For instance if the **Americans with Disabilities Act** (USA, 1992) protects those people (including new-born babies) with a wide range of disabilities from discrimination, since there is no major moral distinction between a baby in the womb and a new-born, then a handicapped foetus is also entitled to be protected.

Key quote

'To put it another way, they will have a narrative history, and their lives can go better or worse for them. To put it another way, most of them would not be better off not existing ... consequently, the best interest of these babies is served by maximal treatment.'

GREGORY PENCE, *CLASSIC CASES IN MEDICAL ETHICS* (SECOND EDITION), PAGE 191

There should at the very least be no *automatic* reason to abort a handicapped child in the womb.

Some reactions to handicap are more to do with a fear of being in that position oneself. There are those who say they would rather not exist than live as a handicapped person. But this is a dangerous argument. It would be like saying to someone who had not been able to go to university because they were not intelligent enough that they must therefore be living a miserable life. People can and do make the most of the kind of bodies given to them. There need not be any direct correlation between **intelligence and happiness**. Down's syndrome babies, for example, often have IQs between 30 and 70, which is sufficient to live a life with a sense of history, and they can, in their own terms, respond emotionally given sufficient love and care.

Finally, there is the broad principle which underpins the sanctity of life, which is that all human life should be treated with care and love. It is the basis for medicine and enshrined in the oldest doctors' ethic, the **Hippocratic Oath**, not wilfully to kill. Christian ethics looks to the example of Christ, whose life and teaching particularly singled out the weak, the ill and the marginalised as examples of those the Kingdom of God welcomed. **Compassion** as a Christian principle means to 'suffer with' and it warns against treating others as things or objects.

Kant's secular version of the sanctity of life puts it very simply: never treat people as a means to an end but an end in themselves. Thus the care for the handicap is not a question of preference but one which accepts life, in whatever form, as part of the human condition.

c) Threats to the mother's life

Key question

Is a mother's life necessarily more valuable than her unborn baby?

Until the mid-twentieth century, the only grounds for abortion were when a pregnancy threatened a mother's life. Even back in the sixteenth century Thomas Sanchez argued that an embryo could be aborted in an **ectopic pregnancy**. He used as the basis for his argument Augustine's just war argument, where reasonable force might be used to defend one's self against a life-threatening aggressor. The argument in a secular form has already been referred to in Thomson's article, which argues for the mother's right to protect her own interests by using force against physical threat.

Key thought

An **ectopic pregnancy** is where the foetus develops in the fallopian tubes, not in the uterus. This usually proves fatal to mother and baby.

i) Arguments for abortion on the grounds of threats to a mother's life

Cross-reference

See pages 71–73 below for the various parts of the doctrine of double effect.

Sanchez's argument rests on advocating the **doctrine of double effect**. It is possible to imagine a situation where everything possible has been done to save the mother and baby's life, but where, in giving attention to the mother's health, the side-effects of medical treatment have *indirectly* (and so unintentionally) resulted in the death of the baby. Even pro-life and strong sanctity of life advocates such as the Society for the Protection of Unborn Children allow for a **termination** of a pregnancy, although as it is not a deliberate act it is not technically an abortion.

Others argue on **welfare grounds** that threats to a mother's life must take precedence over the foetus' life. This not to say that the foetus' life is any less valuable than the mother's life, but where difficult decisions have to be made then one evil has to be weighed against another. The Church of England takes this viewpoint based on the **lesser of two evils argument**.

> *The undoubted evil of abortion would in this situation represent the lesser of two evils, only resorted to as the appropriate way of caring for the mother if the evil of a significant threat to her life or health cannot otherwise be avoided.*
>
> (Church of England's Board of Social Responsibility, *Abortion and the Church*, page 27)

Utilitarian arguments have the more complex task of weighing up the value of the mother's life against her baby. For preference utilitarians the onus is on the mother to express whether or not she wishes to continue with her pregnancy. In early pregnancies, before the development of any cognitive brain activity, it might safely be assumed that the foetus is not capable of having preferences whether to live or die. In later pregnancies a woman might decide that the quality and range of her preferences are greater and more sophisticated than that of her foetus. Furthermore, she may have existing family and friends with whom she has created significant relationships who have preferences for her not to die.

ii) Arguments against abortion on the grounds of threats to a mother's life

Some of the criticisms of the doctrine of double effect sanctity of life arguments are:

- It doesn't adequately settle the **intrinsic value** of mother and baby. If both lives are deemed to be equally valuable according to the strong sanctity of life principle, then it might be equally reasonable to treat the baby and forfeit the mother's life. There are indeed cases where the mother has known that in saving her child she will die as a result.
- Once the principle of abortion is permitted, even in cases of threats to mothers' lives, then a **slippery slope** is created which replaces physical threats by psychological threats. The *Roe* v. *Wade* case is an example, where the mother threatened suicide if the pregnancy continued. Once this principle is permitted as an exception (as it is in the 1967 Abortion Act), then anything

---

Key quote

'The removal of tubal ectopic pregnancy is not generally regarded as an abortion procedure since the primary *intention is to protect the mother's life, not to destroy her unborn child.'*

SPUC, *LOVE YOUR UNBORN NEIGHBOUR*, PAGE 48

Cross-reference

See page 47 above for the principle of the cognitive criterion.

which is deemed to threaten the life of the mother becomes grounds for abortion. As evidence for this, opponents to abortion point to the present state of affairs where liberalising laws in Europe and the USA, at first for threats to lives, has now resulted in abortion for reasons as weak as 'threats to my career' or 'threats to my freedom'. Statistics illustrate that the vast majority of cases are not life threatening.

Cross-reference

See Helen Watt, *Life and Death in Healthcare Ethics*, page 10.

Some of the criticisms of the preference utilitarian quality of life arguments are:

- It is unreasonable to suppose that a foetus can express the same kind of sophisticated preferences as an adult mother. However, it is reasonable to assume that the foetus wishes to live. Some natural law thinkers, such as Helen Watt, argue that preference utilitarians such as Peter Singer have confused a foetus 'having interest in' with 'taking interest in'. It is true that an early embryo (note *not* a pre-embryo) does not have the mental/physical facilities to *take* interest in anything, but it does *have* a general interest that its life should be preserved and nurtured.
- In some cultures if the baby is a boy a social preference may be to favour the birth of the baby at the cost of the mother's life (assuming she is capable of carrying out the pregnancy to birth).

5 Normative ethical responses to abortion

Abortion raises many basic issues to do with medical ethics. Beauchamp and Childress (*Principles of Biomedical Ethics* [1994], pages 37–38), for example, suggested **four principles**: respect for **autonomy** (freedom to exercise one's will), **non-maleficence** (avoiding harm), **beneficence** (producing benefits) and **justice** (distributing benefits, risks and costs fairly). Each of the normative ethical systems should be judged against these principles.

a) Natural law

Cross-reference

Read pages 10–11 above on the natural law sanctity of life argument.

Natural law arguments, as we have seen, argue that as a primary precept an innocent life should always be protected. Once the foetus is considered a person, whether at conception or at brain activity for example (for those who prefer delayed ensoulment), its life becomes sacrosanct.

The Roman Catholic Church rules out delayed ensoulment for the following natural law reasons:

Key quote

'If embryos are living, whether viable or not, they must be respected just like any other human person.'

DONUM VITAE (1987),
CHAPTER 1, PARAGRAPH 4

- God is the first cause of all human life as it is he who gives it life.
- Life therefore is a gift.

Key word

In natural law everything has its purpose or **telos**. Aquinas suggested that humans have five related primary ends. The spiritual *telos* is the worship of God. See page 10 above.

Key word

A fortiori means literally in Latin 'from the stronger'. An a *fortiori* argument suggests that if x is wrong/right then y is even more so.

Key quote

'The foetus, though enclosed in the womb of its mother, is already a human being ... If it seems more horrible to kill a man in house than in a field, it ought surely to be deemed more atrocious to destroy a foetus in the womb before it has come to light.'

JOHN CALVIN, COMMENTARY ON THE LAST FOUR BOOKS OF MOSES (1563)

Cross-reference

Read pages 14–15 above on the different types of utilitarianism.

- Life at every stage offers the potential to become more fully actualised as a human being, capable of loving and worshipping God.
- God therefore is also the final cause or **telos** of all human life.
- Although the embryo is not a fully flourishing person (any more than a one-year-old is) it has the potential to become so.
- Human life is to be seen as a **pilgrimage** in which the image of God emerges from the simplest physical form to the complex form *we* call 'person'.
- Humans therefore have an absolute responsibility to protect human life so that it may develop and flourish to its end or *telos*. For that reason the Protestant Reformer **John Calvin** (1509–64) argued that just as it would be wrong to attack a defenceless man in his home, it must *a fortiori* be wrong to attack an even more defenceless foetus in the womb.

Does natural law permit any exceptions? Some suggest that as natural law permits the killing of combatants in war, then by analogy an unwanted foetus might be considered an aggressor or trespasser in the womb of the mother. If so, then the foetus is no longer an innocent and subject to protection. But the analogy would only work in extreme cases (such as rape) and even then it hardly seems reasonable for the foetus to *intend* to harm the mother.

On the other hand the **doctrine of double effect** allows for some flexibility. For example, if a woman's life is threatened by an ectopic pregnancy or where a mother has uterine cancer, both may be treated if the primary intention is to treat the mother's health even if the unintended but foreseen *side-effect* kills the baby. Technically, though, this is not an abortion (it is not deliberate killing) but a **termination**. In Roman Catholic teaching, every effort should be made to preserve the life of the child.

b) Utilitarianism

Utilitarian arguments all balance the good of keeping a child and the good of having an abortion. As we have seen, utilitarians vary as to what they think the 'good' is which should be maximised.

- **Hedonic utilitarians** argue that each case should be judged according to the amount of pain or happiness caused. There are many considerations here such as the emotional pain of bringing up an unwanted child, the financial costs of feeding and caring for another child which might affect the happiness of existing children and the restrictions placed on a woman who may wish to pursue a career. These all have to be balanced against the psychological harm caused by the loss of a child (guilt, regret and reactions of others), the physical dangers caused by the abortion itself and the possible inability to have children in the future.

Some might also consider the possible pain the foetus might go through – especially in the later stages of foetal development. This has become an increasingly significant part of the debate. Many scientists suggest that **sentience** in the sense of feeling pain occurs around twenty weeks, in which case at the very least the baby should be given an anaesthetic before being aborted.

- **Preference satisfaction utilitarians** argue that it is not just a question of balance of pain/happiness but what is desirable. Preference utilitarians take the preferences of the foetus more seriously than hedonic utilitarians, but only where they consider it would be reasonable for a foetus to have preferences. It would make sense, therefore, in cases of severe disability not to give a high value of life to the foetus as its desires would be far less than in a healthy foetus. It might even be considered that society would be better off without unwanted children or children who are a great drain on the financial and emotional well-being of society.

- **Ideal utilitarians** might reject the quality of life arguments of the preference utilitarians and opt instead to balance ideals such as justice. They might for example consider that abortion merely as a form of contraception as a result of carelessness is hardly just grounds for terminating a life – especially in the later stages of pregnancy. On the other hand abortion on the grounds of rape or threats to a mother's life are justified measures against unwanted pregnancy. In either of the cases the question of justice cannot remain a purely private decision but must be consistent with the application of justice in other aspects of society.

- **Welfare utilitarians** argue that abortion has to be placed within the context of other medical needs. Although they might agree with the hedonic utilitarian that mental and physical concerns all have to be weighed up, it might also be considered that there should be careful counselling by a doctor and perhaps even a period of time to consider a decision before abortion itself. It might even be necessary for a doctor to over-rule a patient's preference in the best interests of the patient.

Cross-reference

Read pages 13–15 above for Peter Singer's preference utilitarian views on abortion.

A general criticism of all utilitarian arguments is the vagueness of the 'threat' or 'pain' posed by a possible pregnancy as sufficient grounds for abortion. This is the problem of the slippery slope. Opponents argue that good reasons for abortion can quickly deteriorate to the trivial. For example the 1967 Abortion Act permits abortion on certain grounds as exceptions but, in practice, the statistics suggest that any woman who asks for an abortion is given it.

c) Virtue ethics

One reason why abortion causes considerable political disagreement is that it asks us to consider what kind of society we wish to be.

Virtue ethics is not just about an individual's character but also the character of society. Do we want a society which uses killing (if that is how it is regarded) to solve social problems? And finally as abortion is also a medical procedure, it must also include the character and motives of the doctor.

- **Mother.** Virtue ethicists might argue that having an 'unwanted' child by avoiding abortion is not only a courageous act but also generous if followed by adoption. As we have seen, many feminists argue that, although there is no necessity to become a mother, there is less justification to kill or terminate a life.
- **Society.** Some have argued that allowing abortion cultivates a 'culture of death'. Virtue ethics addresses the cold application of principles, whether they are consequential or deontological, from the point of view of the characteristics or traits we admire. As the philosopher Frankena has said, 'Principles without traits are impotent but traits without principles are blind.' As we have seen, feminists are divided over whether abortion enables women to choose their own destiny respectfully in society or whether, in fact, it places undue pressure on them to have abortions when they would rather continue with the pregnancy.
- **Doctor.** Beauchamp and Childress' **four principles** of doctors' ethics require also the right intentions such as courageousness, loving-kindness and open-mindedness. A doctor therefore might have to balance his or her own views on abortion when acting in the best interests of a woman who wants an abortion by using these virtues to act skilfully and professionally.

But as always with virtue ethical approaches the question is, how are the virtues to be decided? Some feel that there are particular female virtues which are undervalued by society and that until these are better represented abortion ethics, whether pro-life or pro-choice, will fail to deal with women's actual needs.

d) Revealed ethics
i) Strong sanctity of life Christians

Strong sanctity of life Christians base their ethics primarily on the authority of the **Bible** and conclude that the Bible extends the command to 'love one's neighbour' to the child in the womb from the moment of conception. As all humans are made in the image of God (Genesis 1:27), the deliberate termination of an innocent life is a capital offence (Genesis 9:6) because only God can give and take away life (Job 1:21). Christ's life and death was so that Christians 'might have life and have it abundantly' (John 10:10). A key passage for conservative Christians is **Exodus 21:21–25**, which distinguishes between hitting a woman, which causes her to miscarry the baby

---

Cross-reference

William Frankena, *Ethics* (second edition), page 65.

Key thought

Beauchamp and Childress' **four principles** of doctors' ethics are: respect for autonomy, non-maleficence (avoiding harm), beneficence (producing benefits) and justice (distributing benefits, risks and costs fairly).

Cross-reference

Read Michael Wilcockson, *Medical Ethics*, pages 4–5, on the virtues and doctors' professional practice.

Cross-reference

The main elements of the strong sanctity of life argument are set out on pages 11–12 above.

Key quote

'If men strive together, and hurt a woman with child, so that there is a miscarriage ... If any harm follows, then you shall give life for life.'

EXODUS 21:22–23

Key quote

'Personhood in the sense of "the state of being a person" admits no degrees.'

SPUC, *LOVE YOUR UNBORN NEIGHBOUR*, PAGE 43

Cross-reference

The main elements of the weak sanctity of life argument are outlined on pages 12–13 above.

Key quote

'We do not believe that the right to life, as a right pertaining to persons, admits of no exceptions whatever; but the right of the innocent to life admits surely of few exceptions indeed.'

THE CHURCH OF ENGLAND, *ABORTION AND THE CHURCH* (1993), PAGE 27

Key people

Joseph Fletcher (1905–1991) embraced Marxism as a young man but was able to transfer its radical views of society to Christianity. He was ordained as a priest and taught his radical theology and philosophy for many years, during which time he published his influential book *Situation Ethics* (1966). Later in life he abandoned Christianity but wrote on a wide range of ethical matters.

Key word

Antinomianism means no laws or rules.

alive (punishable with a fine), and causing her to miscarry and kill the baby (punishable by the death penalty). Abortion, therefore, is murder and intrinsically wrong.

This view is confirmed elsewhere in the Old Testament, where abortion and infanticide are treated as pagan and immoral acts (see 2 Kings 15:16 and Amos 1:13). Strong sanctity of life arguments support the vitalist position that a human person is created at the moment of conception. In Psalm 139:13–16 the writer says that God 'knitted' him together in his mother's womb and in the New Testament John the Baptist, in the womb of Elizabeth, recognises Jesus who is in Mary's womb by leaping (Luke 1:15) for joy when the two mothers meet.

ii) Weak sanctity of life Christians

Weak sanctity of life Christians argue that abortion should be permitted only in rare cases where there is threat to the mother's mental or physical health. This view cuts across many Christian traditions and is the official view of the Church of England and the Methodist Church. Weak sanctity of life arguments might also support a delayed ensoulment view for early terminations but also warn that it is dangerous to make the life of the foetus so absolute that it becomes an idol. It therefore holds a *prima facie* view that the potential life of the foetus should be protected unless, as in the case of rape, it is more rational to prioritise the needs of the mother and existing family over the baby.

iii) Liberal or radical Christians

Liberal or radical Christians argue along consequential lines that the primary consideration is love or **agape**. **Joseph Fletcher** called this view **situationism**. Fletcher's example of the rape of an unmarried, schizophrenic girl is given at the start of this chapter. Fletcher rejects the rigid deontological legalism or 'formalism' of Christians who place rules before people, but nor does he advocate **antinomianism** and instead he suggests that each case should be judged according to **four working principles**. In the case of the raped girl Fletcher argues that her mental health is paramount and furthermore 'no *unwanted and unintended* baby should ever be born', based on the four principles:

- **Pragmatism** considers what should be done to make the situation most loving. This is the heart of the Christian life. Abortion for rape, handicap and threats to a mother's life cannot be either right or wrong until considered against the command to love.
- **Relativism** ensures that there are no absolute duties which make people less important than rules. But for relativism to mean anything it must 'be relative to something' (*Situation Ethics*, page 44)

Key quotes

'In short, theory divorced from practice is ivory tower stuff, and practice without theory is bumbling.'

JOSEPH FLETCHER, IN *JOSEPH FLETCHER: MEMOIR OF AN EX-RADICAL*, PAGE 66

'We love because God loves us first.'

1 JOHN 4:7–12

and that is love. Love recognises 'human creatureliness'; this may not be a problem for early abortions but for late abortions the value of mother and baby requires difficult calculations to be made.

- **Positivism** is the view that as religious laws (such as the Ten Commandments) are not God-given or natural but human responses to God's love then there is no intrinsic reason why abortion should not be an option for the Christian.
- **Personalism** considers that all humans are to be treated as persons because as God is personal and humans are made in his image, then 'personality is the first order concern in ethical choices' (*Situation Ethics*, page 50). Therefore if abortion is chosen for good reasons, it cannot be the lesser of two evils, because this would be to deny the validity of the loving action.

e) Kantian ethics

The great strength of Kantian ethics is that it seeks to solve moral dilemmas according to reason and not emotion.

The Kantian position would almost certainly reject abortion if the reason was that having a child was inconvenient. This would be especially true if the foetus is considered to be a person or even a potential person. The practical imperative ensures that it would be quite wrong to treat the foetus as a means to an end. This is reinforced by the categorical imperative which universally forbids the killing of an innocent person.

However, although Kantianism usually rejects exceptions, is there a case to be made for abortion in extreme situations in what we have called 'hard cases' and women's unique argument for autonomy?

Cross-reference

Read pages 50–56 above for the discussion of 'hard cases'.

- **Rape and threats to mother's life**. If in the case of rape and threats to a mother's life the foetus is seen as an aggressor then a possible Kantian response might be to consider the protection of the mother based on the universal duty to 'always protect the innocent first'.
- **Feminism and autonomy**. Autonomy is essential to Kantian morality. As we have seen, some feminists have argued that a woman has a right to decide on her own reproductive autonomy because as she is the owner of her body she is in a unique position of deciding what is best for her. The categorical imperative might be expressed as 'women must always do what is best for their bodies'. As Christine Overall argued, making a woman keep the foetus would be like compelling her to give up one of her organs against her will. If the foetus is considered to be part of the mother's body there is nothing to justify the reduction of her autonomy of this kind.

Cross-reference

Read pages 43–45 above on the feminist arguments for and against abortion.

However, unless the Kantian takes the view that the foetus is not a person, both the hard cases exceptions view and the feminist autonomy argument illustrate the problem Kant faces when two duties appear to make *equal demands*. Given that it is very unlikely that in the hard cases position a foetus actually has evil intent to threaten the mother's life, it has to be treated as an innocent person. In the same way the feminist autonomy argument has to down-grade the status of the foetus to liken it to an organ in order for the justification to be acceptable.

Summary diagram

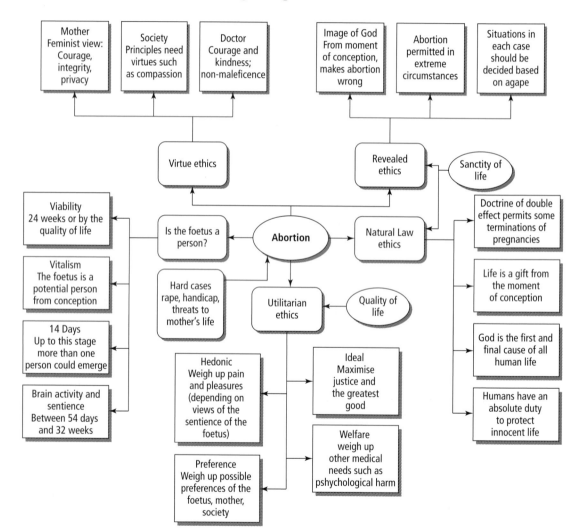

Study guide

By the end of this chapter you should have considered abortion from a variety of different moral viewpoints. These should include the rights of the mother as well as the rights of the foetus. In addition you should have formed a view as to the status of the foetus as an actual or potential person. This should also mean reading Chapter 1 and considering such issues as ensoulment and viability. You should also be able to discuss the problem of 'hard cases' from various normative ethical points of view.

Revision checklist

Can you explain:

- the natural law response to abortion
- the use of the double effect to justify terminations but *not* abortions
- the religious response to abortion in strong and weak sanctity of life terms
- Fletcher's four working principles in relation to abortion
- the preference utilitarian consideration of the foetus' preferences v. preferences of the mother.

Do you know:

- what it means to say a woman has a *prima facie* right to privacy
- what RU-486 is and the moral and medical issues associated with it
- the law on abortion and the harm criterion (physical and mental)
- what welfare utilitarianism is and how it can be used to assess abortion.

Can you give arguments for and against the claim that:

- a foetus is a person at conception
- rape or foetal handicap are sufficient reasons for abortion
- a woman's right over her body justifies abortion
- virtue ethics is effective in deciding whether to have an abortion or not.

Essay question

1) Analyse the view that Kantian ethics are of little use in the debate about abortion.

Kant's position should be briefly summarised as his desire to give proper place to the human good will as the basis for all moral decisions. The good will is what makes us human and different from animals. In order to test that the good will is genuine it must be tested rationally by universalising it to become a duty applicable to all. It might be argued that these qualities are considered to be good and important ones for all moral decision making because they give value to human autonomy and make us responsible for our own actions. They also seek to be consistent and to treat all people as equals and not as a means to an end. The question is whether these qualities are helpful in the question of abortion.

It might be argued that in a debate as emotive as abortion it is good to be governed by reason. Kant's rejection of emotion according to situation as motivation for acting wisely could be considered as an entirely appropriate means of avoiding selfish, rash and hasty decisions. This might give good reasons to reject abortion especially if the foetus is considered even a potential life as abortion means treating it and all other humans as a thing and not a person. The question is whether Kant adequately deals with hard cases. Is the argument that rape or threats to the mother's life make the foetus an 'aggressor' enough to justify using lethal force? Can feminist-Kantian arguments be made for reproductive autonomy along the lines that 'a woman has a duty always to do what is best for her body' to justify abortion? It might be felt that Kant's categorical imperative should be replaced by a *prima facie* system of duties which doesn't suffer the problem which Kant's does of clashing duties and allows there to be a hierarchy of duties according to situation.

Further essay questions

2a   Outline the moral arguments for abortion as a consequence of rape.

2b   'The only justified reason for abortion is when a pregnancy is a threat to the mother's life.' Discuss.

3   Assess the view that if abortion is permitted so is infanticide.

4   'A human embryo/foetus has an absolute right to life and should be protected at all times.' Discuss.

4 EUTHANASIA AND DOCTORS' ETHICS

Chapter checklist ✓

The problem of euthanasia is reviewed and the place of palliative care considered, beginning with the moral problems raised by suicide. The main distinction between cutting short a life and allowing a person to die is discussed with reference to consequential and deontological ethics. The chapter concludes by looking at different types of euthanasia and the responses of a range of normative ethical systems.

Case study
'Devoted husband kills wife'

In May 2007 a newspaper headline read 'Devoted husband in "mercy killing" of depressed wife is found guilty of murder' (*The Daily Telegraph*). Frank Lund had been happily married to his wife for 33 years but she was severely depressed caused by an acute form of irritable bowel syndrome and had taken a large dose of pills. He bought the tablets for her but soon after taking them she began to be sick. He was afraid she would not die and because he had promised her that she would not wake up in hospital he put a plastic bag over her head and smothered her with a pillow.

The case is significant because groups campaigning for euthanasia did not give their support to Lund. Why was this? The answer is that Patricia Lund's condition was not life-threatening and therefore Frank Lund's action was the direct and immediate cause of her death.

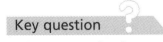

Key question

Euthanasia means literally 'a good death' but should a person be allowed to choose when they die?

1 A problem of definition

The case therefore raises a basic problem of distinguishing between the right to suicide, assisted suicide, euthanasia, murder and manslaughter (or involuntary homicide). This is not just confusing for those involved in making medical ethics decisions but also for what it implies about the way we view the value of life and the role of society.

- **Suicide** is when a person dies as a direct result of their own voluntary action.
- **Assisted suicide** is when a person dies as a direct result of their own voluntary action but with the help of another person. This is different from voluntary euthanasia only in so far as the person may have many reasons for wanting to die; their condition doesn't have to be life-threatening.
- **Physician-aided suicide** is when a person dies as a direct result of their own voluntary action but with the help of a doctor or physician.
- **Physician aid in dying** is when a person's death is hastened but not directly caused by the aid (e.g. medication) of a doctor or physician.
- **Voluntary euthanasia** is when a person's death is directly caused by another person (perhaps a doctor) on their request. Most arguments today assume that the person requesting to die is suffering from *an underlying life-threatening condition* and is in great pain.
- **Passive euthanasia** is when a doctor or physician withdraws life-sustaining treatment which indirectly causes death. Alternatively the physician allows a patient to die by 'letting nature take its course'.
- **Non-voluntary euthanasia** is when a doctor or the courts decide that life-sustaining treatment is no longer justified.

Many of these terms appear to be interchangeable. For example, is passive euthanasia the same as physician aid in dying? Many people who support the view that a doctor may give **palliative care** which indirectly hastens death nevertheless resist calling this euthanasia. In their own mind this distinguishes between treatment, which is **passive** (indirect killing), and care, which is **active** (directly reducing pain and killing).

Although the distinction between suicide and euthanasia is the involvement of another person, the fundamental issue is whether it is morally licit or permissible for a person to take their own life.

2 The law and euthanasia

Key question

What reasons should be given to make euthanasia legal?

Until 1961 suicide in the UK was a criminal offence. Although the **1961 Suicide Act** decriminalised suicide it *did not* make it morally licit. As the Suicide Act has direct consequences for euthanasia, it is worth noting its two major clauses:

Key word

Palliative care is the use of drugs and medicine to relieve pain but without directly causing the death of patients.

a) 1961 Suicide Act

1 The rule of law whereby it is a crime for a person to commit suicide is hereby abrogated.
2 (1) A person who aids, abets, counsels or procures the suicide of another or an attempt by another to commit suicide shall be liable for a term not exceeding fourteen years.
  (2) If on the trial of an indictment for murder or manslaughter it is proved that the accused aided, abetted, counselled or procured the suicide of the person in question, the jury may find him guilty of that offence.

Many think that law now supports the principle of autonomy. But, in fact, the Act reinforces the principle of sanctity of life by criminalising any form of assisted suicide. On the other hand, the Act does not hold the vitalist position that all life is equally valuable and should be preserved at all costs because there are cases when allowing a person to die is the better course of action.

b) The right to self-determination

Key question

Does a person have a right to ask doctors to assist in the termination of their life if she requests it?

This distinction was famously illustrated in the **Diane Pretty** case in 2002. Diane Pretty, who was paralysed from the neck down with motor neurone disease, had asked her doctors to assist in her suicide. Her lawyers had presented the case based on the **right to self-determination**. But her case was not upheld even when taken to the European Court of Human Rights. The reason given was that although the law recognises the right to life, it does not consider its corollary is the right to die. Most importantly the courts decided that Mrs Pretty was not suffering from a life-threatening condition – if she had been, then doctors might have been able to argue that they could assist in her dying, even though they could not have helped in the direct *cause* of her death.

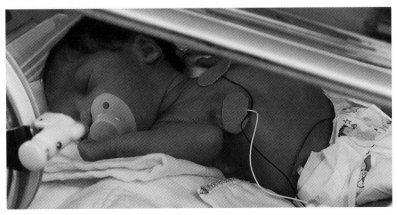

Who should decide if a sick premature baby should be allowed to die?

On the other hand the case of **Baby Charlotte** in 2005, who was born prematurely and with severe brain damage, illustrates that the law does not consider life to be absolutely sacred. Against the wishes of her parents, the High Court ordered the doctors not to resuscitate the baby if she fell into a coma. The principle was that her underlying condition did not justify the medical assistance she was being given just to stay alive.

c) Physician aid in dying

Many consider that the law has led to considerable confusion and that one way of developing the present situation is to create a new Act which would permit **physician aid in dying**. The proposal states that there should be a bill to:

> *Enable a competent adult who is suffering unbearably as a result of a terminal illness to receive medical assistance to die at his own considered and persistent request; and to make provision for a person suffering from a terminal illness to receive pain relief medication.*
>
> (*Assisted Dying for the Terminally Ill Bill*, 2004)

One of the major objections to proposals of this kind is the fear that it will suffer from the **slippery slope** whereby what begins as legitimate reasons to assist in a person's death will also permit non-lethal conditions. This, it is claimed, will pollute society, as Plato and Aristotle argued. In a letter to *The Times* (24 September 2004) a group of eminent academic lawyers and philosophers, including John Haldane and Alasdair MacIntyre, argued that:

- supporters of the Bill slide from making the condition one of *actual* unbearable suffering from terminal illness to merely the *fear*, discomfort and loss of dignity that terminal illness might bring
- if quality of life is grounds for euthanasia for those who request it then logically this could be extended to those who don't request it (or who are unable to request it)
- the example in the Netherlands shows that the law cannot easily place safeguards against those who simply choose to ignore them. There is the difference between idea and practice in the 'real world'.

But **Helga Kuhse** challenges proponents of the slippery slope argument to provide empirical evidence to support their case. Her conclusion is that the slippery slope argument is used by scaremongers to support their complete ban on all forms of euthanasia. The most frequently cited example of the wedge argument is the active non-voluntary euthanasia practised by the Nazis during the holocaust years as a form of **eugenics**, where the deaths of millions were justified as part of the 'improvement' of

Key question

Although another ruling permitted the parents to make the final choice was it right to let Charlotte survive even though she is severely brain damaged and needs constant care?

Cross-reference

For the moral pollution argument see pages 31–32 above.

Key people

Helga Kuhse is senior honorary research fellow in bioethics at Monash University, Australia. With Peter Singer she founded the Centre for Bioethics.

Key word

Eugenics means literally 'the production of good off-spring'.

society. Kuhse concludes:

> *Whilst the Nazi 'euthanasia' programme is often cited as an example of what can happen when a society acknowledges that some lives are not worthy to be lived, the motivation behind these killings was neither mercy nor respect for autonomy; it was, rather, racial prejudice and the belief that the racial purity of the* Volk *required the elimination of certain individuals and groups. As already noted, in the Netherlands a 'social experiment' with active voluntary euthanasia is currently in progress. As yet there is no evidence that this has sent Dutch society down a slippery slope.*

(Helga Kuhse, in Peter Singer [editor], *Companion to Ethics*, page 302)

d) Euthanasia law outside the UK

i) Netherlands

Often people argue that voluntary euthanasia arrangements should be brought in line with the principles determining legal abortion. The situation in the Netherlands is frequently referred to because it most clearly expresses the balance between the popular will, medical practice and legal control. The case is for physician-assisted suicide.

Cross-reference

For a full account of the situation in the Netherlands see Singer, *Rethinking Life and Death*, pages 143–47.

- Mercy killing is illegal, but where there is a **conflict of duties** between the doctor's medical ethics and the demands of the patient euthanasia may be permitted.
- Only a medical practitioner may be permitted to carry out euthanasia.
- The patient must make his request to die persistently and explicitly.
- The patient's request must be freely made, well informed and without coercion.
- The patient's condition must be one where there is no foreseeable room for improvement and where there is unbearable pain. All other alternatives for relieving pain should have been considered.
- A doctor should seek the advice and second opinion of another independent doctor.
- The Dutch parliament regularised this procedure in 1993. The doctor must report his action to the public prosecutor who then judges each situation case by case. A doctor may be prosecuted if the above criteria have not been adhered to.

ii) USA

In the USA the movement is towards 'proxy empowerment' and developing the use of living wills. The movement is towards physician-assisted suicide. Physician-assisted suicide is strongly resisted by the pro-life movement.

iii) Australia

In Australia there is no uniform law; however, a doctor may discontinue life-support at the request of the patient. This does not constitute, for the purposes of law, assisted suicide. In the state of Victoria an Act of 1988 permits a person to appoint a proxy. In South Australia a person may use an advance directive under the 1983 Natural Death Act refusing 'extraordinary treatments' should they become incapacitated.

3 Allowing to die and cutting short a life

Key quote

'I will give no deadly medicines to anyone if asked, nor suggest any such counsel.'

THE HIPPOCRATIC OATH

The problem of euthanasia is that it has to straddle both principle and practicalities. Those who consider that there should not be a right to terminate an innocent life nevertheless argue that there are circumstances when some form of assisted dying is permissible. On the other hand others consider this to be morally confusing and argue that there are circumstances when 'cutting short' a life is not only permissible but good.

The Moor case illustrates the tension between those such as Dr Moor who argue that allowing to die is not the same as killing and those such as the detective who consider that there is either killing or not killing. The former position is largely supported by deontologists who support the **doctrine of double effect** and the second view by the consequential **utilitarians**.

Case study
Dr David Moor

His trial concerned the death in 1977 of George Liddell, an 85-year-old former ambulance worker who had recently been discharged from hospital after treatment for bowel cancer. He was bedridden, having suffered a stroke and a heart attack, and was doubly incontinent, deaf, diabetic and anaemic.

The prosecution case hung upon a morphine injection Dr Moor gave to Mr Liddell on the morning of his death. When the investigation began the doctor had not disclosed the injection to police or NHS officials. He later gave details, saying that he had been panicked by media attention into withholding the information.

Outside the court, Dr Moor repeated his philosophy, saying: 'In caring for a terminally ill patient, a doctor is entitled to give pain-relieving medication which may have the incidental effect of hastening death. All I tried to do in treating Mr Liddell was to relieve his agony, distress and suffering. This has always been my approach in treating my patients with care and compassion. Doctors who treat dying patients to relieve their pain and suffering walk a tightrope to achieve this.' He insisted that the morphine he gave Mr Liddell was to relieve his pain and was in no way a lethal dose.

Detective Superintendent Colin Dobson of Northumbria Police said: 'To a police officer and the criminal justice system, the terms mercy killing and euthanasia are meaningless. If you shorten someone's life by minutes, that's murder, and by law we had to approach our investigation from this viewpoint.'

('Cheers as GP is cleared of murdering patient', *The Times,* 12 May 1999)

Dr Moor was acquitted of murder in 1999.

a) Consequentialism: end and means

For most modern consequentialists all that matters in order to judge a situation is that the outcome is good or bad. Therefore an **omission**, such as failing to give a patient some drugs, is morally equivalent to giving patient drugs if both actions have the effect of killing. Likewise some argue that a doctor who **refrains** from acting is no different from the one who acts if the intention (i.e. the desired outcome) is the same, just as in the same way the doctor who complies with a patient who **refuses** treatment directly assists in his suicide.

But is the consequentialist position entirely consistent?

If A chooses to shoot B then we classify this as an intended act; if C sees A and fails to stop A shooting B then this is an intended omission. Is C at all **blameworthy**? C could claim that by not acting he was simply complying with another principle (e.g. never involve one's self in other people's affairs). Although the consequentialist claims to judge just the outcome, he does nevertheless assume that there are some significant non-consequential factors such as the duty of the doctor to be responsible for his patients.

b) Deontology: doctrine of double effect

A fairly typical expression of the doctrine of double effect is that a person may licitly perform an act which he foresees will produce good *and* evil if:

- the action in itself from the outset is good
- the good effect and not the evil is intended
- the good effect is not produced by means of the evil effect
- there is proportionately good reason to permit the evil effect.

Key quote

'Thus an act or omission which, of itself or by intention, causes death in order to eliminate suffering constitutes a murder gravely contrary to the dignity of the human person and to the respect due to the living God, his Creator. The error of judgement into which one can fall in good faith does not change the nature of this murderous act, which must always be forbidden and excluded.'

CATECHISM OF THE CATHOLIC CHURCH, PAGE 491

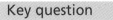
Key question

Does a person ever get to the stage where their life ceases to be worthwhile?

Key word

Deontologists argue that an
action is good if it is based on
duties on rules.

So for example a consequentialist might argue that there is no
moral difference between a patient who refuses treatment without a
doctor and dies, than if a doctor is involved. The **deontologist**
might well agree that in both cases the doctor is equally responsible
but the quality of intention is far from trivial. For example there is a
difference between the pacifist who refuses to fight on principle
and the coward who fails to fight. The doctrine of double effect
takes seriously the relationship established between the patient and
doctor. Therefore refraining or acting in a patient's death is only
permissible if the primary intention is *not* to kill, even if this
hastens death.

- **Purity of intention**. Consequentialists are unimpressed by the
  quality of intention argument. If the deontologist argues that he
  has foreseen a possible outcome then it does not matter how
  'good' his intentions are or what kind of person he is: an evil
  act is an evil act. But the deontologist considers the quality of
  intention to be very important. There is a significant difference
  between the grandson who visits his grandmother because he has
  to and the one who does so because he wants to. In the latter
  case the outcome is enriched by **virtue** and likewise deceit can
  degrade an apparent act of kindness.
- **Arbitrariness**. Consequentialists object to the deontologist's
  distinction between intended foreseen effects and unintended
  foreseen effects. For example in the well-known example of the
  trolley bus, five people are lying on one track and one on another.
  At the moment the points are switched to the track with five
  people on it. For the utilitarian the choice is simple: change the
  points and save the five. But the deontologist argues that life is not
  that simple. For example if I have one healthy person and five sick
  people and I could use the organs of the healthy person to cure
  the five, do I have a duty to sacrifice the one? The deontologist

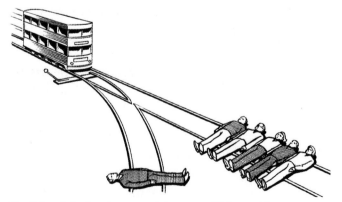

Should the train be allowed to carry on in its course to kill five people?

argues that it is logically possible to have *prior* intentions – I could refrain and allow the trolley bus to kill five people on the grounds that it would be more evil *intentionally* to kill one person. But for most consequentialists this defence is irrational and arbitrary.

- **Ordinary and extraordinary means.** Consequentialists consider that the deontologist's rigid refusal ever to use direct killing can lead to more suffering, loss of dignity and confusion over exactly what constitutes 'extraordinary' means. For example, in the natural law tradition a person who refuses food and water in order to die has deliberately committed suicide, which is condemned in Roman Catholic theology as a mortal sin. But a person is within their rights to refuse surgery on the grounds that it is over and above what is needed ordinarily for bare existence.

- **Proportionality and quality of life.** The consequentialists point out that the final element of the double effect includes the consequential principle that the evil of the unintended action must not be greater than the intended one. In other words, if prolonging life would bring about disproportionate suffering, then the deontologist should surely permit direct killing. The use of QALYs or 'quality adjusted life years' in some hospitals is thought to be an **empirical** means of determining the quality of life of a patient in terms of the resources needed to maintain a life. Deontologists agree that outcomes are important but argue that the consequentialist underestimates the importance of means and the very subjective nature of a QALY; namely who decides what constitutes a worthwhile life?

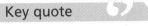

Key quote

'*Competent patients have a right to refuse any treatment, including life-prolonging treatment.*'

THE BRITISH MEDICAL ASSOCIATION (*MEDICAL ETHICS TODAY*, 1993, PAGE 149)

Key word

Empirical means gaining knowledge through observation and experience rather than logic or theory.

4 Non-voluntary euthanasia

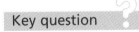

Key question

When does a human being cease to be a person? Consider again the problems of personhood on pages 4–8.

Cross-reference

Read page 18 above on paternalism.

In non-voluntary euthanasia a decision is made on behalf of the patient on the strength of the situation. The landmark case of **Tony Bland** in the UK was after the Hillsborough football disaster in April 1989. Bland was placed on a life-support and although able to feed and breathe was in a deep coma. Finally after lengthy legal debate his life-support was turned off. The significance of the case is that it acknowledged that doctors cannot be expected to maintain a life (however defined) at all costs. The moral issue is whether acting **paternally** and prolonging the life of 'brain dead' patients is necessarily in their best interests.

a) PVS and the problem of defining death

The Bland case and others like it have set up a precedent which has significantly shifted not only how we understand death but the value of life as well. In the past death was defined as when the heart ceased pumping blood round the body, accompanied by the cessation of other vital bodily functions. Today, a person can be kept 'alive' in this sense for long periods of time even though, as in the Bland case, important parts of the brain have ceased to operate. Being 'pink and supple' does not necessarily equate with being alive. Coma patients in this state can perform a number of involuntary actions and contrary to what many people think the patient is not necessarily lying inert in bed. The new definition of death is when there is no brain activity. So, a patient who is in a **persistent vegetative state** (PVS) where they have lost part of the brain (i.e. the cerebral cortex) would theoretically be deemed dead even if his body was functioning. But recent research has revealed how difficult making such a diagnosis is. Not only can it take some time to determine whether the patient is indeed brain dead but it is now apparent that the brain can function at very low levels, just enough to provide vital hormones for the body.

b) Deciding on the patient's best interests

In practice being in a PVS or being declared 'brain dead' is not always taken to mean that the patient is dead (if that were the case then there would be no debate). The issue in broad terms is whether sustaining him on life-support is in the best interests of the patient. In other words, 'life' is not just a biological fact but also a moral or evaluative judgement. The same problem of defining death and balancing it against the best interests of a patient also occurs when taking organs from a dead patient. The **dead donor rule** is used by some to define death to be both lack of brain and body function. This rules out any form of euthanasia.

Perhaps in the end each case has to be viewed separately on its own merits.

5 Normative ethical responses to euthanasia

a) Kantian ethics

Kant argued that it can never be a duty to commit suicide. Suicide treats the person as a means to an end (in violation of the practical imperative) and fails to consider the person's duty to protect the innocent. A duty to kill oneself would therefore undermine the stability of society on which the duty to protect life depends. If suicide is wrong then all forms of active euthanasia must also be rejected. Furthermore it cannot be a universal duty of all doctors to kill their patients even if they were all terminally ill because this would make life contingent on health, which consequently detracts from the dignity of a person whatever physical state they might be in.

Key quote

'The ability to make complex judgements about benefit requires compassion, experience and an appreciation of the patient's viewpoint.'

THE BRITISH MEDICAL ASSOCIATION (*MEDICAL ETHICS TODAY*, 1993, PAGE 170) ABOUT TREATMENT OF PVS PATIENTS

Key thought

The **dead donor rule** is when there is no brain activity and no body function. Read Michael Wilcockson, *Medical Ethics*, pages 117–19.

Cross-reference

Kant's argument on suicide is discussed in more detail on pages 30–31.

b) Utilitarianism

The consequential/utilitarian arguments have already been considered, especially their rejection of deontology. Utilitarianism's particular criticism is that the deontological distinction between 'allowing to die' (permitted) and 'cutting short' a life (intrinsically wrong) is false. Utilitarians, as we have seen, consider the strong sanctity of life natural law position to place too much store on the significance of intention, the arbitrary nature of foreseen but unintended side-effects and the increased cause of suffering produced by the doctrine of ordinary and extraordinary means. Finally, utilitarians argue that the principle of proportionality contained in the doctrine of double effect shows that deontologists are really consequentialists. For all these reasons utilitarians such as Peter Singer and Helga Kuhse argue that euthanasia can only be discussed rationally once all forms of the sanctity of life position are abolished. Helga Kuhse comments:

> *When we refrain from preventing the deaths of handicapped infants, comatose patients, and the terminally ill and suffering, by classifying the means necessary for keeping them alive as 'extraordinary', 'not medically indicated', 'disproportionately burdensome', and so on, we are resorting to an equally spurious device in order to preserve our sanctity-of-life ethics unscathed. If we want to go beyond definitional ploys, we must accept responsibility for making life and death decisions on the basis of the quality of life question; we must drop the sanctity of life doctrine and work out a quality of life ethic instead.*
> (Helga Kuhse, *The Sanctity of Life Doctrine in Medicine: A Critique* [1987], pages 206–7, 220)

- **Hedonic utilitarianism** establishes the basic position which Hume outlined that as happiness is directly related to the ability to decide our own future then a person who decides to 'retire from life does no harm to society' because he will have sufficiently good reasons to wish to die. The hedonic utilitarian might agree with Hume that if 'adding to life' by living longer does not make life *more* worthwhile, then cutting it short does not make it *less* worthwhile. Finally euthanasia, like suicide, is not a crime because there is no 'victim' – the only crime is for society to be too cowardly to accept it. Equally a person might wish to use a QALY as a contemporary version of Bentham's calculus to determine the quality of their life; or a doctor might use this in non-voluntary euthanasia for a PVS patient.
- **Ideal/rule utilitarianism**, whilst agreeing with the hedonic utilitarian position, might argue that respect for patient autonomy is only part of the calculation. For example a doctor might consider that it would not be in the **best interests** of his patient to request euthanasia. He might for example argue that only

Cross-reference

Read page 71 above on consequentialism and euthanasia.

Cross-reference

Read pages 33–35 for David Hume's view of suicide.

Key quote

'If suicide be a supposed crime, 'tis only cowardice can impel us to it.'
DAVID HUME, 'OF SUICIDE'.

life-threatening conditions should be considered grounds for voluntary euthanasia as well as taking into account the feelings of relatives. A rule-based system would therefore avoid the charge that euthanasia would inevitably lead to a slippery slope ending in eugenics. Of course a rule cannot ensure that euthanasia will not be abused by a doctor or even relatives, but there is no *logical* reason why a utilitarian position on euthanasia will lead to the cheapening of life.

- **Preference utilitarianism** takes seriously the view that given the choice whether to die in pain or painlessly most would prefer to die without anguish. Furthermore most would not want to see their friends or family die in pain. But preference utilitarians might go further and argue that there might be very good reasons why someone might wish to use euthanasia other than to avoid pain. If someone knew that they were suffering from a crippling disease (such as Huntington's or Alzheimer's) then as an act of generosity to others and relief to themselves they might choose to die before they became a burden to themselves and their families.

- **Welfare utilitarianism** considers the minimum conditions under which a life can be said to flourish. Welfare utilitarian doctors might have very few objections to physician aid in dying and passive euthanasia where their role is to hasten death in a very sick or comatose patient. However, they might wish to take into account the effects of allowing euthanasia as standard medical practice: it might engender a climate of fear (an old person in hospital might feel that euthanasia was an obligation should they become very ill); it might confuse the aims of medicine if killing were to become considered good medicine; and it might make doctors less careful in treating their patients.

c) Virtue ethics

Virtue ethics is particularly useful when discussing the doctor–patient relationship. A momentous decision to terminate a life depends very much on a patient's trusting dependency on his doctor.

A virtue ethical approach is cautious in treating rules and duties as absolutes. Some would argue that even though the doctor has a duty of care to a patient, this does not mean keeping him or her alive at all costs; active or passive euthanasia could both be good medicine. Prudence (*phronesis*) is the skill of the doctor to choose between the extremes; as Arthur Clough's poem expresses it, 'Thou shalt not kill; but need'st not strive officiously to keep alive', that is, the extreme of excess (the officiousness of keeping alive at all costs) and deficiency (such as cowardice through inaction and allowing further suffering). The quotation illustrates that although doctors

Key quote

'Euthanasia and suicide are two aspects of the same evil; the relegation of life to a lowlier status than well being ... Those who must live the suicidal temptation are not helped by those who seek to elevate their despair into a virtue.'

DANIEL JOHNSON, *THE TIMES*, OCTOBER 1991

Key quote

'Thou shalt not kill; but need'st
not strive officiously to keep alive.'
ARTHUR CLOUGH (1819–61),
THE LATEST DECALOGUE

have a *prima facie* duty of beneficence, without the **corresponding virtue** of benevolence or compassion it becomes impossible to know how to make beneficence work properly in practice. Virtues, therefore, *enhance* the quality of care given to a patient on an individual basis and *enable* the doctor to balance consequences with his professional duties in every situation.

For these reasons the medical profession supports a virtue ethical approach which considers **palliative care** or possibly passive euthanasia to be more appropriate for the doctor than active voluntary euthanasia:

- Real care for the sick and dying is to be found in a caring environment. The **hospice movement** allows a person to die in dignity and in a loving environment. Nevertheless, the British Medical Association argues for passive euthanasia, where in severe acute cases prolonging life would be 'unacceptable'; however, even when treatment is withdrawn, 'Care must always continue until the very end of the patient's life' (British Medical Association, *Medical Ethics Today*, page 159).
- A doctor's relationship with his patient is always one of hope; the inclusion of the possibility of voluntary euthanasia or even physician aid in dying puts an intolerable burden on him. Euthanasia is contrary to his training as a doctor where the principle of **beneficence** as the practice of benevolence means giving pain relief, not direct killing. The option for a doctor to kill his patient (even on request) might be too easy and remove his duty to find suitable pain management (*Medical Ethics Today*, page 154).

Thus many doctors fear that even a limited change in legislation would bring about a profound change in society's attitude to euthanasia. By removing legal barriers to the previously 'unthinkable' and permitting people to be killed, society would open up new possibilities of action and thus engender a frame of mind whereby some individuals might well feel bound to explore fully the extent of these new options. Once previously prohibited action becomes allowed, the argument goes, it may also come to be seen as desirable – if not by oneself, then as something which might be recommended for others.

(British Medical Association,
Medical Ethics Today, page 151)

d) Natural law

Cross-reference

Read pages 71–73 above on
deontology and euthanasia.

The deontological/natural law arguments have already been considered, especially their rejection of consequentialism. Natural law's particular criticism is that the consequentialist fails to make the important distinction between 'allowing to die' (permitted) and 'cutting short' a life (intrinsically wrong). Without this distinction the primary precept of self-preservation and protection of innocent life would be a major threat to the well-being of society and undermine a doctor's duty to care for his patients. A summary of the natural law views on euthanasia are:

Cross-reference

Read pages 31–32 above. This view is supported by Plato, Aristotle and Aquinas.

- **Social stability**. Suicide/euthanasia of all kinds undermines the social stability of society because it undermines the purpose of the citizen to maintain its laws and it is a sign that society has failed in its duty to care for all its members.
- **Duty to God**. Aquinas states that a primary natural law duty is to worship God, but both he and Augustine argue that suicide (and therefore euthanasia) is an abrogation of one's duty to protect an innocent life. All active forms of euthanasia or physician-aided dying are illicit and intrinsically wrong.
- **No refusal of treatment**. The doctrine of ordinary and extraordinary means does not permit a person to refuse ordinary treatment. In *Evangelium Vitae* (1995) the Pope makes a distinction between: **ordinary treatment** (obligatory), where life is prolonged if it does not cause extra burdens on the patient and **basic care** includes food and water, which are necessary to sustain life, not necessarily to enhance or even to prolong it; and **extraordinary treatment** (not obligatory), where treatments do not have high expectations of success (such as surgery) or could be dangerous (such as experimental therapies).
- **Duty to protect innocent life**. The natural law argument is that whatever state of consciousness a person is in they cannot cease to be a person. Non-voluntary euthanasia for a PVS, incompetent, seriously disabled people or very sick babies is not permitted on the grounds that death is defined only as the cessation of the heart and brain (dead donor rule). Furthermore the natural law sanctity of life argument also rejects euthanasia on the grounds that only self-defence is sufficient reason to kill; therefore a doctor has a duty to protect a patient from committing suicide, and assisted suicide/euthanasia is murder.

Key quote

'Discontinuing medical procedures that are burdensome, dangerous, extraordinary, or disproportionate to the expected outcome can be legitimate.'

CATECHISM OF THE CATHOLIC CHURCH, PAGE 491

Cross-reference

Read pages 10–11 on the natural law sanctity of life argument.

Only the double effect argument permits allowing to die in certain circumstances as a side-effect of pain-relieving treatment, but as this lacks the intention to cause direct death, it cannot be called euthanasia. Even passive euthanasia is wrong if the intention is to cause death. This is the position held by the Catholic Church in its *Declaration on Euthanasia* (1980).

> *Thus an act or omission which, of itself or by intention, causes death in order to eliminate suffering constitutes a murder gravely contrary to the dignity of the human person and to the respect due to the living God, his Creator.*

(*Catechism of the Catholic Church*, page 491)

e) Revealed ethics

Revealed ethical arguments in Christianity are largely against euthanasia because of the Bible's condemnation of suicide and the strong sanctity of life position on the duty to protect all innocent life.

Cross-reference

Read pages 11–12 above for a fuller account of the strong sanctity of life argument and pages 28–30 on suicide.

i) Strong sanctity of life arguments against euthanasia

The following is a brief summary of arguments presented in earlier chapters:

- **No right to dispose of an innocent life.** The Bible presents a consistent view that as humans are made in the image of God (Genesis 1:27) then life is 'set apart' and intrinsically good. Life therefore is a gift from God and not ours to dispose of (Job 1:21) and should be honoured and respected. The taking of an innocent life is murder (Exodus 20:3). Given the choice of life or death we must choose life (Deuteronomy 30:19). God commands us to love and that means enduring pain and suffering (1 Corinthians 13:6).
- **Suicide is blasphemy.** Suicide and therefore all forms of euthanasia are blasphemous because it is a deliberate rejection of God's gift of life. It is also blasphemous because it rejects God's redemption through his victory over death through the resurrection of Christ. To deliberately choose death is in effect to deny that redemption is possible. This is why the figures of King Saul (1 Samuel 31:4) and Judas (Matthew 27:3–5), who both committed suicide, are examples of those who regarded themselves as beyond redemption.

ii) Weak sanctity of life arguments for euthanasia

Cross-reference

Read pages 12–13 above for a fuller account of the weak sanctity of life argument.

The Christian weak sanctity of life argument does not consider that killing an innocent person out of love is morally equivalent to murder. Murder implies some ulterior motive such as revenge, cruelty, greed or hatred. Suicide, or more particularly euthanasia, as an act of love in exceptional circumstances is not morally wrong.

- **No one has a duty to endure a life of extreme pain.** Although Paul calls Christians to be a 'living sacrifice' (Romans 12:1), this does not mean enduring extraordinary pain or suffering. Sometimes the sacrifice means recognising that this life has to be relinquished out of love for others, as Samson did (Hebrews 11:32–38).
- **Life is a gift not a burden.** If life is given to us as a gift, it is also given so that we may use it responsibly and dispose of it as we wish. It would not be a gift if the giver still had ownership of it. Therefore being a good steward of life (Genesis 1:28) means knowing when and how it is appropriate to bring it to a close.

Summary diagram

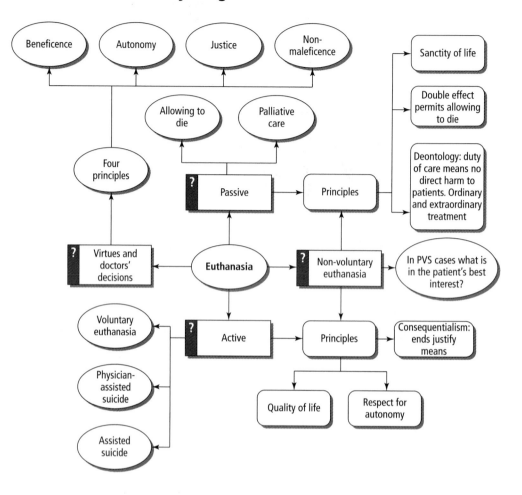

Study guide

By the end of this chapter you should have considered the problems of trying to define the moral and legal distinctions between different types of suicide and euthanasia. You should be clear about the differences between passive and active euthanasia and the significance of these distinctions for doctors and their patients. Finally you should be aware of the debate between the consequentialists and the deontologists and the significance of the double effect in the debate about cutting short a life and allowing to die, and ordinary and extraordinary means.

Revision checklist

Can you explain the moral difference between:

- allowing to die and cutting short a life from a consequential (utilitarian) position
- allowing to die and cutting short a life from a deontological (natural law) position.

Can you define:

- suicide
- physician-aided suicide
- voluntary euthanasia
- passive euthanasia
- non-voluntary euthanasia.

Do you know:

- what the 1961 Suicide Act states
- the law on voluntary euthanasia.

Can you give arguments for and against:

- palliative care when dealing with the very sick and dying
- allowing very premature babies to die
- the use of virtue ethics for doctors in their treatment of the terminally ill.

Essay question

1 a) Explain the practical and moral differences between active and passive euthanasia.

b) 'Utilitarianism is the best method of assessing whether euthanasia is morally acceptable.' Discuss.

The essay may deal with active and passive euthanasia in two parts. Active euthanasia is the direct intended termination of a life. It might be distinguished from assisted suicide because with euthanasia the underlying condition must be life-threatening, whereas assisted suicide could occur for a number of reasons. The Lund case could be referred to. Active euthanasia is voluntary and is in response to a person's request to die. The moral problems are how to define what constitutes a quality of life that is so poor that death is a merciful act. The Pretty case illustrates the problem of the right to self-determination. The sanctity of life argument could be referred to. Passive euthanasia is indirect killing usually by removing life-support which then causes death and is done in the best interests of the patient. The moral problems might include: the issue of determining minimal life (e.g. the Bland case); quality of life (Baby Charlotte case); and fears of a slippery slope justifying eugenics.

In the evaluative answer a contrast could be made between utilitarian and natural law deontological thinking. For example the utilitarian is critical of the distinction between intended and unintended but foreseen consequences that deontologists use to relieve suffering but not directly cause death. The utilitarian considers this to be irrational, arbitrary and likely to cause more suffering. The example of the trolley bus could be used to discuss the acts and omissions problem. But it could be argued that utilitarianism might lead to some unsatisfactory outcomes. Hume's argument for suicide illustrates the unfeeling side, which respects a person's autonomy to die when they wish. There is also confusion between utilitarians – for example between the aims of act and welfare utilitarians about what the 'ends' are and the long-term effects of euthanasia on family and society.

Further essay questions

2a   Explain what is meant by the 'sanctity of life'.
2b   Assess the view that Christians should reject all forms of euthanasia.

3   How valid is the use of the 'double effect' to justify the death of a terminally ill patient through the use of powerful drugs?

4   'Virtue ethics offers the best solution for doctors dealing with the issue of euthanasia.' Discuss.

5 KILLING AS PUNISHMENT

Chapter checklist ✓

The chapter begins with the famous case of the Sonnier brothers who brutally kidnapped, raped and murdered two girls. The central question is whether the death penalty is an appropriate punishment by the state for heinous crimes. This raises the question as to what punishment is for and why some people consider retribution based on the idea of just deserts justifies capital punishment whereas others would only consider execution if it acted as a deterrent. Finally, others argue that all forms of capital punishment are wrong because the primary aim of punishment must be to reform and rehabilitate the criminal. Various normative ethical responses are surveyed.

1 Capital punishment

Key quote 🔊

'Depend upon it, Sir, when a man knows he is to be hanged in a fortnight, it concentrates his mind wonderfully.'

DR JOHNSON, 19 SEPTEMBER 1777, IN JAMES BOSWELL, *LIFE OF JOHNSON* (1791)

The issue of capital punishment or state-sanctioned killing as a form of punishment raises many of the same kind of issues as war and peace (Augustine and Luther both saw war as an extension of capital punishment) only in this case the threat is from individuals within society. However, the context in which capital punishment is considered is sufficiently different to pose quite new considerations. Here the problems are to do with the individual, his relationship with the state and the process of law. In other words the issue of judicial killing, the most extreme of all state sanctions, concentrates the mind on the reasons and purpose of punishment in general.

a) Heinous crimes

Case study
The case of Patrick Sonnier

The case is significant because it involved a Roman Catholic nun, Sister Helen Prejean, whose experience helped to persuade many Christian churches that capital punishment is always

wrong. The case of Patrick Sonnier forms the basis for her book *Dead Man Walking* (1996).

On 7 November 1977 the *New Iberian* newspaper reported that two young people, both from loving Roman Catholic families, David LeBlanc, 17, and Loretta Bourque, 18, had been shot at close range in the back of the head three times with a .22 rifle. The editorial had concluded: 'It's hard to imagine that there may be somebody in this fine community of ours who could contemplate, much less carry out, this vilest of vile deeds.' On 2 December 1977 two brothers, Elmo Patrick Sonnier, 27, and Eddie James Sonnier, 20, were accused of having posed as security officers, kidnapped the two teenagers and handcuffed them. They drove them 20 miles and then in the woods Loretta was raped. The brothers ordered both to lie on the ground and then in cold blood shot them. At the trial it was revealed that both men had a long history of offences and came from a poor background. Eddie at first said that Patrick had committed the murders and raped the girl. Eddie said he had had sex with her because she was willing. Later, Eddie confessed he had killed the teenagers but his confession was rejected and Patrick was sentenced to death.

This case and many others like it from around the world not only raise questions about the use of capital punishment, but the nature and aims of punishment itself.

- Is there any crime so bad which permits the state to kill? Does Patrick Sonnier deserve to die for his crime?
- Patrick comes from a very poor, white family. They rarely have enough to eat and so both the men have turned to crime from early on in their lives. To what extent should factors like these excuse (or mitigate) a crime?
- Has the execution of a man like Patrick Sonnier deterred others from murder and rape?
- Is the use of execution a sign that society has failed in its responsibilities to all its citizens?
- Article 5 of the UN Declaration of Human Rights states the 'right not to be subjected to torture or to cruel inhuman or degrading punishment'. Should all civilised societies reject the use of the death penalty?

b) History of capital punishment legal reforms

The history of capital punishment over the past two hundred years in Britain is of particular importance because it illustrates how public attitudes to punishment and justice have changed.

- The 1837 Act reduced the number of capital offences to sixteen.
- The 1841 Act abolished hanging for rape.
- In 1868 the last public hanging was held.
- In 1922 the 'Infanticide Act' (hanging for mothers who killed their new-born children) was abolished.
- In 1933 'The Children and Young Persons Act' (hanging for those children under eighteen who had committed capital offences) was abolished.
- In 1965 the 'Murder (Abolition of Death Penalty) Act' was passed for a trial period and confirmed in 1969.
- In the 1988 'Crime and Disorder Act' removed treason and piracy (the two remaining grounds for capital punishment) from the statute books.

PROFILE

The hanging of Derek Bentley in 1953 sparked off widespread abolitionist feeling amongst the general public. Bentley had been an accomplice to a burglary that had resulted in the shooting of a police officer. At the time of the shooting he had been in police custody, but Christopher Craig, who had actually shot the round, was too young to be charged with the capital offence. An increasing sense of injustice coupled with a tide of popular moral repulsion swelled sufficiently to bring parliament to the stage where the abolition of the death penalty was considered to be the only logical step to reform the law. Bentley's pardon was finally granted posthumously in August 1998.

c) Present situation

Amnesty International reports that: more than two-thirds of the countries in the world have now abolished the death penalty in law or practice. The numbers are as follows:

- Abolitionist countries for all crimes: 91
- Abolitionist countries for ordinary crimes only: 11
- Abolitionist countries in practice: 35
- Total abolitionist countries in law or practice: 137
- Retentionist countries: 60

Key words

Abolitionist and **retentionist** refer to countries who have abolished the death penalty and those who have kept or reintroduced it.

- During 2007, at least 1252 people were executed in 24 countries. At least 3347 people were sentenced to death in 51 countries. These are the figures reported to Amnesty International – the true figures are certainly higher.
- Executions are known to have been carried out in the following countries in 2007: Afghanistan, Bangladesh, Belarus, Botswana, China, Egypt, Equatorial Guinea, Ethiopia, Indonesia, Iran, Iraq, Japan, Kuwait, Libya, North Korea, Pakistan, Saudi Arabia, Singapore, Somalia, Sudan, Syria, USA, Vietnam, Yemen.
- China may have executed between 470 and 600 people in 2007.

United States of America

The death penalty was reintroduced in certain states from 1977 onwards.

- From 1997 to 2007 there have been 1099 executions. A third (380) have been carried out in the state of Texas.
- Fifty-three executions in 2006 was the lowest annual total for a decade.
- The number of people sentenced to death (but not necessarily executed) in 2006 was the lowest since 1977.

Treaties

Second Optional Protocol to the International Covenant on Civil and Political Rights
Aiming at the abolition of the death penalty, adopted by the UN General Assembly in 1989 and of worldwide scope. It provides for the total abolition of the death penalty but allows states to retain the death penalty in time of war if they make a reservation to that effect at the time of ratifying or acceding to the Protocol.

The Protocol to the American Convention on Human Rights to Abolish the Death Penalty
Ratified (i.e. formally agreed) by nine states and signed by two others.

(Source: based on www.amnesty.org/en/death-penalty)

Key word

A **treaty** is a formal agreement negotiated between countries.

2 Aims and justification of punishment

What moral imperatives justify the use of punishment? In most ordinary moral statements there is usually a relationship between a concrete situation and the reasons that justify acting in a particular kind of way. A utilitarian might, for instance, argue that stealing is generally wrong because it causes a great deal of anguish and pain. Kantians might, for example, argue that taking other people's property without permission cannot be consistently and universally combined with respect for persons and a stable society. But justifying the moral grounds for punishment is not always easy or obvious.

We can distinguish at this stage between two forms of punishment: **moral punishment** suggests that moral reasons can justify different types of punishment; **legal punishment** suggests that within the judicial process (through statute or common law) the state sanctions various forms of punishment. The two categories are closely and intimately related to each other. The discussions amongst legal philosophers are complex, but in the case of capital punishment the distinction is particularly significant for it is the *legal* process of killing as punishment which distinguishes it from killing as a private act based on personal moral conscience.

a) The problem of punishment as suffering

Before we return to the precise moral grounds for punishment, we must first establish what it means to punish. Punishment usually suggests that there is some blame, fault or liability, which a person has incurred through an act or omission. The punishment awarded is therefore a penalty for a moral or legal failure and by penalty we usually mean a deprivation or suffering of some sort (usually of liberty, property or life). Punishment should be carefully distinguished from **revenge**. For despite their similarities, revenge is the result of personal vendetta whereas punishment is based on moral and/or legal authority. Punishment is considered to be just whereas revenge is not. The conclusion of many philosophers is paradoxical. Although the need for punishment at first appears to be self-evident, the *moral* reasons are often obscure.

The justification for killing as punishment, therefore, must take place in the wider discussion of the aims of punishment.

b) Retribution, deterrence and reformation

The three aims of punishment are: **retribution, deterrence and reformation**. Modern thinking on punishment tends towards a consolidated view where no one aim is sufficient to provide a comprehensive account.

A further useful distinction between the different aims of punishment is whether the punishment is **backward looking** or **forward looking**. Punishment which is backward looking considers only the crime itself whereas forward looking punishment considers the long-term beneficial effects to society as a whole.

Key question

Why is punishment often seen as a moral contradiction?

Key quote

'Why is the claim that a man has done what he ought not to have done in itself a reason for making him suffer? ... The question has taken several forms, and no satisfactory answer has ever been given.'

TED HONDERICH,
*PUNISHMENT: THE
SUPPOSED JUSTIFICATIONS*,
PAGE 217

3 Retribution

Key question

Should people always be paid back in kind for what they have done wrong?

Key words

Lex talionis is Latin, meaning 'law of retaliation' or, as it is expressed in the Old Testament, 'an eye for an eye'.

Just deserts implies that there is a law of nature, which demands punishment that is equal to the crime

Vindication is proof that the law has been applied through punishment and justice achieved..

a) Punishment as retribution

Of all the aims of punishment retribution most clearly expresses what many people instinctively feel is the basis of punishment. It has an ancient history from the law codes of the Babylonian Hammurabi (1728–1686BC) to the Old Testament and is often referred to as the **lex talionis**. Its basic position is that a **grievance**, whether an individual's or society's, requires **satisfaction** on the part of the victim. The victim's entitlement that the criminal should be punished is for no other reason than that the criminal is owed his **just deserts**; failure to punish causes an injustice to the victim and society. Retribution in its classic form is backward looking; it considers that it is a law of nature that an offence requires an equal measure of punishment. This is why retribution is often made into a public spectacle (as in a hanging) to demonstrate to society that the victim has paid for the law which he has broken. Retribution therefore acts psychologically as a form of **vindication** that the law has been applied and acted upon.

i) Modern versions of retributivism

However, strict application of the *lex talionis* has proved problematic. Taken at face value it would suggest that a man who steals should have things stolen from him; a person who rapes should be raped; the person who murders another should be killed. This version of the *lex talionis* is often regarded as crude, although the basic intuition that punishment should recompense victim and society is considered to be true. Contemporary retributivists have therefore suggested following versions of the 'goods' which have been violated, which give more subtle reasons for punishment:

- **Rights retributivism** means paying for rights which have been infringed. Rights retributivism argues that because other citizens have exercised their rights with responsibility and so voluntarily restricted many of their own wishes that when a person has abused the rights of others by behaving irresponsibly they should lose the same rights they have abused. Another way of thinking of this argument is that it depends on a basic sense of 'fair play'.
- **Contract retributivism** recognises the social context and justification of law and punishment. By contract we mean the self-imposed restrictions which all citizens take on in order to permit other freedoms. It follows that anyone who has subscribed to the contract that fosters these freedoms has equally agreed in advance to the removal of the same freedoms should he break with the contract.
- **Restorative retributivism** argues that where an offender's bad actions have resulted in the unfair distribution of goods,

punishment restores the balance of goods. Goods have to be interpreted as the *satisfactions* associated with goods and not the goods themselves (this would pose insuperable practical problems).

ii) Respect for persons

Kant's influential argument for retribution is particularly important because he places the treatment of the criminal first. Based on the principle of the **golden rule** the criminal is treated in the same way as he has treated his victims. In other words Kant argues that it is reasonable for the criminal to be judged by the same principle as he has judged his victims.

- His punishment is rationally consistent with the moral imperative he has acted by (i.e. if he has stolen from others, he must now have his goods taken from him).
- His punishment is therefore not treating him as a means to an end, as a deterrent or example to others, but as a person.
- Finally, his punishment therefore **annuls** the offence and heals the harm caused to the victim.

b) Capital punishment as retribution

The retributive arguments have a long and ancient history particularly in the West because of the support of Christian teaching. Throughout the modern debates and particularly in the eighteenth and nineteenth centuries the retributive debates have frequently made use of the *lex talionis* in passages such as Genesis 9:6, which says a person who sheds blood shall have his blood shed, and Romans 13:4, which talks of executing God's judgement with the sword for wrongdoers. The Church has supported capital punishment on these grounds and as a means of maintaining the social order.

The newer forms of retributivism have also supported the death penalty.

- **Rights retributivism** supports the notion that where a person has brutally removed the basic rights of others (life and dignity, for example) it follows that he has forfeited his own right to live and deserves to die. Those who support the fair play argument add that even though the criminal ought by rights to die, there may be other reasons why this may not be carried out (for example the victim's relatives may not want it).
- **Contract retributivism** argues that where a citizen has blatantly broken his side of the social contract at a fundamental level, for example through an act of treason, by smuggling drugs (as in Malaysia), by blasphemy or through murder, then society is right to regard his action with severity. The threat of the death penalty is a sign of the seriousness by which the social contract is held. A

Cross-reference

For a fuller discussion of Kant on retribution read pages 102–3 below.

Key thought

The **Golden Rule** is found in many cultures and can be summarised as 'do to others as you would have them do to you'.

Key word

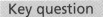

To **annul** means to cancel out.

Key question

Does capital punishment help to maintain society's respect for human dignity?

Key quotes

'Whoever sheds the blood of man, by man shall his blood be shed; for God made man in his own image.'

GENESIS 9:6

'But if you do wrong, be afraid, for he does not bear the sword in vain; he is the servant of God to execute his wrath on the wrongdoer.'

ST PAUL, *LETTER TO THE ROMANS* 13:4

citizen knows what the law is and if he chooses to break it, he can expect to receive his just deserts.

- **Restorative retributivism** defends capital punishment for the reasons mentioned so far but emphasises the psychological desire to replace the sense of loss caused by particularly horrendous crimes. Unlike the traditional absolute 'like for like' just deserts argument, restorative retributivism permits punishment to be in *proportion* to the suffering caused to society and victim. If, as Kant argues, the harm caused by murder can only be restored by capital punishment then the state has a duty to kill the offender.

c) Criticisms of capital punishment as retribution

The problem with retributivism is that it offers little objective evidence or reasoning as to why taking a life should be a form of justice. Those who use retributivism have, in the end, to appeal to some form of non-verifiable intuition (we just know) or psychology (another person's suffering cures my own) or mystical (it is in the nature of things) or religious (God demands it) grounds for retribution.

i) Offender's motives or intentions

Key question

Does an evil act imply an evil intention?

Key words

Mitigation means alleviation and in law is used to refer to factors which can be used to justify a lesser punishment.

Mens rea is the Latin phrase meaning a 'guilty mind' and used to refer to the criminal whose act is the result of an evil intention.

But to what degree does retributivism take into account the state of mind of the offender who commits the crime? If there were to be grounds for **mitigation** such as age, deprived social status, mental ability (e.g. low IQ) and clinical depression then the bedrock of traditional retributivism would be severely compromised.

- Kant argues according to the principle of **mens rea** that an evil action implies an evil mind; someone who murders or rapes or tortures does not do it by accident. Retribution therefore appears to have a strong sense of **equity** by treating all like cases the same. But this is not entirely satisfactory. Many people would accept that the moral intentions of a child of three are quite different from those of a 14-year-old and therefore the cases must be treated differently. Likewise a person on the brink of death through starvation who steals bread from a shop has a very different motive from someone who steals because it saves them money.
- However, if retribution *does* take some account of mitigation then it is open to **inconsistency** where factors which are deemed appropriate in one case are not in another. This confusing state of affairs would not achieve the aim of retribution which is to give a clear indication that immoral behaviour will not be tolerated.

The history of the move away from capital punishment shows an increasing awareness that motives, psychological state and provocation are not evil but confused or distorted. This point was made in the famous Leopold and Loeb case (1924). **Clarence Darrow**, their defence lawyer, argued that despite the atrocity of their crime both young men should not be executed due to their **diminished responsibilities**. In fact he went even further and questioned whether anyone has sufficient free will ever to warrant the death penalty. In his summing he argued:

> *The principal thing to remember is that we are all the products of heredity and environment, that we have little or no control, as individuals, over ourselves, and that criminals are like the rest of us in that regard.*
>
> (Clarence Darrow)

Key thought

If **diminished responsibility** does indeed exist does this mean that we do not have free will? Read Mel Thompson, *Ethical Theory*, Chapter 3.

ii) Inconsistency

In an attempt to take into account motives and intentions the historical development of capital punishment has increasingly led to great inconsistency. The retributive aim founders most here where a lack of objective assessment makes it impossible to determine the level of responsibility which establishes a person's guilt. The Bentley case has come to illustrate the importance which many people place on degrees of responsibility and guilt. This is not to say that reduced responsibility mitigates *all* retributive punishment but it calls into question its fairness and ability to establish social control and respect for the law.

Cross-reference

See page 85 above for the Bentley case.

iii) Trivial reasons

Honderich argues it is questionable to what degree any citizen is really so consciously aware of being part of the contract that any action can really be seen as a deliberate attempt to undermine the status quo. In reality it is the legislators and not the people who are the designers of the contract and its laws. For example, the **Waltham Black Act** has shown how capital punishment has been used for what are now regarded as comparatively trivial offences. For these reasons **contract retributivism** does not achieve the degree of objectivity sufficient to justify taking a person's life.

Key question

Is illegally smuggling drugs into a country a good reason to receive the death penalty?

Key thought

The **Waltham Black Act** (1723) sets out 50 possible capital offences: forgery of birth, baptism, marriage certificates, arson, attempted murder of parents, picking a pocket of more than one shilling.

iv) Anger is not sufficient reason

Restorative retribution has no objective or empirical basis. It might be possible literally to allow the victims of murder (or the state on their behalf) to settle on some punishment such as money or death which they feel would adequately recompense for the hurt suffered because of the crime. But it is very hard to judge whether capital punishment would actually have the desired effect in seeking fairly to recompense for grievances and anger experienced throughout society. Satisfying hurt or anger is not a good reason for making such a serious judgement as to whether another person should live or die.

Key people

John Rawls (1921–2002) was one of the most influential political philosophers of the twentieth century. He spent all his working life at Harvard University. His book *A Theory of Justice* (1971) has provoked considerable discussion. He argued that as a question of social justice no one should be better off than anyone else because everyone in society has a duty to everyone else. Justice is forward looking and seeks to maintain the social contract. Read Mel Thompson, *Ethical Theory*, pages 75–76.

Cross-reference

See pages 89–90 above for the views of contract retributivists.

Key quote

'Rather than being a violation of the wrongdoer's dignity, capital punishment may constitute a recognition of human dignity.'

LOUIS POJMAN, IN LOUIS POJMAN AND
JEFFREY REIMAN, *THE DEATH PENALTY:
FOR AND AGAINST*, PAGE 61

Two other related criticisms are:

- Anger is the beginning of the **slippery slope** to vengeance. Retribution is supposedly based on an objective of just deserts independent, as Kant argued, of emotional judgement. Therefore any argument for capital punishment that places the satisfaction of anger in any form as its primary consideration cannot be a sound rational basis for legal judgements which include taking a person's life.
- **John Rawls** argues that the inclusion of anger illustrates that just deserts is not natural or objective but an invention of society. Anger is created whenever someone breaks the social contract which society has itself created at some time. Rawls' criticism, though, is rejected by **contract retributivists** because he fails to consider why capital punishment should be considered sufficient reason to maintain the contract for rational not emotional reasons.

v) Inhumane treatment

Kant argued that the death penalty reinforced society's respect for persons because the victim comes to see how the principle on which they acted (murder, for example) is being equally and consistently applied to him. But even those who support capital punishment in theory argue that though the state has a *right* to kill those who have murdered, it does not have a *duty* to do so. For example, according to the *lex talionis*, in theory a multiple murderer ought to be executed several times, being revived just before he dies, so as to be equivalent to the number of murders he has committed. But many find such cold-blooded treatment repellent because of its unnecessary cruelty.

The death penalty is therefore seen as morally unacceptable on the grounds that it is always inhumane.

Case study
The execution of Patrick Sonnier

The warden is standing over in the right-hand corner next to a red telephone.

'Have you any last words, Sonnier?' he asks.

'Yes, sir, I do,' Pat says, and he looks at the two fathers, but addresses his words to only one of them. 'Mr LeBlanc, I don't want to leave this world with any hatred in my heart. I want to ask your forgiveness for what me and Eddie done, but Eddie done it.' Mr LeBlanc nods his head. Mr Bourque turns to Mr LeBlanc and asks, 'What about me?'

> *Pat is in the chair now and guards are moving quickly,*
> *removing the leg irons and handcuffs and replacing them*
> *with leather straps. One guard had removed his left shoe.*
> *They are strapping his trunk, his legs, his arms. He finds my*
> *face. He says, 'I love you.' I stretch my hand toward him. 'I love*
> *you, too.'*
>
> *A metal cap is placed on his head and an electrode is*
> *screwed in at the top and connected to a wire that comes from a*
> *box behind the chair. An electrode is fastened to his leg. A strap*
> *placed around his chin holds his head tightly against the back of*
> *the chair. He grimaces. He cannot speak anymore. A grayish*
> *green cloth is placed over his face ... I*
> *hear three clanks as the switch is pulled with pauses in*
> *between. Nineteen hundred volts, then let the body cool, then*
> *five hundred volts, pause again, then nineteen hundred volts.*
> *'Christ, be with him, have mercy on him,' I pray simply.*
>
> *I look up. His left hand has gripped the arm of the chair*
> *evenly but the fingers of his right hand are curled upward ...*
> *Warden Maggio looks up at the clock and announces the time*
> *of death; 12:15 am. His eyes happen to look into mine. He*
> *lowers his eyes.*
>
> (Helen Prejean, *Dead Man Walking*, 1993, pages 120–21)

Many argue that according to the *International Bill of Human Rights* capital punishment should be rejected on the grounds that not only does it disregard 'the right to life' (Article 3) but more significantly under Article 5 everyone has 'the right not to be subjected to torture or to cruel inhumane or degrading punishment'. As the example from *Dead Man Walking* illustrates, capital punishment is regarded by many as cruel and barbaric and unacceptable in a modern civilised society.

4 Deterrence

a) Punishment as deterrence

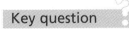

Key question

Does capital punishment stop people from committing murder?

Deterrence has a **forward-looking** view of punishment because it views punishment essentially as a means of enabling society to function fully in the future. This view is not ruled out by the retributivist as an aim of punishment, but the difference is that the deterrent view does not punish the offence for its own sake. The deterrent argument is classically the lynchpin of the **utilitarians** and especially its founding father **Jeremy Bentham**. In his most influential work on the topic, *An*

Key people

Jeremy Bentham (1748–1832) was a British philosopher who developed utilitarianism as a rational means of reforming the law so as to protect the interests of the poor and the sick. A law should be revised or abolished according to one simple test: that it produces the greatest happiness for the greatest number. Read Mel Thompson, *Ethical Theory*, Chapter 9.

Key people

Cesare Beccaria (1738–94) was an Italian aristocrat and criminal lawyer. In 1764, at the age of 26, he published his great work *Dei delitti e delle pene* 'Of Crimes and Punishment', which was very quickly translated into many languages and influenced many, including Jeremy Bentham. Although he argued that capital punishment might be used to deter others from committing a crime, he regarded it as barbaric.

Key quote

'No other punishment deters men so effectually from committing crimes as the punishment of death. This is one of those propositions which is difficult to prove, simply because they are in themselves more obvious than any proof can make them. It is possible to display ingenuity in arguing against it, but that is all. The whole experience of mankind is in the other direction.'

SIR JAMES FITZJAMES STEPHEN,
'CAPITAL PUNISHMENTS',
IN *FRASER'S MAGAZINE*, 1864

Introduction to the Principles of Morals and Legislation (1789), Bentham argued that:

- punishment is unnecessary if the offence will not recur
- punishment is only appropriate to dissuade others from behaving in the same way
- punishment is, therefore, to protect society for the future.

The utilitarian principle is bound to regard punishment in itself as undesirable because it deliberately inflicts some kind of pain on the offender. According to the utilitarian principle of maximising happiness and avoiding pain, any deliberate infliction of pain can only be justified provided it results in greater happiness, desires, preferences or satisfactions.

The strength of this view is that it is able to look at each case with some degree of independence. It exercises a **minimising policy**, i.e. that punishment should inflict the least amount of pain possible. Its form of punishment and justice is always **distributive** and for the benefit of all, not a minority. And finally it allows the offender the opportunity to reform and seeks to prevent crime rather than wait for harm to be done.

b) Capital punishment as deterrence

The modern debate begins with an influential essay by **Cesare Beccaria**, 'Of Crimes and Punishment' (1764), where he argues that the only rational and morally sound basis for capital punishment is deterrence. However, Beccaria goes on to say this view has to be modified by several factors: capital punishment does not deter; an enlightened and civilised society should work for prevention of crime, not punishment; capital punishment is inconsistently and indiscriminately employed. The utilitarian deterrence argument is therefore faced with a dilemma.

- On the one hand the utilitarian argues that not to use capital punishment would be to cause an injustice to the potential victims of crime if one does not execute actual criminals; citizens can expect to be protected from harm and especially threats to their lives.
- On the other hand there is no guarantee that capital punishment does deter.

i) Deterrence and fairness

Capital punishment as deterrence poses the problem of fairness for utilitarians. This is because although the threat of punishment can be justified to deter criminals from committing harm to society, it cannot easily justify why causing actual harm as punishment should be fair.

As an answer to this problem some have advocated the **unfair advantage argument**. The unfair advantage argument begins by restating the retributivist's view, which says that the criminal should pay back what he unfairly gained through his crime and, in addition, should be punished for the unfair advantage he took by avoiding the laws that other citizens have worked hard to maintain. The unfair advantage argument differs from the traditional retributivist *lex talionis* argument because the punishment is not so much aimed at removing the harm caused to the victim but restoring to society the advantages of keeping to the law.

Furthermore the unfair advantage argument has to assume that punishment is effective in deterring other people from committing crimes. In the case of heinous crimes which are judged to undermine the very fabric of society, the threat to the potential criminal that he might forfeit his life must be enough to deter and therefore capital punishment can be considered fair as it reinforces the advantages of keeping to the law.

ii) Public example

The symbolic nature of deterrence also requires that in order for it to be as effective as possible capital punishment should be public and visually dramatic. During the nineteenth century, for example, the process and *ritual* of hanging was so refined that it took on the guise of a dramatic morality play. Through it the crowds could watch as the prisoner, led by the chaplain to the gallows, delivered his moralising 'sermon' (often taught to him by the chaplain) warning them not to copy his example of crime; the execution then followed.

iii) Evidence and best bet argument

For pro-capital punishment arguments to be true, deterrent effects must be **empirically** demonstrated. Opinion remains divided as to whether existing research is able to substantiate the deterrent claim. Differences in methodology and approach are likely to impact upon end results and sceptics argue that the use of statistics is nothing more than a **post hoc justification** for pre-held convictions, where moral philosophers and policy makers pick and choose the research that best fits their agenda.

For example, those who defend a capital punishment policy might point to the fact that between 1990 and 2006 the number of executions in the United States has increased and the murder rate has declined (Death Penalty Information Center). However, a more complex picture emerges by comparing those states which have the death penalty with those which do not: non-death penalty states have consistently lower murder rates.

However, even if the evidence is ambiguous, some argue for a **best bet** position. The best bet argument suggests that where the evidence is unclear about the effectiveness of capital punishment as

Key word

Post hoc justification means finding evidence to match an existing belief.

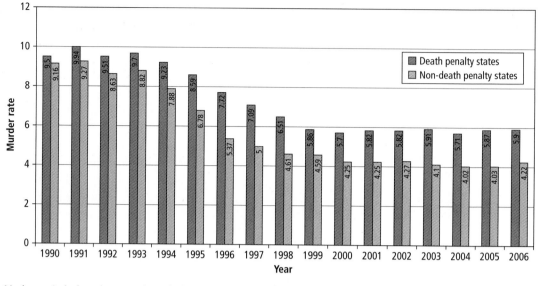

Murder rates in death penalty states and non-death penalty states
(Source: Death Penalty Information Center, www.deathpenaltyinfo.org)

Cross-reference

The **best bet argument** rejects
the acts and omissions principle
illustrated by the thought exercise
of the trolley bus dilemma. See
pages 72–73 above.

deterrence we are still gambling with people's lives. Therefore it is a
better bet using the death penalty as deterrence to save *innocent*
people's lives rather than preserving the lives of those who are guilty
and by so doing failing to deter actual murderers from taking
further innocent lives.

c) Criticisms of capital punishment as deterrence

Criticisms of the deterrent position fall into two kinds: observational
and philosophical. The deterrent argument for capital punishment
stands or falls on the factual evidence whether it does or does not
deter. Of course it *may* do so, but with what certainty, for how
long and with what degree of reliability? Does the threat of
capital punishment make the good citizen better but wash over the
habitual offender? Statistics without considerable justification can be
manipulated to suit diametrically opposed views. However, there are
moral arguments against the use of capital punishment as deterrence
which exist independently of the factual evidence.

i) Lack of evidence

Abolitionists such as Amnesty International cite the situation in
Canada where, 17 years after abolition, the murder rate is 27 per
cent lower than in 1976. Amnesty International quotes the
conclusions of a report made by the United Nations in 1988:

> *This research has failed to provide scientific proof that executions have
> a greater deterrent effect than life imprisonment. Such proof is unlikely
> to be forthcoming. The evidence as a whole still gives no positive support
> to the deterrent hypothesis.*

*The fact that all the evidence continues to point in the same direction is persuasive **a priori** evidence that countries need not fear sudden and serious changes in the curve of crime if they reduce their reliance on the death penalty.*

(Amnesty International, *When the State Kills*, pages 10–14)

The problem with statistical data often provided by pro-death penalty groups is that the social conditions that establish homicide rates are complex and the number of executions carried out is only one amongst many interrelated variables (for example employment levels, ethnic mix and age structure). To single out the death penalty as the one reason why homicide rates have fallen is to remove its predictive power and question the empirical reliability of the whole deterrence argument.

Cross-reference

See pages 95–96 above in favour of the best bet argument.

Jeffrey Reiman rejects the best bet argument that given the indecisive evidence for capital punishment as deterrence it is better not to use it than risk the death of innocent lives and moreover the lesser punishment of life in prison is also likely to have just the same deterrent effect. As the utilitarian principle states that less pain is always preferable when promoting the greatest happiness then prison is a more preferable option than capital punishment.

And if life imprisonment were sufficiently probable to pose a real deterrent threat, it would pose as much of a deterrent threat as death. And then it seems that any lengthy prison sentence – say, twenty years – dependably imposed and not softened by parole, would do the same.

(Jeffrey Reiman, in Louis Pojman and Jeffrey Reiman, *The Death Penalty: For and Against*, page 105)

ii) No duty to use capital punishment

Supposing the evidence for deterrence could be demonstrated unequivocally to work, would this inevitably lead one to advocate capital punishment? Do I become culpable if I refrain from carrying out executions (i.e. my failure to act has resulted in the death/murders of innocent people) because I believe that all deliberate killing in a civilised society is wrong? Therefore I have no *prima facie* duty to use capital punishment. The question is whether a society that holds this view is blameworthy for future deaths caused by lack of capital punishment. One line of defence might be to call on the **acts and omissions** doctrine. I might reasonably argue that I cannot be blamed for something which I have not done. So, for instance, I cannot be blamed for failing to help those who have died from starvation after drought in a distant country when I am not in a position to do so. Or in another situation if, as a pacifist, I refrain from fighting a war can I be blamed for the deaths of my compatriots?

Cross-reference

Read pages 119–120 below for further discussion on pacifism, acts and omissions and blame.

So, if in the case of capital punishment I hold that killing people is wrong then it follows that I must not directly cause the death of a

Key quote

'Although moral beliefs are not in any straightforward way true or false, there is something both objectionable and absurd about trying to argue for a moral view by saying how harmful its widespread rejection would be.'

JONATHAN GLOVER,
*CAUSING DEATH AND
SAVING LIVES*, PAGE 111

criminal and in refraining from doing so I cannot be directly blamed for any subsequent murder victims because of my omission.

But the acts and omissions doctrine does not convince most consequentialists and natural law moralists. An omission which results *knowingly* in a lesser good must be treated as a blameworthy act. If one rejects the acts and omissions doctrine, as Jonathan Glover does, then the case for capital punishment on the conclusive evidence that it does deter further deaths must be used.

iii) Unfairness and victimisation

The most often cited objection is that it is open to unfairness and despite its humanitarian concern for the individual, it could justify some forms of punishment which retributivists would find abhorrent.

Consider the following thought experiment. A judge decides to execute an innocent man because it is widely believed that he is guilty of committing several murders; his death will satisfy the local community and act as a deterrent against the murder of innocent people in the future. As the real murderer is now deterred from committing any more killings and happiness is restored, the judge's decision is justified.

But as many have argued, this is not only unfair but undermines the principle of protecting the innocent in favour of the ends justifying the means, and gives far too much power to those in authority. Reflecting on this thought experiment Alasdair MacIntyre concludes:

> *For by allowing the principle of utility to override our existing principles – such that a man ought not be hanged for a crime which he has not committed – we remove one more barrier to using the concept of the general happiness to license any enormity. That it can be so used has been amply demonstrated in this century; in particular the high-minded are apt to use totalitarianism as a justification to excuse their responsibility for involvement in such large-scale crimes of their societies, such as Auschwitz or Hiroshima.*
>
> (Alasdair MacIntyre, *A Short History of Ethics*, page 240)

However, the accusation of victimisation need not be insuperable for utilitarians. **Rule utilitarians** for example (such as J.S. Mill) might respond that if there is general disapproval of punishing the innocent then the introduction of a rule forbidding this kind of deterrent punishment would avoid the possibility of the 'punishment' of the innocent and reassure the public of their own safety.

iv) Negative deterrence

The sociologist **Emile Durkheim** observed that intense or excessive punishment such as capital punishment may not make people more

Key people

Emile Durkheim (1858–1917) was one of the founders of sociology. He was editor of the journal *L'Année Sociologique* and wrote on suicide, crime, education and religion.

Key quote

'There had been many such sights … they were far more calculated to awaken pity for the sufferers than respect for that law.'

CHARLES DICKENS, *BARNABY RUDGE* (1840–41), CHAPTER 77

Key quotes

'For the human being can never be treated merely as a means to the ends of another and thus be joined with objects of the right regarding things, against which his innate personhood protects him.'

IMMANUEL KANT, *GROUNDING FOR THE METAPHYSICS OF MORALS*, 6:331

'It is not the severity of the penalty inflicted, but the certainty both of detection and of the exaction of the penalty required by law, whatever this may be. If ... there is always a hope of reprieve, the death penalty will be less of a deterrent than a life sentence without possibility of reprieve.'

WILLIAM TEMPLE, 'THE DEATH PENALTY' (*THE SPECTATOR*, 25 JANUARY 1935)

law abiding; it may make them distrustful of the whole judicial system.

The intensity of punishment is the greater the more closely societies approximate to a less developed type – and the more the central power assumes an absolute character.

(Emile Durkheim, 'Two Laws of Penal Evolution', in *L'Année Sociologique* 4, 1899–1900)

The spectacle of a hanging can equally have the effect of turning people *against* the death penalty and making them regard the law as barbaric and unjust. George Orwell famously wrote of his repulsion when watching an execution in his essay 'A Hanging' (1931) and in July 1840 the two celebrated writers William Makepeace Thackeray and Charles Dickens, having witnessed the hanging of Francois Courvoisier, turned their literary skills to the abolitionist cause.

For deterrence to be effective an execution needs to be public, yet evidence is that people find executions morbidly salacious and in the nineteenth century public hangings were an excuse for bad behaviour from the crowds. For these reasons hanging in Britain became a private affair in 1868 conducted within the prison. The last vestige of religious meaning was abolished in 1927 when chaplains were forbidden to read the burial service. If capital punishment is considered too repulsive to be carried out publicly then it suggests that the lesser punishment will have a greater deterrent effect in a civilised society.

v) An offender's minimal right to life

Deterrence might also be rejected according to Kant's 'practical imperative', which states that people should never be used as a means to an end. If the reason for an execution is to deter others then the offender is being treated as a means to an end (the greater good). Any minimal respect for him as a human being ought to respect his right to life.

The response to this line of argument is that if this is true for capital punishment then all forms of deterrence are questionable. But punishment works on some degree of dehumanising the culprit as a warning to others; if it did not do so then it would not put off others from committing offences against society. For the utilitarian, as there are no natural human rights, then an offender might lose any legal rights he has by his gross infringement of the social contract. The essential question remains for the utilitarian whether capital punishment is ever proportionate as deterrence for the good of the many.

vi) Uncertainty and stays of execution

William Temple, who was instrumental in the abolition of the death penalty in Britain, argued that the effectiveness of deterrence depended on the certainty on which a crime would receive capital punishment. The problem lies with the severity of the punishment and the reluctance which a society may feel in using it. Whilst these moral uncertainties exist the potential criminal knows that the likelihood of receiving the punishment is greatly reduced and so the effectiveness of deterrence is greatly diminished.

5 Reform

a) Punishment as reform

Key question

How far should we go to 'reform' a criminal?

Reformative punishment is **forward looking** and shares many of the characteristics of deterrence. Where it differs is in its consideration of the status of the offender. It sees punishment as both the means and opportunity to return the offender back into society as a useful member. It shares some of the retributivist's desires to allow the offender to feel that he has paid off or atoned for his guilt, but goes further in seeing this as a positive process for the future. Some aims of reform are less extravagant and hope at least to make the offender more *law abiding* (even if this is just a fear of being caught and punished again). Other reform aims might include a more compassionate or benevolent understanding of the **motives** or **factors** which led to the offence. The reformer looks in particular at the mental and physical state of the offender. These factors not only mitigate the crime but also suggest that society is obliged to help the offender overcome his or her difficulties. Our knowledge of psychology has helped us sympathise with the offender who has not acted entirely through his own conscious will but is affected by repressed experiences from his past (or other psychological imbalances).

b) Capital punishment and reform

The only arguments which can be made for capital punishment as reform fall under the deterrent argument. As we have seen, the retributivist has also regarded the reform of the offender as an important part of the process of atoning for guilt and as an example to others. However, the reformist position has been one that looks less at the victims of crime and more at the humanity of the offender.

The reformist position inevitably leads to a broadly anti–death penalty position.

i) Forgiveness

Cross-reference

Read pages 8–13 above on the sanctity of life.

Capital punishment is rejected because no one is so wicked that they cannot live some kind of worthwhile existence. The Christian **sanctity of life argument** endorses the view that if all humans are

Key quote

'Almighty God, the Father of our Lord Jesus Christ, who desireth not the death of a sinner, but rather that he may turn from his wickedness and live.'

THE CHURCH OF ENGLAND, BOOK OF COMMON PRAYER (1662)

Key people

William Temple (1881–1944) was Archbishop of Canterbury and was especially interested in the education and welfare of the poor and disadvantaged. He was influenced by neo-Hegelianism which underpinned much of his social philosophy – notably his popular book *Christianity and Social Order* (1940).

created in the image of God, then God desires that all human beings should be capable of forgiveness and redemption. The Christian moral imperative is to save the sinner, not to kill them.

ii) Killing with killing

Reformists consider that capital punishment rests on a moral contradiction, namely the killing of a person (even though they may be guilty) because they have killed. If deliberate killing is intrinsically wrong, which is why it is being punished, then it is equally wrong to permit the state to kill and even less satisfactory to place itself above personal moral behaviour. **William Temple** argued, in an influential article, that the state most effectively upholds the principles it seeks to protect by avoiding the very means which it condemns.

> *It is often said that execution for murder is justified because murder, being an outrage upon the sanctity of life, calls for a quite unique retribution or repudiation. That in itself may be true: but the State will do most to promote regard for the sanctity of life by paying regard to that sanctity itself … This is an argument which in any special application is incapable of being tested; but the principle of it rests both upon a very wide observation of instances and upon the understanding of human character possessed by those who have most deeply penetrated its secrets.*
>
> (William Temple, 'The Death Penalty', in *The Spectator*, 25 January 1935)

c) Criticisms of reform and capital punishment

Many argue that the role of punishment is not to indoctrinate moral values but to enable the criminal to pay off his debts to society (or to deter others). The reformist position is flawed in two ways. First, whose values does the reformer intend to instil? Second, is prison the right environment to impart them? Reform also assumes that offenders necessarily feel that they have done something morally wrong; if prison is to educate it is to indicate that what a culprit has done is legally wrong. A society based on liberal thinking entitles a person to hold his own moral views and values.

Key question

Should the aim of punishment be to make people morally better?

- Reform could be construed as an unnecessary infringement of personal autonomy.
- The issues raised by **psychology** are open to considerable discussion; there are Orwellian worries that if prison is seen to be the place to have these imbalances 'corrected', then any misdemeanour might give the state the excuse needed to turn out 'balanced' citizens (through indoctrination).
- Reform is another form of **victimisation** because it focuses too much on the criminal and not enough on the victim of crime. In

Key people

C.S. Lewis (1889–1963) was a professor of English at Oxford University but also an influential and popular writer on Christianity. His book *The Humanitarian Theory of Punishment* (1953) justified retributive justice and capital punishment along similar grounds as Kant.

doing so it makes the criminal the object of concern when what matters is dealing with the crime and its effects on others.

● Others, like **C.S. Lewis,** accuse such 'humanitarian' forms of punishment of diminishing the offender's sense of just deserts and in doing so reducing his dignity.

6 Normative ethical responses to killing as punishment

a) Kantian ethics

Key quotes

'Only the law of retribution (Ius talionis) [i.e. lex talionis] can determine the quality and quantity of punishment.'
IMMANUEL KANT,
THE METAPHYSICS
OF MORALS, 6:332

'Justice ceases to be justice at all if it gives itself away for any price.'
IMMANUEL KANT,
THE METAPHYSICS
OF MORALS, 6:332

Kant's philosophical argument for capital punishment may be found in his book *The Metaphysics of Morals* (1797) in which he sets out his non-metaphysical but transcendental (or universal) argument for the traditional retributive justice.

Kant begins by utterly rejecting any form of utilitarian argument for punishment. He gives the example of offering a murderer an alternative to the death penalty: being used in a risky medical experiment which would be for the 'greater good' of furthering human knowledge and which if the criminal survived would allow him to continue his life. But a suggestion of this kind is quite unacceptable because what undermines or 'gives itself away', as Kant puts it, is that punishment can only be for one reason alone and this is to underpin justice.

> *Penal law is a categorical imperative, and woe to him who creeps along the twisting paths of the doctrine of happiness in order to find that, for the advantage it promises, frees him even in the slightest degree from his punishment, according to the Pharisaic motto: 'It is better that one man should die than the entire people perish.'*
> (Immanuel Kant, *The Metaphysics of Morals*, 6:332, in '*Toward Perpetual Peace*' [edited by Pauline Kleingeld], page 129)

Cross-reference

See pages 88–93 above on retributive justice and respect for persons.

The point of retributive justice, as we have seen, is that according to the categorical imperative it would be inconsistent, irrational and inhumane to treat the criminal any differently from the moral principle which he chose to justify his crime. Therefore, as Kant argues, even if all the inhabitants on an island were to desert it leaving the last murderer in prison, he still ought to be executed, even though he poses no threat to society:

> *Even if civil society were to dissolve … the last murderer to be found in its prison would have to be executed first, so that everyone receive what his deeds merit and have so that the blood-guilt not adhere to the people that did not press for this punishment. It would adhere to the people because it can be regarded as a participant in this public injury of justice.*
> (Immanuel Kant, *The Metaphysics of Morals*, 6:333, in '*Towards Perpetual Peace*', page 130)

The main points of Kant's argument are:

Key quote

Kant's categorical imperative: *'Act as if the maxim of your action were to become through your will a universal law.'*

- Retribution precedes any good done to the offender. By this Kant rules out any reformative or deterrent aims of punishment *in the first instance*. An offender is punished because he 'has committed a crime' and deserves it.
- Justice and righteousness are the bedrock on which human value or dignity depends. Because Kant's view of morality is universal according to the categorical imperative and murder is always the most heinous infringement of human liberty, then it follows that in permitting a murderer to live one is undermining the essential values on which society is founded.
- A murderer ought to be executed in order to see that **just deserts** have been awarded. No other punishment is suitable; killing cannot be exchanged with anything else.
- Failure to punish condemns a society, otherwise it might be construed that in failing to punish it is condoning murder. A judge is **categorically obliged** (there is no distinction between moral and legal obligation) to apply the law and ignore mitigating circumstances.
- Kant appeals to an almost mystical notion that blood for blood satisfies a very deep human **psychological** need when he says, '**blood-guilt** not adhere to the people'. There is certainly a long tradition to which the Bible witnesses (e.g. after Abel's murder by Cain: 'the voice of your brother's blood is crying to me from the ground', Genesis 4:10) that the death of the offender in some way **atones** for the death of his victim. There is circumstantial evidence, often cited by those who are pro-capital punishment, that even the offender realises this and *wants* to die. There is a great deal made of this in the mid-nineteenth century when the priest's job with the condemned was to elicit a confession of guilt. This not only offered the possibility of salvation but by acknowledging the guilt of his crime the criminal removed the stain of the offence from society.

b) Utilitarianism

Cross-reference

See pages 93–94 above for the utilitarian argument for deterrence.

As we have seen, the utilitarian argument rejects the traditional retributive argument because it does not consider there is any intrinsic or natural basis for just deserts. Utilitarian arguments, therefore, are largely in favour of capital punishment only if it can be shown to deter actual criminals from carrying out heinous crimes against others.

i) Retribution and preference utilitarianism

Some utilitarians do support a retributivist position. Preference utilitarians might argue that capital punishment for certain heinous and terrible crimes can only be satisfied if the criminal receives back what pain he has inflicted on society. This shares something of Kant's 'blood-guilt' psychology but avoids suggesting that this is in any way a natural or intuitive good.

ii) Retribution and rule utilitarianism

Cross-reference

See page 89 for rights retributivism.

Some rule utilitarians such as J.S. Mill have argued that capital punishment serves to maintain respect for the law along the same lines in which the **rights retributivists** argued that disregard for another person's basic rights cannot be good for society. Rule utilitarians also argue that a retributive (as well as deterrent) aim of punishment serves to reward the good and leads to greater efficiency in the application of law, ultimately increasing society's welfare and happiness. These are Mill's arguments in his famous address to Parliament in 1868 in favour of capital punishment:

> ... to deter by suffering from inflicting suffering is not only possible, but the very purpose of penal justice. Does fining a criminal show want of respect for property, or imprisoning him, for personal freedom? Just as unreasonable is it to think that to take the life of a man who has taken that of another is to show want of regard for human life. We show, on the contrary, most emphatically our regard for it, by the adoption of a rule that he who violates that right of another forfeits it for himself, and that while no other crime that he can commit deprives him of his right to live, this shall.
> (J.S. Mill, *Parliamentary Debate on Capital Punishment Within Prisons Bill* [1868]; reprinted in Peter Singer, *Applied Ethics*, page 102)

On the other hand utilitarians have often been wary of rules because, as we have already seen, a rule which always imposed capital punishment on certain crimes could be considered unduly cruel and vindictive and fail to allow for alternatives.

iii) Deterrence and act utilitarianism

But for many utilitarians retributive punishment is undesirable in itself because, according to the utilitarian maxim of maximising happiness and avoiding pain, any deliberate infliction of pain could only be justified provided it results in greater happiness. The strength of this view is that it is able to look at each case with some degree of independence and take into account mitigating circumstances. As it exercises a **minimising policy**, i.e. that punishment should inflict the least amount of pain possible, then it might be argued that if capital punishment could be shown to deter others then its use might be justified.

Utilitarian arguments in favour of capital punishment might include:

- The finality of capital punishment secures peace of mind.
- Prison is insufficient because the prisoner might escape, the prison system might be altered with new legislation or a more

sympathetic view of parole might permit a prisoner to be
released later.

Utilitarian arguments against capital punishment might include:

- In practice there are very few cases where prisoners have escaped
  and reoffended.
- The utilitarian could be just as secure in mind that the prisoner
  has been locked away for ever without having to add unnecessary
  pain through execution.
- The **side-effects** of capital punishment make it undesirable, such
  as the painful effects on the executed man's friends, family and
  other prisoners.
- The **brutalising** effect executions have on society as a whole
  and knowledge of the actual process of an execution may cause
  many people great unease about the society they live in.

Cross-reference

Read pages 98–99 and Durkheim's
quotation above.

c) Virtue ethics

At the heart of Aristotle's theory of the virtues is the community or
polis. Humans live naturally in communities and therefore the moral
life is one where each individual operates for the good of the *polis*
by contributing the very best that he can. To be virtuous is to
develop those excellences (*arete*) of character, which lead to the
individual and the community flourishing (*eudaimonia*). Aristotle
argued that a just society (and the good person) is one where all the
virtues are practised.

The notion of **just deserts** therefore follows, that those who are
virtuous should be rewarded and those who are vicious should be
punished. But justice is more than merely distributing goods or
rewarding the good; for Aristotle justice also describes a society
which is at one with itself spiritually and physically. This is why he
rated friendship as the most important virtue, for friendship
describes the way in which any human relationship works in all
its complexity.

The question, therefore, is whether capital punishment is
appropriate to maintain justice.

i) Virtue ethical arguments for capital punishment

Capital punishment might be used as a just desert for those whose
vicious actions undermine the welfare of the *polis*. As virtuous
action is to be rewarded, those who have been harmed by criminal
behaviour have the satisfaction that evil citizens have been removed
from society. Justice recognises that the better person should be a
privileged member of society just as it is only right to prefer the
better player for a football team and to exclude those who have
forfeited their rights by failing to behave as good citizens.

As virtue ethics is equally concerned with good practice (*phronesis*) they might also argue against the excessive cruelty of the execution itself. Very few would argue for a strict application of the *lex talionis* principle, i.e. a rapist should be raped or a violent murderer brutally killed, so capital punishment should not inflict unnecessary suffering on the victim and should use a humane form of execution.

ii) Virtue ethical arguments against capital punishment

Just as Aristotle argued that suicide is wrong because it causes a loss of a valuable citizen to the state then equally it might be argued that capital punishment is a sign that society has in some way failed. Virtue ethicists today might support the reform view of punishment that capital punishment appears vindictive and supports the very vices that it condemns. It is bad *practice* and sends out the wrong signals about behaviour in the community. Christian virtue ethicists might argue that the three cardinal virtues of faith, hope and charity cannot be applied if the criminal has been executed.

d) Natural law

According to Aquinas the *telos* or final state of every action includes self-preservation, progress and reproduction, to live in an ordered society and self-perfection in the pursuit of justice. It follows therefore that punishment serves a purpose to ensure that these ends are achieved. But more fundamentally natural law claims that there is a law of nature which rewards the good and punishes the wicked. Natural law supports the retributivist position of just deserts. The point was made by Leibniz:

> *One may say nevertheless that the damned ever bring upon themselves new pains through new sins, and that the blessed ever bring upon them-selves new joys by new progress in goodness: for both are founded on the* principle of the fitness of things, *which has seen to it that affairs were so ordered that the evil action must bring upon itself chastisement.*
>
> (G.W. Leibniz, *Theodicy* [1698], quoted in Louis Pojman and Jeffrey Reiman, *The Death Penalty: For and Against*, page 14)

i) Rights retribution

Key question

Is it possible for someone to do something so bad that they cease to be considered human?

Cross-reference

The problem of collective responsibility for killing in war is discussed on pages 124–125 below.

Nevertheless, it is not obvious how natural law permits the deliberate cold-blooded taking of any human life. Aquinas deals with this in two stages. First, no individual may pass judgement on another or else the action would become one of revenge. The process of judgement has to be collective so that if there is blame then it cannot be apportioned to any one individual. Second, people who carry out terrible crimes which break the fundamentals of natural law (such as the deliberate killing of an innocent person) can no longer be protected by the same rights which protect the innocent. Aquinas argues:

By sinning man departs from the order of reason, and consequently falls away from the dignity of his manhood, in so far as he is naturally free, and exists for himself, and he falls into the slavish state of the beasts, by being disposed of according as he is useful to others ... Hence, although it be evil in itself to kill a man so long as he preserve his dignity, yet it may be good to kill a man who has sinned, even as it is to kill a beast. For a bad man is worse than a beast, and is more harmful, as Aristotle states ... it is lawful to kill an evildoer in so far as it is directed to the welfare of the whole community, so that it belongs to him alone who has charge of the community's welfare. Thus it belongs to a physician to cut off a decayed limb, when he has been entrusted with the care of the health of the whole body. Now the care of the common good is entrusted to persons of rank having public authority: wherefore they alone, and not private individuals, can lawfully put evildoers to death.

(Thomas Aquinas, *Summa Theologica* 2.2, Q. 64, Articles 3 and 4)

<blockquote>
Key quote

'For a bad man is worse than a beast, and is more harmful, as Aristotle states.'

THOMAS AQUINAS, *SUMMA THEOLOGICA* 2.2, Q. 64
</blockquote>

Aquinas maintains, as do many people today, that there are some crimes which are so heinous and of such magnitude that however one regards the mitigating circumstances, that person has demeaned himself to such an extent that he has abrogated any rights which might be due to him as a human being. Aquinas justifies his execution as part of the natural order of things; just as (by analogy) we are entitled to kill animals for food and protection, so we may also take a criminal's life where his actions show him to be no more than an animal and also threatens society's well-being. Aquinas' natural law preserves the traditional backward-looking 'guilt-desert' principle as well as the forward-looking deterrent argument.

ii) Capital punishment in principle but not in practice

The **Roman Catholic Church**'s natural law view is expressed in the encyclical *Evangelium Vitae* (The Gospel of Life, 1995). John Paul II wrote that execution is only appropriate 'in cases of absolute necessity, in other words, when it would not be possible otherwise to defend society. Today, however, as a result of steady improvement in the organisation of the penal system, such cases are very rare, if not practically non-existent.' The position is one set out also in the *Catechism of the Catholic Church*:

<blockquote>
Key quote

'The Church has acknowledged as well-founded the right and duty of legitimate public authority to punish malefactors by means of penalties commensurate with the gravity of the crime, not excluding, in cases of extreme gravity, the death penalty.'

CATECHISM OF THE CATHOLIC CHURCH, PAGE 488
</blockquote>

Preserving the common good of society requires rendering the aggressor unable to inflict harm. For this reason the traditional teaching of the Church has acknowledged as well-founded the right and duty of legitimate public authority to punish malefactors by means of penalties commensurate with the gravity of the crime, not excluding, in cases of extreme gravity, the death penalty. For analogous reasons those holding authority have the right to repel by armed force aggressors against the community in their charge.

(*Catechism of the Catholic Church*, page 488)

Both statements are very wary about the use of the death penalty and whilst maintaining the retributive principle place the emphasis in favour of punishment as protection/deterrence. Where possible, punishment should be reformative both for the good of the offender and for society (as atonement).

In other words, the present Roman Catholic view allows for the wicked to be punished but limits capital punishment to be used in very rare cases. Total exclusion of capital punishment would weaken the Church's view of war and the principle of legitimate killing of the wicked in that context.

e) Revealed ethics

The Christian Church has over the centuries held diametrically opposed views regarding the death penalty. In England over the past two hundred years the abolitionist cause was both hindered and eventually won by the views of the Church. In the USA today, where capital punishment is practised and much debated, the pro-capital punishment cause is part of the credo of many conservative Christians.

i) Pro-capital punishment

The issue here is the relationship between the Old and New Testaments. Those who advocate the death penalty refer to Genesis 9:6, 'Whoever sheds the blood of man, by man shall his blood be shed; for God made man in his own image', and Romans 13:4, 'But if you do wrong, be afraid, for he does not bear the sword in vain; he is the servant of God to execute his wrath on the wrongdoer.' Often referred to are Jesus' words to the penitent robber (Luke 23:39–43) who dies on the cross next to Jesus. As some commentators argue, Jesus does not absolve the man of his crime nor condemn the nature of his punishment but he does promise him eternal bliss as a reward for his repentance.

The pro-capital punishment argument also refers to events where God kills as the punishment for sins. Genesis 6 recounts the destruction of mankind through a flood; the inhabitants of Sodom were destroyed because of gross acts of inhospitality (possibly rape); Ananias and Sapphira were struck down because they failed to disclose to the Apostles all the money they had made on the sale of some property (Acts 5:1–11).

There are any number of cases in the Old Testament which required the death penalty: adultery (Deuteronomy 22), dishonour to parents (Exodus 21:15), a stranger who enters the temple (Numbers 1:51) and magic (Leviticus 20:27).

Key quotes

'Whoever sheds the blood of man, by man shall his blood be shed; for God made man in his own image.'

GENESIS 9:6

'But if you do wrong, be afraid, for he does not bear the sword in vain; he is the servant of God to execute his wrath on the wrongdoer.'

ROMANS 13:4

ii) Anti-capital punishment

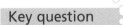

Key question

What principles do some Christians give for rejecting the use of capital punishment?

But for many the shift from the Old Testament to the New Testament marks a significant understanding in the way in which society is to be governed. So, whereas capital punishment was acceptable in Israel's early history for a society which marks itself out as being very different from its neighbours, Jesus' message was based on a new understanding of God's relationship with humans. In Jesus' Sermon on the Mount (Matthew 5–7) Jesus often begins his teaching by saying, 'You have heard it said ...' (referring to the laws of the Old Testament), balancing it with 'But I say to you ...' to modify and sometimes to cancel previous laws.

For example Jesus' emphasis on compassion, forgiveness and rehabilitation marks a decisive swing away from the Mosaic law of vengeance depicted in the Old Testament. In fact Jesus specifically replaces the *lex talionis* (Exodus 21:23–25) with an ethic of reconciliation:

Key quotes

'You have heard that it was said, "An eye for an eye and a tooth for a tooth." But I say to you, Do not resist one who is evil. But if anyone strikes you on the right cheek, turn to him the other also.'
MATTHEW 5:38–39

'Let him who is without sin among you be the first to throw a stone at her.'
JESUS IN THE GOSPEL OF JOHN 8:7

> *You have heard that it was said, 'An eye for an eye and a tooth for a tooth.' But I say to you, Do not resist one who is evil. But if anyone strikes you on the right cheek, turn to him the other also.*
>
> (Matthew 5:38–39)

Jesus' treatment of the woman caught in adultery (John 8:3–11), where Jesus commutes her death penalty because, as he says, none of us is perfect enough to make a judgement of this kind (John 8:7), confirms the view that Christianity cannot support capital punishment in practice, even if in theory there is a logical reason why it could be applied, because punishment must primarily be to reform and rehabilitate.

iii) The problem of authority and judgement

A more thorny theological issue is to what degree humans, the Church or the state have God's authority to carry out his judgement. Peter is told:

> *And I tell you, you are Peter, and on this rock I will build my church, and the powers of death will not prevail against it. I will give you the keys of the kingdom of heaven, and whatever you bind on earth will be bound in heaven, and whatever you loose on earth will be loosed in heaven.*
>
> (Matthew 16:18–19)

The power invested in Peter to bind and loose is taken to mean the forgiveness and condemnation of sins. But there is no consensus over what *degree* is permitted to the Christian community. There are three possibilities.

● **Maximum authority**: in which the community acts as God's agents on earth, and taking the lead from Genesis 9 this authorises man to carry out punishment (and capital punishment). If God's kingdom is to be established on earth then in the face of evil extreme action has sometimes to be exercised.

- **Minimum authority**: the community acts only in so far as it prepares the individual for the coming of God's final judgement. Jesus' death on the cross takes on human guilt so that retributive justice is now redundant.
- **Restrained authority**: the previous model dwelt too much on final judgement, leaving too little to be exercised in the present. In Romans 13 Paul depicts a long-term view of society which requires institutions, laws and punishments (the reference to the 'sword' in Romans 13:4 should not be taken literally but as a symbol of authority). The Christian community is given authority to judge but not so that it creates terror (the danger with a maximum model), but with mercy and restraint. In the story of Cain, Cain was pardoned by God although he deserved to die for having killed Abel (Genesis 4:15). The natural desire to seek vengeance is transmuted into a life where Cain atones for his own sin.

Summary diagram

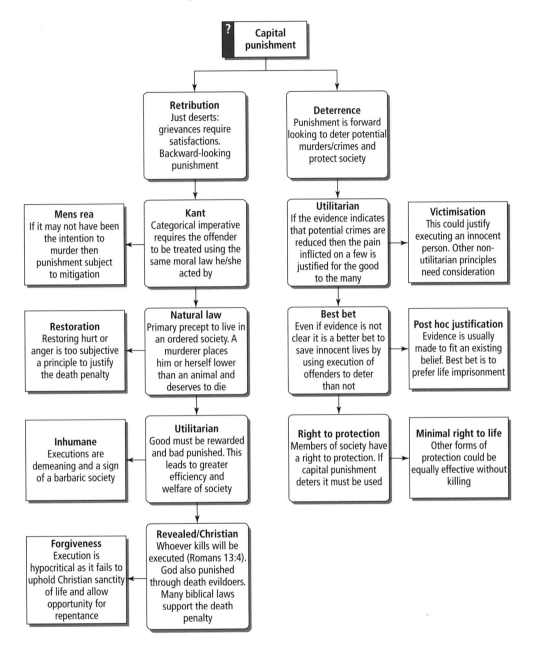

Study guide

By the end of this chapter you should have considered why retributive justice justifies the use of capital punishment: the natural law view that it is a just desert for a heinous crime; Kant's argument that it is consistent with the categorical imperative; more recent justifications of social contract retributivists, rights retributivists and

restoration retributivists. You will have considered the utilitarian
deterrence argument and considered whether even if the evidence is
inconclusive it would still be the best bet to use capital punishment
for murder. You will also have assessed the views of those opposed
to capital punishment that punishment is to reform and rehabilitate
offenders based on Christian views of forgiveness and the view that
humans never have the authority to take a life in cold blood.

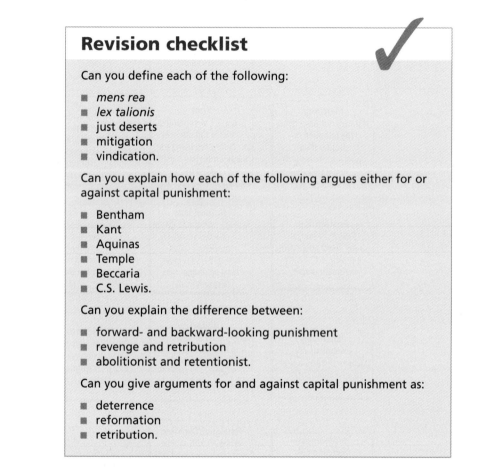

Revision checklist

Can you define each of the following:

- *mens rea*
- *lex talionis*
- just deserts
- mitigation
- vindication.

Can you explain how each of the following argues either for or
against capital punishment:

- Bentham
- Kant
- Aquinas
- Temple
- Beccaria
- C.S. Lewis.

Can you explain the difference between:

- forward- and backward-looking punishment
- revenge and retribution
- abolitionist and retentionist.

Can you give arguments for and against capital punishment as:

- deterrence
- reformation
- retribution.

Essay question

1) 'Without capital punishment murderers would gain an unfair advantage over law-abiding citizens.' Discuss.

The essay might begin by considering what is meant by a just desert
in terms of a grievance caused by a heinous crime and the
satisfactions required to rectify the fault. The argument therefore is
an analysis of retributive justice. You might explain that the crime
committed has given the offender an advantage (e.g. money,
revenge, power) which has been unlawfully gained at the expense
of the victim and law-abiding members of society as a whole. The
principle of *lex talionis* applied to murderers justifies capital

punishment on the grounds that the harm caused to the victim must be paid back, like for like. Furthermore non-natural law justification might be based on a rights retributivism – that it is 'fair play' to repay loss of rights with the right to demand the death penalty – or a contractual retributivism which considers that society is right to remove freedom and life from those who have done the same to society.

Analysis might consider whether the unfair advantage position actually justifies the death penalty. Kant's argument doesn't in fact argue for the death penalty but rather the satisfactions of the moral pain caused. This suggests that the *lex talionis* is never strictly applied (for example rape is not matched with rape) but administered in proportion to the hurt caused to society/victim. Discussion might consider Rawls' view that as the just deserts principle is not objective but subjective and contingent, then there are other ways of maintaining the contract other than by execution. Some discussion might focus on what 'advantage' means and if mitigating circumstances are included then retribution/death penalty is too inconsistent to justify taking another person's life in cold blood.

Further essay questions

2a Explain Kant's use of the categorical imperative to justify capital punishment.

2b 'Kant's argument for capital punishment contradicts his view that all human life is valuable.' Discuss.

3a Explain the natural law teaching on retribution and capital punishment.

3b 'In a society where there is a good prison system Christian ethics cannot justify the death penalty.' Discuss.

4 Assess the view that even if capital punishment could be shown to work as a deterrent, there would be no moral obligation to use it.

6 WAR AND PEACE

Chapter checklist ✓

The first part of this chapter considers the relationship between use of lethal force at a personal level and publicly by the state. Three views are considered: war realists, militarists and pacifists. War realists accept an uneasy relationship between private and public morality, whereas militarists consider that war expresses important moral values. Holy war is considered as an example of militarism. The eight propositions of the 'just war' argument are outlined as well as two types of pacifism (absolute and contingent). Several normative ethical systems and their views on war and peace are considered.

1 Why war?

Key question

What single reason justifies the use of war?

There are many reasons for war. These might include:

- maintaining the social order
- adding/keeping territory
- revenge
- expression of power
- protection of the innocent
- combating evil
- expressing one's beliefs.

For many people today a response to the question 'why war?' is that it is reasonable to use force to defend oneself (family, nation, property) against an illicit aggressor. Ingrained in the natural law tradition, for example, is the notion that the innocent should be protected. The innocent are those who have not caused harm to others.

But for others war is more than this. War is an **expression** of a ruler's, nation's or people's values. The use of force against an aggressor is to express certain values, which war reinforces.

From these two positions emerge three different purposes and justifications for war:

- **War militarism**: war as an expression of certain values.
- **War realism**: war as an instrumental means of achieving certain ends.
- **Just war**: just war could be either militarist or realist, but maintains the proposition that the innocent should be protected and that the means of war should be proportionate to the end.

2 Public and private values and the use of lethal violence

War is about the use of violence often with the intention of killing. The paradox that war poses for some is that although they may condemn the private use of violence and killing, they permit the use of war by the state. However, if it is wrong to kill at the private level, then it is *a fortiori* (so much more so) wrong at the public level where in war the number of people killed are likely to be many more.

a) Private use of violence

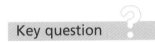

Key question

Is it always wrong to use violence as an individual?

The question is: when is it reasonable to use force and when is it appropriate to use violent means? Both share the use of physical pain and injury but the difference is that force is restrained by purpose whereas violence is unconstrained and has no limits.

For example, there is a difference between a burglar who makes a forced entry into a house in order to steal property and a vandal who deliberately destroys house and property for its own sake. In other words an individual might legitimately use force to protect himself or others and this might involve the *possibility* of violence. As violence has no purpose and may involve the deliberate taking of life it can have no justification, especially at the private level.

But the problem is whether, even if unintended in the first instance, private use of force may involve lethal violent means in order to protect oneself or others from harm. Some argue that it is never right to do so because, when it comes to killing, no individual is in a position to make a just and fair judgement.

Key question

If the use of lethal violence is wrong at a personal level, how can war be justified?

b) Public use of violence

Many argue that the public use of violence in war is justified because the central issue is maintaining or establishing **social order**. As this is something which cannot be done by the individual, the **war realist** and **just war argument** (JWA) both recognise that war is sometimes a necessary **instrument** of state.

Key thought

The **just war argument** proposes that war may sometimes be justified even though it is never morally good in itself.

Key people

Group Captain **Leonard Cheshire** (1917–92) was a British RAF officer who won many honours fighting in the Second World War, including the Victoria Cross due to his work as a bomber pilot.

Key quote

'If it's myself who is being attacked, it may be a counsel of perfection that I turn the other cheek and allow myself to be killed but if the aggressor is killing someone else, or worse still, a whole group of others, then it cannot be a counsel of perfection for me to refrain from going to their defence ... my clear duty in charity is to defend the victims.'

LEONARD CHESHIRE, *WHERE IS GOD IN ALL THIS?*
(1991), PAGES 72–73

Cross-reference

See pages 128–34 below for a full account of the just war argument.

Key quote

Revolution is necessary *'not only because the ruling class cannot be overthrown in any other way but also because the class over-throwing it can only in a revolution succeed in ridding itself of all the muck of ages and become fitted to found society anew'.*

KARL MARX AND FREDERICK ENGELS (*COLLECTED WORKS*, VOL. 5), PAGE 53

3 Pacifism

Key word

Teleological comes from the Greek *telos* meaning a final state.

i) War realist

- The **war realist** argues that where the state is concerned the complexities of private morality cannot and should not be transferred wholesale into the public arena. So, I might as a private citizen choose never to punish my children but allow them to find out their morality by trial and error. But this would never work on a large scale without chaos and possible violence. Public morality has to think in terms of the country as a whole and largely to disregard the individual. **Leonard Cheshire** recognises that personal morality cannot exist in isolation; I have a duty to others which means sacrificing my own sense of what is ultimately right.

- The **JWA** on the other hand argues forcibly for continuity between a private morality and its consistent application in the affairs of state. The present formulation of the JWA has been most often cited when the West was involved in the Falklands War, the Gulf War and to some extent in the conflict in Bosnia.

ii) Militarist

The **militarist**, on the other hand, sees the use of war as an expression of personal morality. The Ayatollah Khomeini famously said, from his perspective as a Muslim leader, 'A religion without war is a crippled religion', and Marx and Engels, the founding fathers of modern communism, not only regarded revolution as a means to establish communism but also as an expression of what communism stands for: the overthrow of the ruling class by the workers.

iii) Pacifist

The **pacifist** also argues for the continuity of private and public morality. If violence is wrong at the personal level, then there is no justification for its use in the public sphere. Michael Wink, a Christian pacifist, is typical of this position when he says, 'Non-violence is not an option for Christians. It is the essence of the gospel.'

Pacifism as **absolute pacifism** shares the same idealistic outlook as the militarist. The essential difference is that it regards all war as *intrinsically* wrong. The issue for the pacifist, therefore, is not the rights or wrongs of war but the means by which the individual can ensure justice without recourse to violence. However, pacifism may also be taken as a broad term for all those whose **teleological** aim is to establish peace whilst acknowledging that the means may, sometimes, require the use of war. **Contingent pacifism** therefore argues that peace is sometimes achieved by other means and not only the absence of violence.

a) Absolute pacifism

In the West absolute pacifism has its origins in the Christian tradition. The picture which emerges of the very early Christians was a group who rigorously practised the teachings of Jesus. His main teaching on pacifism is found in the **Sermon on the Mount** (Matthew 5–7). Here he taught that the Christian should love his enemies, turn the other cheek when wronged, settle disputes out of court and check anger before it escalates into violence. Paul's letter to the Romans (Romans 12:14–21) indicates just how deeply ingrained this attitude was at a very early stage.

Before Christianity became established as the state religion of the Roman empire, theologians such as **Tertullian** regarded pacifism as the characteristic of Christian practice. The story of Jesus **disarming Peter** is often quoted to support Christian pacifism when Jesus condemned Peter for drawing his sword to defend him at his arrest in Gethsemane. Moreover not only did Jesus tell Peter not to use a sword to defend him but to accept his arrest without resistance.

i) Quakers and conscientious objectors

Quakers or The Religious Society of Friends are typical of many Christian radical protestant groups who reject all forms of violence and in particular war. The Quaker is encouraged to see the element or spark of God in each person and actively to overcome all that which causes conflict between people. This can never on any account include the use of violence.

> The Spirit of Christ by which we are guided is not changeable, so as once to command us from a thing as evil, and again to move unto it; and we certainly know, and testify to the world, that the Spirit of Christ, which leads us into all truth, will never move us to fight and war against any man with outward weapons, neither for the kingdom of Christ, nor for the kingdoms of the world.
> (*A Declaration from the Harmless and Innocent People of God called Quakers*, presented to Charles II in 1660)

During the First World War, Quakers and others were often imprisoned as **conscientious objectors** to war. **Charles Raven**, for example, risked condemnation from other Christians by placing conscience before traditional church teaching and loyalty to the state. His experience of two world wars and the atomic bombs at Hiroshima and Nagasaki not only indicated to him the

---

Key people

Tertullian (c.160–225) was converted to Christianity before 197 and became a prolific and influential theologian of the African Church. He distinguished Christianity from pagan teaching and to that end taught that it was better to die a martyr than become involved in military service.

Key quotes

'Put your sword back into its place; for all who take up the sword shall perish by the sword.'
JESUS' WORDS TO PETER
MATTHEW 26:52–53

'But how will a Christian man war, nay how will he serve even in peace, without a sword, which the Lord has taken away? ... The Lord, in disarming Peter, unbelted every soldier.'
TERTULLIAN, *ON IDOLATRY*, 19, QUOTED IN ROBIN GILL, *A TEXTBOOK OF CHRISTIAN ETHICS*, PAGE 260

Key people

The **Quakers** were founded by George Fox in the mid-seventeenth century. He stressed the primacy of Jesus' teaching and largely rejected church buildings and organisation. Quakers stress the 'inner light' by which God works directly through the soul.

Key word

A **conscientious objector** is a person who refuses, for moral reasons, to fight in a war when called by the state to do so.

Key people

Charles Raven (1885–1965) was Regius Professor of Divinity at Cambridge University and an outspoken critic of war.

indiscriminate nature of war but that Christian conscience and duty must be primarily to one's neighbour, not to the state:

> ... *if we are really prepared under any imaginable circumstances to murder the whole population of a hundred square miles by a single explosion, it becomes difficult to feel that our churchgoing and prayers, our duty toward our neighbours and our talk about love, service and sacrifice can be anything but cant and hypocrisy.*
>
> (Charles Raven, *The Theological Basis of Christian Pacifism* [1952] quoted in Robin Gill, *A Textbook*, first edition, page 345)

ii) Martin Luther King Junior

Key people

Martin Luther King Junior (1929–68) was an American black Baptist minister in Montgomery, Alabama. In 1955 he was involved in the boycott of racially segregated buses and then helped to lead the civil rights movement. He was awarded the Nobel Peace Prize in 1964 and was assassinated in 1968.

Martin Luther King is famous for his pacifist response to issues of conflict. King used marches and peaceful protests to promote justice and stated that Christians have a duty to oppose unjust laws. Non-violent resistance is equated with biblical principles such as **agape** and **justice**. King is aware of the problem of **utopianism** held by certain pacifists and he knows that pacifism brings with it its own dangers and sufferings. But suffering, he argues, is 'a creative redemptive love towards all men'. King's pacifism shares the Quaker view of the natural goodness of humanity and desire for justice within every human heart.

His pacifism did not mean (as is sometimes thought) inaction, but rather direct **non-violent** action. His language is strongly eschatological and he knew that in the process of change there would be casualties. His own life and death acts as an icon for the pacifist movement. Those who support this line of reasoning point to its moral consistency, its sense of moral virtue and the long-term stability achieved through evolutionary change rather than sudden revolution. King's methods were influenced by **Mahatma Gandhi's** (1869–1948) teaching on *ahimsa* or non-violence (or non-harming), that political transformation can be achieved through peaceful but forceful means such as strikes, sanctions, protest and civil disobedience.

Key quote

'[The] reason why we should love our enemies is that love is the only force capable of transforming an enemy into a friend. We never get rid of an enemy by meeting hate with hate.'

MARTIN LUTHER KING JR, *THE STRENGTH TO LOVE* (1961), PAGE 54

Cross-reference

Read page 143 below on Christian eschatology. King often referred to the Kingdom of God on earth as the 'beloved community'.

b) Criticisms of absolute pacifism

Criticisms of absolute pacifism are that it has an overly optimistic view of human nature, that in resisting the use of force it can cause the innocent to suffer and that it can avoid being responsible for the lives of others.

i) Failure to acknowledge the sinfulness of human nature

Key people

Reinhold Niebuhr (1892–1971) was an American theologian and professor of applied Christianity at the Union Theological Seminary in New York City. He was critical of the optimism of liberal theology and social policy and stressed the place of human original sin.

The influential Christian theologian **Reinhold Niebuhr** argued that pacifists have failed to give a realistic account of human nature in a fallen world which has not yet achieved the Kingdom of God. Humans are driven by self-interest and therefore Christians are obliged to use force to restrain those who have evil intentions.

Key quote

'Most modern forms of Christian pacifism are heretical ... They have rejected the Christian doctrine of original sin ... They have the absurd idea that perfect love is guaranteed a simple victory over the world.'

REINHOLD NIEBUHR,
MORAL MAN AND
IMMORAL SOCIETY (1932)

Key people

G.E.M. (or Elizabeth) Anscombe (1919–2001) was a British analytic philosopher and an authority on the philosophy of Wittgenstein. As a committed Roman Catholic, she also developed modern versions of virtue and natural law ethics.

Cross-reference

G.E.M. Anscombe, 'War and Murder', in *Nuclear Weapons: A Catholic Response*, Walter Stein (editor), quoted in Michael Palmer, *Moral Problems*, pages 150–51.

Key quotes

'Pacifism therefore allows the wicked no limits to their wickedness.'

G.E.M. ANSCOMBE

'And in this way pacifism has corrupted enormous numbers of people who will not act according to its tenets. They become convinced that a number of things are wicked which are not.'

G.E.M. ANSCOMBE

Niebuhr argues for the use of force as a necessary component in maintaining peace and working for the victory of good over evil, justice over injustice. The use of violent resistance may be used if limited by the principle of discrimination along lines outlined in the just war tradition. He distinguishes between times when non-violence works and times when force is necessary to respond to a perceived evil.

ii) Failure to protect the innocent

We have already seen that critics accuse some forms of pacifism of promoting evil. The philosopher **G.E.M. Anscombe** bases her argument on the natural law principle that the innocent should always be protected. The only consideration is whether attacking someone would be unjust based on the principle that 'murder is the deliberate killing of the innocent whether for its own sake or as a means to some further end'. Her argument can be summarised as follows:

- **War can be bad.** It is true that some forms of war often fail to protect the innocent and those who do it fail to be punished. Often war glorifies such acts. War in these cases is morally wrong.
- **The non-innocent deserve to be attacked.** The central aspect of war is that those who attack the innocent have committed an intrinsically or object wrong. As such they deserve to be attacked. Anscombe argues: 'What is required, for the people attacked to be non-innocent in the relevant sense, is that they should themselves be engaged in an objectively unjust proceeding which the attacker has the right to make his concern; or, the commonest case, should be unjustly attacking him.'
- **The wickedness of pacifism.** Pacifism has corrupted the minds of many because it fails to distinguish 'between the shedding of innocent blood and the shedding of any human blood'. This means that wickedness potentially can have no limits because the pacifist has no reason to use force to limit it.
- **Modern warfare is not more dangerous.** It is true that wars have always involved massacres. But the pacifist's argument that modern technology makes war more dangerous is not true; it is probably less costly in loss of lives than in the past. However, it is true that in war bad things do happen, but as that need not necessarily be the case not all war is bad.

iii) Failure of the acts and omissions distinction

In order for absolute pacifism to be morally coherent, the pacifist has to draw a distinction between an act (i.e. refraining from violence) and omission (i.e. the consequences of not using violence). In order for the act of not using violence to be good then it has to be a sufficient condition of the omission that it does not entail any responsibility. For example, if I carry out the duty of the Ten Commandments not to steal, then regardless of the consequences of such an action, what I have done must be good in itself. A pacifist is good therefore by refraining from the use of violence, even if he can see that it might have apparently bad consequences. Those who defend the acts and omissions distinction point out that I cannot be held responsible for every action I perform which has undesirable side-effects because that would mean that every time I fail to give to a charity sending money to starving people, I would be responsible for any deaths that might follow.

- **Bad consequences**. Peter Singer argues that an omission in the sense of refraining is morally equivalent to an act if it has the same consequences. If therefore it is wrong to kill innocent people then by refraining from assassinating a tyrant who is murdering all those who oppose him, the pacifist has to 'bear some responsibility for the tyrant's future murders' (Peter Singer, *Practical Ethics*, page 308).
- **Reasonable ability to act**. Responsibilities are contingent on our roles and ability to act. If for example I am a strong swimmer and I can save a drowning man, then I have a responsibility to act for the best outcome. Failure to act would be justified only in so far as it would not be in my powers to do so or that the effects would be so indirect as to be very hard to measure. A pacifist's claim would therefore have to be based on lack of physical strength or that the use of violence would have no reasonable grounds for direct good.

iv) Moral self-indulgence

It may appear that the pacifist who resists being involved in any form of violence is exercising a great deal of moral control – perhaps even being prepared to die rather than betray his principle. But as Gordon Graham argues, such a position places the principle before the welfare and lives of others. This may seem to be a tough judgement on conscientious objectors and others who have had to suffer for their beliefs, but as Graham concludes, 'so too do any casualties of war whose lives or liberty they might have prevented' (*Ethics and International Relations*, page 55).

c) Contingent pacifism

The contingent pacifist's position develops the notion that if I am in a reasonable position to use violence proportionately to achieve peace then I am obliged to act. If I do not have the reasonable means (i.e. lack of skill, lack of resources, lack of strength) then my duty to non-violence must take priority (sometimes referred to as preferential pacifism). There are various types of contingent pacifism.

Key thought

Counsel of perfection is derived from Jesus' teaching in the Sermon on the Mount: 'You, therefore, must be perfect, as your heavenly Father is perfect' (Matthew 5:48).

Key quote

'This is my commandment, that you love one another as I have loved you. Greater love has no man than this, that a man lay down his life for his friends.'

JESUS TO HIS DISCIPLES
JOHN 15:12–13

Cross-reference

Read pages 168–71 below for a more detailed Christian response to nuclear pacifism.

i) Personal pacifism

Augustine was clear that pacifism was the hallmark of the Christian's *personal* relationship with others. If I am attacked then I must not use violence but love my neighbour as myself and turn the other cheek. However, this **counsel of perfection** does not extend to others. Once a situation involves threats to an innocent life and I am in a reasonable position to act, then I have a duty to do so. Whereas my duty to myself is self-centred and cannot justify force, I have a duty to protect the weak and even, in the imitation of Jesus himself, lay down my life for others as an act of self-sacrificial love.

ii) Nuclear pacifism

The contingent pacifist does not share the optimism of the absolute pacifist. While society still contains evil people, then the use of force can sometimes be justifiable. But even those who argue that war might be used to defend territory or human rights in extreme circumstances draw the line at nuclear warfare. Nuclear warfare is unacceptable because it cannot be controlled and will inevitably cause the death of innocent people on a massive scale. Moreover nuclear war (or wars using other weapons of mass destruction) is always disproportionate to any end and could never result in peace. Its effect on the social order would be devastating.

4 War realism

The realist view of war is quite often presented, as one might expect, by those who have had first-hand experience of war itself – as combatants or senior politicians. Leonard Cheshire's quotation above (page 116) represents a view which goes back to Augustine, which makes a distinction that is fundamental to the realist: personal moral perfection is a very different affair from the morality which is necessary in governing a state. Cheshire had served in Bomber Command during the Second World War and had experienced the devastation which war brings. For instance, after the controversial aerial bombing of German cities such as Dresden and Hamburg, Air Marshal Harris said: 'There was nothing to be ashamed of in the sort of thing that has to be done in every war, as of war itself.'

Harris' remark reminds his critics that in war nothing is clear cut. Strategically and indeed morally his action was justified because it was the enemy who had perpetrated the evil which men had the responsibility of eradicating. Realism does not celebrate war and at no stage does it say that it is intrinsically good. It is justified, as we have seen, as a *public* act because of the necessity of maintaining law and order.

Key people

Martin Luther (1483–1546) was the founder of the German Reformation. Before leaving the Catholic Church he was a priest and monk and taught theology at Wittenberg. He was tried by Rome for heretical teaching and broke with the Catholic Church in 1520. Central to his teaching was his sense of the sinfulness of human nature and God's grace acquired through faith.

Key quotes

'I observe that it amputates a leg or hand, so that the whole body may not perish … therefore, such a war is only a very brief lack of peace.'

MARTIN LUTHER, *WHETHER SOLDIERS, TOO, CAN BE SAVED*

'For rulers are not a terror to good conduct, but to bad. Would you have no fear of him who is in authority? Then do what is good, and you will receive approval, for he is God's servant for your good. But if you do wrong, be afraid, for he does not bear the sword in vain.'

ST PAUL, *LETTER TO THE ROMANS* 13:3–4

'Be subject for the Lord's sake to every human institution, whether it be to the emperor as supreme, or to governors as sent by him to punish those who do wrong and to praise those who do right.'

1 PETER 2:13–14

Key people

Karl von Clausewitz (1780–1831) was born in Prussia and at the age of twelve joined the Prussian army. He eventually achieved the rank of major general. He served in many campaigns including the Napoleonic Wars (1806–15). He was director of the Military Academy of Berlin and during this time wrote his influential work *On War*, which he never completed.

a) Martin Luther's religious duty to the state

Luther's argument in *Whether Soldiers, Too, Can be Saved* (1526) depends on his essential distinction between the **two kingdoms**: the kingdom of this world and the spiritual kingdom to come of the true Christian. At first it seems that a soldier's life is very alien to the love ethic of the New Testament. But on reflection, and in a wider context, the good which he achieves justifies his role. Romans 13:3–4 justifies the use of the sword, through which God carries out his judgement using man. Luther also refers to John the Baptist's words of moral exhortation to the soldiers, 'now the abuse does not affect the office'. Even Jesus suggests that war has its place on the earthly plane, 'if my kingship were of this world, my servants would fight' (John 18:36).

War cannot be wrong if it is the will of God, because then Moses, Joshua and David would be condemned for using violence. Instead they are praised. The New Testament sanctions the use of war in obedience to earthly authorities through whom God operates.

So, Luther argues in an extreme case, even if the ruler is a tyrant he must be obeyed because he still has reason enough to respond to the will of God. The only grounds for civil war would be against a madman who, because he has lost his reason and ability to respond to God, is no longer able to do good. A Christian's duty is always to the state:

> *A tyrant, however, may do things that are far worse than the insane man does, but he still knows that he is doing wrong. He still has a conscience and his faculties. There is the hope that he may improve … We can never hope that an insane man will do this for he is like a clod or a stone … If injustice is to be suffered, then it is better for subjects to suffer it from their rulers than for the rulers to suffer it from their subjects.*
>
> (Martin Luther, *Whether Soldiers, Too, Can be Saved*, in Robin Gill, *A Textbook of Christian Ethics*, revised edition, pages 297–98)

b) Karl von Clausewitz's consequentialist view

Karl von Clausewitz believed it was possible to have a theory of war – unlike many of his contemporaries, or those who argued that strategy depended on the genius of the leader. Because he had direct experience of fighting in war his **instrumentalist** consequentialist theory took into account the many uncertain factors in battle (both physical and psychological effects). He noted that war frequently had to deal with 'the continuous interaction of opposites' (*On War*, page 136). As a realist he argued that there is no neat way of fighting and justifying war.

Clausewitz argued, therefore, that the moral arguments which govern war have to be part of a **dialectic** between the physical circumstances which have led to war and how a war ideally should be fought. One of his key observations was that at every level of war, from government, to senior generals, to the forces on the ground, there is a constant tension between **ends and means**. For example in every war there is always a dialectic between the **moral factors** (morale, bravery, courage, leadership, determination) and the **physical factors** (danger, resources, the weather). As he says, 'war is a trial of moral and physical forces by means of the latter'. War is learnt through experience; it is both a science and an art.

i) Absolute but not total war

Many have argued that Clausewitz advocated **total war** but Clausewitz's view is more subtle than this; he did not use the term total war but absolute war. What he meant was that war should always aim to be victorious using whatever means necessary to achieve its end as a 'dominant consideration'. But this goal should always be balanced by using the least possible force for maximum effect. However, as Clausewitz notes, wars are not just fought on the battlefield. Other forces control war such as the views of politicians, war theorists and public opinion, which all have to be taken into consideration. Clausewitz indicates that this is far from easy given that the goal of war must be victory:

> How are we to counter the highly sophisticated theory that supposes it is possible for a particularly ingenious method of inflicting minor damage on the enemy's forces to lead to major indirect destruction? … Admittedly an engagement at one point may be worth more than at another. Admittedly there may be a skilful ordering of priority of engagements in strategy; indeed that is what strategy is all about, and we do not wish to deny it. We do claim, however, that direct annihilation of the enemy's forces must always be the dominant consideration. We simply want to establish this dominance of the destructive principle.
>
> (Karl von Clausewitz, *On War*, page 223)

ii) Analogy of the market place

Clausewitz therefore uses the analogy of the market place with war. Whereas others have compared war with art, seeing it in terms of human glory and skill, for Clausewitz war is a competitive process by which a complex set of interests have to be resolved, ultimately with winners and losers.

War is therefore an extension of politics in a world market place.

> We know, certainly, that War is only called forth through the political intercourse of Governments and Nations; but in general it is supposed that such intercourse is broken off by War, and that a totally different state of things ensues, subject to no laws but its own. We maintain, on

Key words

Instrumentalism considers that judgements are good only if they are effective in achieving their ends.

Dialectic comes from the Greek meaning 'to discuss' (as in question and answer). There are many different uses of the term dialectic. In contemporary philosophy it often refers to the way in which opposites can be combined.

Key quote

'Every thing in war is very simple, but the simplest thing is very difficult …'

KARL VON CLAUSEWITZ,
ON WAR, PAGE 119

Key question

To what extent should public opinion or the views of politicians affect the way war is fought?

Key word

Total war is often used to refer to the lack of discrimination between enemy military and civilian targets.

Key quote

'War is a clash between major interests that is resolved by bloodshed – that is the only way in which it differs from other conflicts. Rather than comparing it to an art we could more accurately compare it to commerce, which is also a conflict of human interests and activities; and it is still close to politics, which in turn may be considered as a kind of commerce on a larger scale.'

KARL VON CLAUSEWITZ,
ON WAR, PAGE 149

the contrary, that War is nothing but a continuation of political inter-course, with a mixture of other means.

(Karl von Clausewitz, *On War*, page 402)

Clausewitz suggests that war is therefore a way in which governments 'talk' to each other. We can see this happening today in the case of the first Gulf War (1990), in the bombing of Serbian strategic sites by Nato forces to protect the Albanian people living in Kosovo (March 1999) and the **war on terror** in Iraq and Afghanistan. In all these cases military action is used to reinforce threats by governments.

c) Michael Walzer's communitarian view

In his book *Just and Unjust Wars* (1992), Michael Walzer explores concepts of justice and morality in relation to a range of issues connected with the traditional JWA. He argues that although governments may have to use war as a means to an end (we have given them this right), this does not mean they are exempt from the responsibility of using violence. Statesmen have to share the guilt; their hands are morally dirty and there is no getting away from this. This so-called **dirty hands** view ensures that war will always be a last resort and the use of violence must be in proportion to the given end.

Walzer considers how the realist reconciles public and private morality. A ruler decides to torture a terrorist who knows the whereabouts of a bomb that could kill hundreds of innocent people. We recognise that public figures sometimes have to live in two worlds and our judgements of them don't always allow for this.

When he ordered the prisoner to be tortured, he committed a moral crime and he accepted a moral burden. Now he is a guilty man. His willing-ness to acknowledge and bear (and perhaps to repent and do penance for) his guilt is evidence, and it is the only evidence he can offer us, that he is not too good for politics and that he is good enough. Here is the moral politician: it is by his dirty hands that we know him. If he were a moral man and nothing else, his hands would not be dirty; if he were a politician and nothing else, he would pretend that they were clean.

(Michael Walzer, in M. Cohen [editor], *War and Moral Responsibility*, pages 69–70)

Whereas the realist argues that the use of war is sometimes a necessary aspect of governments, Walzer also considers whether a government is justified in intervening in the affairs of other sovereign states. Here are two questions he poses:

- **Is it just to intervene in a war on behalf of another nation?**
  Walzer rejects J.S. Mill's non-interventionist view that a nation's sovereignty and political autonomy should be respected on the grounds that people can only become free by their own will and rights. Walzer's communitarian political ethic claims that we

Key thought

The phrase 'war on terror' was coined by President George Bush after the attacks on New York and Washington on 11 September 2001 by al-Qaeda terrorists.

Key question

How do we know what the limits to war are?

Key people

Michael Walzer (b. 1935) is a leading American political philosopher. He was professor at the Institute of Advanced Study, Princeton University, and taught at Harvard. His views are sometimes described as belonging to the 'communitarian' position as developed by Alasdair MacIntyre. Although he rejects the war realist position his arguments accept that realism is a necessary element in making moral decisions about war.

Key thought

Dirty hands describes the dilemma where whatever one does is morally wrong but failing to act is morally worse. The existentialist writer Jean-Paul Sartre uses this idea in his 1948 play *Les Mains Sales* (Dirty Hands).

cannot live in isolation from each other and when a nation is invaded by another then it is a moral duty to help defend its rights and freedom.

- **Is it acceptable to intervene in a civil war?** Walzer argues that it is the duty of the international community to support the government of a country in a situation of civil war as they are the 'official representative of communal autonomy in international society'; however, once a dissenting group achieve a similar or equal power of support within that country they have achieved 'belligerent rights', and interveners should step aside.

d) War realist criticisms of pacifists

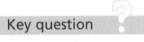

Key question

Why might pacifism cause or prolong war?

War realists are particularly critical of pacifism. Because pacifism is driven primarily by the moral view that all use of violence is wrong, pacifist ideology can distort policy thinking in two ways: it can cause wars and it can prolong wars. For example:

- **Pacifist utopians** (those who believe that humans can achieve a state where there will be no violence and live in co-operation) are accused of *causing* wars by the realist because they insist on consistent private/public moral behaviour. Realists claim that as they are unable to take the necessary strategic or practical steps early enough they in fact cause war. Some realists have called this the 'instrumentality of evil'.
- **Moral utopians** (those who believe that the use of war is a duty to overcome evil) are accused of prolonging wars. Realists point to Vietnam or Somalia or even Bosnia where the use of war on 'humanitarian' and other ideological grounds has resulted in more death and greater confusion. Realists are very wary when countries play the 'moral policeman' and use war as a means to do so.

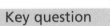

Key question

Why might war realism be more moral than pacifism?

Wars should be governed primarily by practical ends, not moral considerations. Ironically, by employing 'objective instrumentality', the realist argues that his wars are, in the end, more moral. The case of the **Gulf War** (1990–91) and 'Operation Desert Shield' are examples where military strategists argued for further attacks (to remove Saddam Hussein from power), but were hindered by public moral concern – especially as public opinion became sceptical about the real reasons for the war (to protect Kuwait against Iraqi invasion) and considered it was more to do with protecting US oil assets. As a result, it is argued, the Gulf War was never satisfactorily concluded.

5 Militarism

The militarist, like the pacifist, is an idealist. Whereas for the pacifist war is intrinsically wrong, for the militarist war is good and inextricably linked to the establishment of the state and expresses its deeply held values. There is a strong psychological element here which celebrates virtues such as loyalty to the fatherland, the power and strength of the state, commitment to a cause or utter belief in God.

Militarist war is an end in itself. Although we often think that militarism is only practised by fascist dictators, wars often have a militarist dimension to them. Militarism may also be found in the **holy war** arguments, notably within Christianity and Islam. When the motive is a moral crusade, to die for the cause is to die as a martyr and receive its rewards. The enemies are no longer human beings but demonised as representatives of evil. War is not the lesser of two evils, or an instrument for peace, but an outward act of good.

a) War as expression of virtues

For many, war is justified not just in instrumental terms (as a means to an end), but as an end in itself. The **virtues** developed in war are ones which express important values. War is often seen in manly terms as supporting virtues such as courage, strength and love for one's country or friends or God. **Edmund Burke** described the French Revolution as an 'armed doctrine', i.e. an expression of its belief in equality, fraternity and liberty. Others have used phrases such as the 'happy warrior' to describe the soldier in war who is happy to sacrifice his life for the sake of his country's values.

However, as **Aristotle** taught in his version of virtue ethics, the dangers of militarism can lead to excess as well as deficiency of virtues. For example, excess of courage leads to foolhardiness, deficiency to cowardice. If, as Aristotle argued, the point of the virtues is to establish a harmonious community or *polis*, militarism can become so enamoured of war in itself that it fails to achieve this end. Militarism might sanction a state which is happy to dispense with its citizens who will never enjoy the fruit of their labours. Militarism which fails to exercise **phronesis** can be prone to injustice in war, escalation of violence and scant regard for innocent non-combatant life.

b) Holy war

For centuries Christianity did not have a holy war doctrine – even though the Old Testament frequently endorses war against Israel's enemies such as Joshua's attack on Jericho as part of his invasion of Canaan (Joshua 6). The New Testament is at best ambivalent about the use of violence and until the **First Crusade** those who fought in battle had to do penance afterwards in order to receive communion and clergymen were forbidden to fight.

Key people

Edmund Burke (1729–97) was an Anglo-Irish politician and philosopher. He strongly opposed the French Revolution.

Key quote

'Eternal peace is a dream and not even a beautiful one. War is part of God's world-order. Within it unfold the noblest virtues of men, courage and renunciation, loyalty to duty and readiness for sacrifice – at the hazard of one's life. Without war the world would sink into a swamp of materialism.'

HELMUTH VON MOLTKE THE ELDER, IN A LETTER TO JOHANN KASPAR BLUNTSCHLI, 1880

Key word

Phronesis is the Greek word used by Aristotle to mean practical wisdom. By this he meant the skill of living the golden mean between the vices of excess and deficiency.

Key thought

The Crusades were a series of holy wars fought from 1095 to 1291 between Christians and Muslims in the Holy Land (modern Israel). The First Crusade (1096–99) captured Jerusalem, during which many of the residents were brutally killed.

Key quotes

'Let this be your war-cry in combats, because this word is given to you by God. When an armed attack is made upon the enemy, let this one cry be raised by all the soldiers of God: It is the will of God! It is the will of God! ... Whoever shall determine upon this holy pilgrimage and shall make his vow to God to that effect and shall offer himself to Him as a living sacrifice, holy, acceptable unto God, shall wear the sign of the cross of the Lord on his forehead or on his breast.'

POPE URBAN II, SERMON IN 1095

'For I delight in the law of God, in my inmost self, but I see in my members another law at war with the law of my mind and making me captive to the law of sin which dwells in my members.'

ST PAUL, *LETTER TO THE ROMANS* 7:22–23

Key people

Sir Francis Bacon (1561–1626) was an English philosopher, lawyer, scientist, historian and intellectual reformer. He claimed that 'all knowledge is my province' and set about developing an intellectual system which would take seriously empirical knowledge for the benefit of all.

i) Pope Urban II

But in 1095 at the Council of Clermont **Pope Urban II** established the ground rules for a defensive war, which rapidly became the basis in the popular mind for Christian holy war. The 'war of religion' was in the first instance to maintain Christian lands, not to expel or annihilate the infidel. However, the language used by the Pope stressed the religious virtues of soldiers – they were to be 'soldiers of Christ' and death was an act of sacrificial love, in the same way that Christ had died for the world.

Furthermore, whereas St Paul had described the individual's life in terms of a personal war between sin and the spiritual life (Romans 7:13–25), war was now elevated to the public level as part of the Christian spiritual battle to overcome evil.

The soldier was depicted in priestly terms taking vows of penitence and obedience and wearing the cross. As a soldier of Christ he would receive pardon and remission of sins and the promise of life eternal. But if Pope Urban II had intended only to permit a restrained version of religious war, it was, at a popular level, rapidly transformed into a full-blown holy war, where the death of the infidel was sufficient justification.

ii) Francis Bacon

Francis Bacon argued in 'An Advertisement Touching a Holy War' (1629) that holy war should satisfy five criteria:

- to spread the faith
- to retrieve countries that were once Christian, even if there were no Christians left there
- to rescue Christians in countries that were once Christian from 'the servitude of the infidels'
- to recover and purify consecrated places that are 'now polluted and profaned'
- to revenge blasphemous acts, or cruelties and killings of Christians (even if these took place long ago).

However, Bacon is cautious about the actual use of holy war. Towards the end of his essay, he acknowledges that as all human societies have some sense of natural law, Christians must be generous in their treatment of peoples who may have imperfect knowledge of what they have had specifically revealed to them by Christ. Holy war is reserved only for those who live 'utterly degenerate' lives.

iii) Critique of holy war

Subsequent atrocities and the slaughter of innocent women and children – especially of the Jews (who were accused of Christocide or killing of God's Son, Jesus Christ) – is remembered uneasily today by

Key quote

'... few serious Christian thinkers
would now defend a crusading
view of war.'

NEIL MESSER, *CHRISTIAN
ETHICS*, PAGE 56

Christians. Holy war tends to dehumanise the enemy and fails to
distinguish sufficiently between the innocent or non-combatant and
combatant. Whereas in just war it is the cause which is evil not the
combatant, holy war regards all the enemy as evil. Therefore unlike just
war, holy war does not distinguish the means of war from the end.

6 Just war

Although the origins of the just war argument (JWA) may go back
to Plato and Aristotle, in its present form it was developed in
Christian circles as Christians found themselves in a position where
their obedience to the state was in conflict with their traditional
obligation to resist the use of violence. The JWA adopts a number
of the elements of the different war attitudes set out above and
although much of its history has been in the Christian and **natural
law** tradition, there is nothing which makes it an *exclusively*
Christian argument. It has various forms and has been adapted and
added to as warfare, society and differing notions of justice have
developed. It originated with **Augustine** (354–430), who set out the
reasons for going to war, and developed by **Aquinas**, who developed
the first three elements of the JWA. Others, notably **Francisco de
Vitoria** (1480–1546), added the condition of proportionality to
right intention and **Hugo Grotius** (1583–1645) supplied the natural
law principle that the innocent (i.e. non-combatants) should have
immunity *in war*.

Key words

Ius ad bellum is a Latin phrase
meaning the justification for going
to war.

Ius in bello is a Latin phrase
meaning the just means within
war.

Key quote

'There are six criteria under the *ius
ad bellum and it is important to
note that they all have to be
satisfied; four out of six, for
example, does not amount to an
overall pass mark.'

CHARLES GUTHRIE AND
MICHAEL QUINLAN, *JUST
WAR*, PAGE 12

The JWA has two distinct but clearly related elements. The **ius
ad bellum** principle established the argument within the context
of the state and the **ius in bello** principle maintains that war is
primarily instrumental and must be fought with minimum force to
achieve the proper end – peace.

The main just war propositions

Ius ad bellum principles:

1 There must be a just cause (those attacked must deserve it).
2 War must be sanctioned by a legitimate authority.
3 War must be fought with the right intentions (i.e. to achieve
   peace).
4 There must be a reasonable prospect of success.
5 War should be the last resort.
6 The damage done in war must be proportionate to the injustice which has provoked the war.

Ius in bello principles:

7 The actions taken in war must be proportional to their ends.
8 Non-combatants must be given immunity from attack.

PROFILE

a) Just cause

Augustine established that the primary cause for a just war is to restore peace. But other causes might include: avenging injuries, restoring land, putting down a rebellion, removing a major political threat and so on.

i) How is a just cause to be decided?

Critics of JWA have argued that the very notion of a just war is fundamentally flawed, as both parties in war usually consider their cause to be just. Both cannot be just unless it is accepted that there are different views of justice, in which case the JWA serves no distinctive purpose.

Furthermore some critics quote a fundamental principle in law, 'let no one be the judge of his own cause'. But who today is politically neutral enough to give an objective judgement? Some have suggested organisations such as the United Nations, but others argue that the individual state should take responsibility and accountability for its own actions and act independently from other nations.

These two problems with the just cause argument appear insurmountable, but this does not mean the JWA has necessarily failed, merely that deciding on these issues is complex.

ii) Defence only?

The natural law basis of the JWA presents the view that **defensive war** is legitimate whereas **offensive war** is not. This also rules out **pre-emptive strike**. The principle of offence is enshrined in the much-quoted **UN Article 51**.

> *Nothing in the present Charter shall impair the inherent right of individual or collective self-defence if an armed attack occurs against a Member of the United Nations, until the Security Council has taken measures necessary to maintain international peace and security. Measures taken by Members in the exercise of this right of self-defence shall be immediately reported to the Security Council and shall not in any way affect the authority and responsibility of the Security Council under the present Charter to take at any time such action as it deems necessary in order to maintain or restore international peace and security.*
>
> (United Nations, Article 51)

But is offensive war necessarily unjust? The JWA tries to avoid militarism yet the use of pre-emptive strike may make moral and strategic sense (Israel justified her pre-emptive attack on Egypt in the Six Day War [1967] on these grounds). What may be perceived as an offensive first strike could also be justified as a response not to a *physical* attack but to the build-up of a *potential* aggressor's troops or provocative behaviour or some kind of interference in the ideology of the defending country.

Key question

Was the invasion of Iraq in 2003 by the United States and allied forces on the grounds that Saddam Hussein had weapons of mass destruction a 'just cause'?

Key quotes

'War should be waged only as a necessity and waged only that through it God may deliver man from that necessity and preserve them in peace.'

AUGUSTINE, *LETTER 189*

'Just War theory fails almost before it has begun.'

GORDON GRAHAM, *ETHICS AND INTERNATIONAL RELATIONS*, PAGE 60

Key word

Pre-emptive strike means to make the first tactical move in war before the enemy.

b) Legitimate authority

In the earlier formulations the JWA referred to the sovereign. The authority of the sovereign was often considered to be established because he represented God's will on earth and for that reason a war proclaimed by a private citizen or group of citizens could not be considered legitimate authority. JWA was therefore used by governments according to the principle of *vis coactiva* (a compelling law) to quash any attempts to overthrow the state or monarch.

Today legitimate authority usually refers to any democratically elected government.

i) Who decides when an authority is legitimate?

What happens if an authority is not thought to be legitimate? This is especially problematic if the authority is considered to be tyrannical. Neither Augustine nor Luther resolved this problem satisfactorily. Martin Luther (1483–1546), for example, argued vehemently against the German Peasants' Revolt (1524–36) on the grounds that the monarch is still appointed by God even if he is a tyrant.

Dietrich Bonhoeffer, on the other hand, working within the Lutheran tradition, argued that even though Hitler had been elected head of state he could not be a legitimate authority because of his use of total war. Any use of total war demonstrates that the civil authority regards itself in absolute terms and outside judgement (by God or others). An authority which undermines the natural rights of innocent men and women cannot be legitimate; in this case conscience must act as legitimate authority. So, as other commentators have concluded, the absence of an actual ruler is not a necessary condition for the JWA to work. What is necessary for the JWA is the appeal to fundamental natural moral laws and human rights.

ii) Does an insurrection have legitimate authority?

An insurrection is not legitimate if its aims are unrestrained violence, not directed to a just cause and do not have widespread support of the people. But an insurrection against a tyrannical state, which aims to restrain the use of violent force and whose combatants receive the support of the people, may therefore regard itself as a legitimate authority.

This final point highlights an important feature of the JWA amongst those who support it: not all parts of the JWA have to be complete for the argument to work as a whole. Each element helps to regulate every other part. Above all it works as a means of guiding discussion in a logical and orderly way. Gordon Graham comments:

> *The theory of the Just War, in fact, remains a plausible, sustained and sophisticated attempt to regulate the conduct of international affairs by*

Key quote

'Christians in Germany will face the terrible alternative of either willing the defeat of their nation in order that Christian civilization may survive, or willing the victory of their nation and therefore destroying our civilization. I know which of these alternatives I must choose; but I cannot make that choice in security.'

DIETRICH BONHOEFFER,
IN A LETTER TO REINHOLD
NIEBUHR

Key people

Dietrich Bonhoeffer (1906–45) was a German Lutheran pastor who sided against the Nazi movement and worked for the Confessing Church. He was arrested by the Nazis in 1943 and hanged by the Gestapo in 1945.

Key quote

'The call of conscience arises from the imperilling of a man's unity with himself.'

DIETRICH BONHOEFFER,
ETHICS (1955), PAGE 211

ethical principles in the most demanding and difficult context, violent conflict.

(Gordon Graham, *Ethics and International Relations*, page 64)

c) Right intention

The proposition here can be stated in a number of ways. The 'right intention' captures something of the JWA's development in the natural law environment of Augustine and Aquinas. The intention must be for peace – land, rights, self-defence and protection of the innocent are not *in themselves* sufficient reasons for war. In other words, the intention is justified as long as it is proportionate to its end.

i) Subjectivity

How can one judge what a genuine good intention is? Augustine and Aquinas limit the good intention to peace but it might equally be justified to claim back land which has been unlawfully taken by another country, or on humanitarian grounds to intervene in a civil war to protect a group of people from genocide. In recent times this has been known as 'liberal interventionism'. Furthermore there is also a contradiction that if the use of lethal violence is wrong at a personal level then why should it be any different at the public/ national level?

ii) Proportionate to its end

The right intention is based on a best guess that the use of war will be proportionate to its end. But this is very difficult to determine accurately especially given the uncertainties of war. The present war in Iraq (started on 20 March 2003) illustrates how expensive it has become (estimated at $600,000,000 so far). Money of this magnitude could be used to solve other, many more worthy humanitarian causes in the world. There is also a fear that as technology develops more dangerous and lethal weapons that any war is in danger of escalating into total or even nuclear war.

d) Likelihood of success

Likelihood of success is a development of right intention. The **Falklands War** is an example of a gamble which the British government took by sending a Task Force half way round the world. To its critics this was a foolish and expensive move but with hindsight it proved a success because the objective (to take back the islands from Argentine invaders) was achieved. However, whereas in Aquinas' version success simply meant winning the war, today success means how it is to be finished. This includes how a society or country devastated by war is to be reconstructed and made good. This is often termed **ius post bellum**, and as Shirley Williams has said it means having an 'exit strategy'.

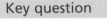

Key question

Is war justified to prevent genocide even if this means interfering with another country's sovereignty?

Cross-reference

Consider Walzer's views on interventionism on pages 124–25 above.

Key quote

'No one in the West who has seen what is happening in Kosovo can doubt NATO's military action is justified. This is a just war based not on territorial ambitions but on values. If we let an evil dictator range unchallenged we will have to spill infinitely more blood and treasure to stop him later.'

CHICAGO ECONOMIC CLUB
(24 APRIL 1999)

Key thought

The **Falklands War** was fought over the disputed sovereignty of the Falkland Islands and South Georgia and South Sandwich Islands between 19 March 1982 and 14 June 1982.

Key word

Ius post bellum means just after war and includes reinstating the rights of those attacked, restoring law and order and punishing war criminals.

Cross-reference

Shirley Williams in Kim and Draper, *Liberating Texts?*, page 138.

e) Last resort

The JWA constantly affirms that the aim of war is to establish peace. This criterion therefore checks that other means of settling conflict have been considered and tried. The means employed are those approved by the pacifist (negotiation, sanctions, appeasement). Not surprisingly the sharpest criticism of the JWA is from the pacifist, who instinctively feels that all wars can be averted. The problem is again a problem of hindsight. If Churchill had formed an appeasement with Germany in the 1930s, the Second World War might have been averted (Churchill himself acknowledged this).

On the other hand, many felt that force was used too hastily both in the **Gulf War** and the more recent Iraq War (Russia and France in particular were vocal critics of the USA and UK). A last resort may prove too late and lose the strategic and political advantages while sanctions and negotiations give the enemy time to muster troops. The pacifist does not always take into account the considerable *indiscriminate* suffering and death sanctions cause. The JWA at least aims to be specific and provide the non-combatant with immunity.

f) Proportionality

Proportionality is an important element of both *ius ad bellum* and *ius in bello* elements of the JWA. There is broad agreement that the use of war must be in proportion to the cause of the conflict. This is problematic – it is by no means easy to judge how many lives lost can justify regaining national freedom or land for the sake of peace.

The *ius in bello* notion of proportionality continues the *ad bellum* principle on the grounds that if it is not applied tactically and strategically in the **conduct of war** itself then justice cannot be maintained. In war proportionality means that combat must be conducted justly, giving immunity to non-strategic sites, non-combatants and prisoners of war. It means rejecting methods in war which are evil in themselves (*male in se*) such as rape, genocide and biological warfare.

i) Judging consequences

Making judgements of proportion in war are to some degree guess work; they have also to distinguish between short- and long-term effects. One celebrated case which illustrates this issue was the sinking of the Argentine cruiser the *General Belgrano* during the Falklands War (1982). The *Belgrano* was torpedoed with a loss of 368 Argentine seamen – what makes the case a continued area of controversy is that at the time it was outside the exclusion zone; it seemed to be moving away from the island and Task Force. By way of defence, the UK government argued that given the skeleton fleet and its distance from the UK, the *Belgrano* posed a possible threat that (had they not acted when they did) would have had terrible

Key thought

The **Gulf War** (2 August 1990–28 February 1991) was a conflict between Iraq and a coalition force from 34 nations, authorised by the United Nations to return Kuwait to the control of the Emir of Kuwait.

Key question

How is proportionality different from the notion of success?

Key quote

'No war is just, the conduct of which is manifestly more harmful to the State than it is good and advantageous; and this is true regardless of other claims or reasons advanced to make of it a just war.'

FRANCISCO DE VITORIA (1486–1546), QUOTED IN A.J. COATES, *THE ETHICS OF WAR*, PAGE 167

Cross-reference

See A.J. Coates, *The Ethics of War*, pages 208–14, for a full account of the issues.

Key thought

Unilateral refers to losses on one side, bilateral to losses on both sides.

Cross-reference

Read pages 154–57 below on nuclear weapons and just war arguments.

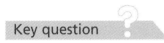
Key question

How does one define who the 'innocent' are in war?

consequences. But it is still a matter of dispute whether this action was disproportionately violent and whether alternative measures could have been taken.

ii) Unilateral and bilateral loss

The Falklands example also raises the question whether loss is to be calculated **unilaterally** or **bilaterally**. The battle of Loos (1915) and the Somme (1916) (where 57,470 men were lost on a single day with little offensive advantage) are two examples where critics question the justification of such action. If the losses have to be put in the context of the whole battle is not the JWA concern for *all* human life compromised (i.e. bilaterally)?

iii) Nuclear weapons

Nuclear weapons and weapons of mass destruction also call into question whether proportionality can ever be maintained in modern warfare. Some argue that the JWA can still be maintained in 'limited nuclear war' only if strategic targets are attacked. Others argue that the just war argument itself can be modified so as to treat all members of the enemy as legitimate non-innocent targets. But for others the prospect of nuclear weapons indicates the basic inadequacy of using the JWA today.

g) Discrimination and non-combatant immunity

Another important part of the *ius in bello* JWA is the protection of innocent life. Fundamental to all natural law arguments is that life is intrinsically valuable. But where war is concerned those who work as combatants know that they might have to sacrifice their lives but the same cannot be said of non-combatants.

The non-combatant immunity argument can be simply expressed: immunity of certain members of the enemy is on the grounds that if A threatens B, then B has the right to defend himself against A. But if not all members of A are directly involved in the threat (i.e. they are non-combatants) then B has no right to act against them.

i) Problem of immunity

The argument in practice is far less clear cut. Are all non-combatants necessarily innocent? Civilians may be involved in the war effort (making arms, clothes, rations, etc.) and therefore part of the causal chain that aids the combatant in war. If this is the case then it would be legitimate to bomb civilians on the grounds that no one is innocent in war. Such a conclusion would abandon the principle of immunity and replace the JWA in favour of total war.

Some have argued that although non-combatants are part of the causal chain of war, they should be distinguished from combatants because it is not their intention to fight and contribute directly to the use of violence. In this sense they are 'harmless' rather than blameless but they should still have immunity. But the distinction between harmless and harmful makes the line between combatant and non-combatant very vague and very difficult for the JWA to work properly.

ii) The problem of targets

Another major criticism is that whereas the notion of the battlefield in the past was clear cut, war nowadays is fought over vast areas and often in cities. It is inevitable that non-combatants will suffer. The response to this has been to invoke the **doctrine of double effect**. The double effect argument can be applied in two ways. First, it might be argued that when choosing a strategic target the *intention* is not to harm non-combatants although there is a likelihood of this happening. The problem here (as with any form of the double effect argument) is that the agent still knows that innocent lives are at risk.

Cross-reference

See pages 71–73 above for the main elements of the doctrine of double effect.

Another form more readily applicable in military terms might be to think of the double effect in terms of 'direct' and 'indirect' consequences. In military terms this helps to decide the moral legitimacy between precision bombing, selective bombing and area bombing.

For many only precision bombing is licit because the indirect consequences on non-military targets, though known, are minimal. But 'targets' do not just have to be military. The horrific 'indirect' results of the area bombing of Hamburg and Dresden during the Second World War were justified by many as a means of undermining the enemy's morale and bringing a swift end to the war. But is it possible to justify the deaths of 40,000 innocent civilians who died in a single night? Not to do so is to advocate a form of militarism very alien to the JWA. The problem remains: how many non-combatant casualties does it take to negate the JWA?

Key word

Theatre of war is the area in which a battle is fought. In the past this was limited to the battle field.

Many feel that the JWA was developed at a time in history when the **theatre of war** could be more precisely defined; as this is not the case today the JWA is no longer appropriate.

7 Normative ethical responses to war and peace

a) Kantian ethics

Cross-reference

For a more detailed account of Kant's moral philosophy read Mel Thompson, *Ethical Theory*, Chapter 10.

Kant's argument against war tackles the well-known response that, although world peace is a good idea in theory, it will never work in practice. In his essay 'Toward Perpetual Peace' (1795) Kant develops the various elements of his moral philosophy to suggest a number of practical ways in which war, for all civilised nations, may be a practice of the past. As a contingent pacifist Kant acknowledges that war is sometimes necessary, but he doesn't think civilised nations have tried hard enough to work for peace.

i) Reason and human nature

Kant agrees with Thomas Hobbes that the natural state of humans is war. Left to our own devices humans would treat territory, property and other people as fair game to anyone who had sufficient power to take it for themselves. This is the state of barbaric peoples. But this state forgets that humans have reason which takes them to a higher level of civilised existence. This is why peace therefore has to be *established*; it does not occur naturally by itself.

Reason is associated with what Kant calls the **good will**. Despite the human desire to act violently, humans also have an innate power to will each other good. The true human being struggles therefore to overcome his lower animal self using reason.

ii) Practical imperative

Kant's practical imperative is one which gives dignity to every person as a rational and autonomous member of the human race. The maxim states, therefore, that it is always wrong to treat a person as a means to an end. This has a number of implications, which he discusses in his essay:

- Every state shall enjoy its own freedom and shall not come under the power of another state. This is because a state is made up of people and therefore to exchange land or territories for whatever reason (as in treaties or exchange of lands) is to treat people as part of the land and not subjects in themselves.
- There must be no **standing armies**, not only because armies need to be active and therefore having an army can incite war, but because the state is using people as a means to an end. Paying people to kill and to be killed treats them as machines and de-humanised, disposable cogs in the machinery of state.

iii) Categorical imperative

The purpose of the categorical imperative is to ensure that every moral action is rational, respects the freedom and autonomy of everyone else (including oneself) and is therefore to be judged as a universal law. In 'Toward Perpetual Peace' Kant argues that the categorical imperative rules out almost all kinds of war.

- The imperative therefore ensures that no **peace treaty** can be established that does not rule out categorically recourse to war in the future. To do so would be to reduce the treaty to a conditional statement. As Kant had established with his argument on promise keeping, there can be no conditional promise – either a promise is a duty or it is not.

Key quote

'The state of peace among men living side by side is not the natural state; the natural state is one of war.'

IMMANUEL KANT,
'TOWARD PERPETUAL PEACE' 8:349

Cross-reference

Read page 18 on Hobbes and Mel Thompson, *Ethical Theory*, pages 73–4.

Key thought

A **standing army** is a professional army which is not disbanded during peace time.

Key quote

'Being hired out to kill or be killed seems to constitute a use of human beings as mere machines and tools in the hands of another (the state), a use which is incompatible with the rights of humanity in our own person.'

IMMANUEL KANT,
'TOWARD PERPETUAL PEACE' 8:345

- No nation should interfere with the constitution or government of another state. The categorical imperative respects the **autonomy** of others to act as they wish – even if this is harmful or evil (because, as Kant argues, this should act as a warning to others). The only exception is in cases of civil war where law and order has collapsed; the purpose is to re-establish civil law and order, nothing else.

iv) Law and the kingdom of ends

The kingdom of ends describes Kant's ideal state where everyone will be a 'legislator', treating each person as an equal with the same rights and dignity. In 'Toward Perpetual Peace' only a republic can satisfy these conditions. He does not imagine a world super state (because he feels that this would lead to competition between peoples) but a **league of nations** working under a common law.

Key quote

'The agreement of the citizens is required to decide whether or not one ought to wage war, then nothing is more natural than that they would consider very carefully whether to enter into such a terrible game.'

IMMANUEL KANT,
'TOWARD PERPETUAL PEACE' 8:351

- With no absolute rulers in a republic there would be no armies and no wars. This is because it would require the consent of the people to fight and as most people do not wish to die (especially when they see the devastation of war) no authority could over-rule the people as the legislating members.
- In a league of nations there would be no law which would sanction the use of war to settle disagreements. The reason why the JWA fails, according to Kant, is that it has no external law by which to determine whether a war is justified. However, in practice nations rarely use the arguments of philosophers and use war (as Clausewitz argued) as an extension of their political means.

Many of Kant's notions have become realities. A **league of nations** was founded after the First World War and was later replaced by the **United Nations** in 1945. His vision of world citizenship is slowly being made possible by the acknowledgement of human rights and international treaties and law. The weakness of his vision of perpetual peace is whether given the inability of people to behave in a civilised and rational way it is an unrealistic utopia.

Key thought

The **League of Nations** was founded as a result of the Treaty of Versailles (1919–20). Its aims included preventing war through disarmament, settling disputes through negotiation and universal welfare.

b) Virtue ethics

As we have seen, virtue ethics supports both war and pacifism. There are many different versions of virtue ethics but broadly speaking they fall into two kinds: pure or virtue orientated virtue ethics and principle orientated virtue ethics.

Cross-reference

For a more detailed account of virtue ethics see Mel Thompson, *Ethical Theory*, Chapter 16.

i) Virtue orientated virtue ethics

In its pure form virtue ethics supports the **militarist** view of war because it expresses many human qualities and virtues which are admired – courage, love for others, loyalty, etc. – although as we have seen, there is a danger with this view that the virtues can

Cross-reference

Read page 126 above on virtues and militarism.

favour only the strong at the expense of the weak. It might also be thought that war only expresses male characteristics and that female virtues might be very different – where reconciliation rather than conflict expresses courage.

On the other hand pure virtue ethics might equally support the **absolute pacifist** position. They might take their lead from Kant that although the desire of any civilised community is peace so that individual citizens can flourish (the state of *eudaimonia*), peace has to be *established* by skilfully learning and exercising a range of virtues. Such virtues might include: self-control against an aggressor, love of one's enemies, diplomacy, integrity and even the courage to suffer and die rather than use violence.

ii) Principle orientated virtue ethicists

Principle orientated virtue ethicists argue that unless the virtues correspond to established principles, then virtues become meaningless. But likewise the application of principles or rules without virtues can be cold, calculating and ineffective. In other words virtues *add* to principles by giving them human value. For example there is a difference between making an apology out of duty and making an apology sincerely. This requires the skill of prudence (*phronesis*), that is, the ability to apply principles by seeking the middle path between extremes.

The principle orientated virtue ethicist therefore might accept the **war realist** position that given human nature wars have to be fought. If for example the **just war** principle is accepted, the corresponding virtues might be a constant reminder that war is not to be fought out of vengeance (the vice of excess) but from a genuine desire for peace. But equally prudence can ensure that the virtue of peace is not applied so timidly (the vice of deficiency) that the skill of the use of force in war becomes ineffective.

iii) Virtues and leadership

A significant and ancient part of war ethics is the role played by the character of the authority who summons and the authority who leads a war. In **Niccolò Machiavelli**'s influential book *The Art of War* (1521) he outlines two kinds of virtuous leaders in war: 'one kind includes those leaders who have accomplished great deeds with an army already organized according to its normal discipline' and the 'other kind includes leaders who have not only overcome the enemy but who ... were forced to produce a good well-disciplined army of their own' (*The Art of War*, Book VII). To accomplish these skills the leader in war leads by example and sets the highest standards.

This is more complex in modern times when political leaders tend not to be military leaders. But as we have seen in **Michael**

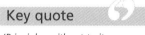

Cross-reference

Look at the example and teaching of Martin Luther King. Read page 118 above.

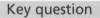

Key quote

'Principles without traits are impotent but traits without principles are blind.'

WILLIAM FRANKENA, *ETHICS* (SECOND EDITION, 1973), PAGE 65

Key question

What skills and character must a leader have in order to conduct a good war?

Cross-reference

See pages 124–25 on Michael Walzer's argument.

Walzer's argument, the politicians who authorise war cannot be morally separated from the consequences of war. This is because virtue ethics operates within the community and their function is to develop the values and skills of living well. But this raises a difficult issue for a leader and that is whether his role legitimises the use of violence, which would be forbidden to ordinary citizens. Walzer gives the example from the end of Homer's *Odyssey*. Odysseus returns home to carry out a ferocious revenge on the suitors and their supporters, an action which involves killing, cruelty, deception, lies and courage and which is effective in restoring him to the throne of Ithaka. The narrative forces the reader to ask whether Odysseus is justified in using such a degree of violence.

Does the use of violence make Odysseus a moral person? The answer is that it does because the suitors had violated the most important moral code (the sacredness of the home) when they 'wickedly abandoned all standards of civilized behaviour, plundering the estate and insulting the wife of our greatest man' (*Odyssey*, Book 24:457). The *Odyssey* frequently illustrates how the gods enforce the family as the essential building block of society. Odysseus' action therefore is necessary as an example of the strong leader who reinforces the values of society.

However, the example from Homer illustrates one of the problems with virtue ethics and that is how the virtues are to be chosen. It is difficult to imagine from a Christian perspective, for example, how compared to Jesus, Odysseus' action could be considered as a model of virtue. While it is true that the 'moral saint' sets an example of virtuous behaviour it is clear that in order for virtue ethics to work satisfactorily we need to have another means by which to work out the moral principles which the moral saint represents.

c) Utilitarianism

Cross-reference

For a more detailed account of utilitarianism read Mel Thompson, *Ethical Theory*, Chapter 9.

Most of the utilitarian arguments have been covered above. As the utilitarian aim is to minimise pain and maximise happiness then the calculation has to be that the use of war is justified if, and only if, it produces greater good than not fighting a war.

i) Just war arguments and utilitarianism

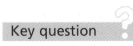

Key question

To what extent is the just war argument utilitarian?

Cross-reference

Singer's argument is on page 120 above.

Although the JWA is couched in natural law terms, the utilitarian would have few disagreements with its aims and methods. The aim is to establish peace using the minimum amount of force necessary to achieve good ends. The principle of non-combatant immunity and proportion *ad bellum* and *in bello* are broadly supported by utilitarianism. Peter Singer's argument outlined above offers an important rejection of the natural law acts and omissions justification of those non-combatants killed knowingly but unintentionally.

ii) Utilitarianism and the problem of means in war

As a consequential system utilitarianism justifies war only if its final outcome is good. But this leaves utilitarianism with a problem as far as the actual waging of war is concerned. This is because utilitarianism is less interested with the intentions and means than the outcome. The problem is one which Bernard Williams famously outlined in his example of Jim and the Indians. However, **Clausewitz's dialectical utilitarianism** offers a neat balance between ends and means by balancing war as a whole (in terms of strategy) and war as it is fought (in terms of tactics).

iii) Absolute pacifism

It is difficult to see how all the various forms of utilitarianism could not prefer peace to war. It is possible that some forms of militarism might appeal to those who enjoy the excitement of war but this has to be balanced against those who are not militarists and would prefer not to die. In the same way, although absolute pacifism would be supported by the utilitarian in so far as it does not cause deliberate harm, the weakness of this absolute position is its failure to protect others against exploitation and aggressors. The **welfare utilitarian** might, for example, argue that absolute pacifism fails to protect access to health, money, shelter and food because of its absolute prioritising of peace. It is more likely that most utilitarians would support contingent rather than absolute pacifism.

d) Natural law

As we have seen the JWA has employed many aspects of natural law. Aquinas' primary principles of natural law state that an act is good if it fulfils one or more of the following:

- self-preservation, progress and reproduction
- self-perfection (the pursuit of justice)
- to learn and live by reason
- to live in an ordered society
- to worship God.

As the JWA makes clear, war cannot be good in itself as it involves deliberate killing. On the other hand war may be permitted if, as a last resort, it: preserves the lives of the innocent; establishes an ordered society; achieves peace – which is the primary end or purpose of society.

As we have seen, **G.E.M. Anscombe**'s argument illustrated the potential wickedness of the pacifist position because of its abrogation of responsibility to protect the innocent against lethal threats to life.

Cross-references

See pages 16–17 above for Williams' example.

See pages 122–24 above for a more detailed account of Clausewitz's utilitarianism.

Key question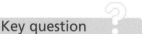

Does utilitarianism support absolute pacifism?

Cross-reference

See page 15 above on the aims of welfare utilitarianism.

Cross-reference

See pages 10–11 above on natural law and the sanctity of life. For a more detailed discussion read Mel Thompson, *Ethical Theory*, Chapter 7.

Cross-reference

See page 119 above for Anscombe's argument.

Cross-reference

The argument set out here is based on Aquinas' *Summa Theologica* 2:2, Q. 40.

Key quote

'All who draw the sword will die by the sword.'

MATTHEW 26:52

Cross-reference

See pages 71–73 above for the full version of the double effect.

Key thought

'**Proportionalism** holds that there are certain moral rules and it can never be right to act against these unless there is proportionate reason which would justify it. The proportionate reason would be grounded in the particular situation, but the situation must generate a reason which is sufficiently strong to overturn what would otherwise be a firm rule.'

PETER VARDY AND PAUL GROSCH, *THE PUZZLE OF ETHICS*, PAGES 141–42.

i) Aquinas' argument

Aquinas' argument from *Summa Theologica* is the foundation for the JWA. In his usual manner he sets out various objections and argues against them in his replies.

- **Punishment for sinful acts**. *Objection*: As Jesus taught that all deliberate killing should be punished by capital punishment (Matthew 26:52), therefore all wars are unlawful and sinful. *Reply*: It is true that it is not legitimate to arm oneself as a private citizen. But arming oneself as a private person by the authority of the state is legitimate for the sake of justice; so this must also be to act according to God's authority. Therefore one is not taking 'the sword' personally, but acting under authority. Therefore 'drawing the sword' is not necessarily sinful and does not deserve punishment.
- **Resistance to evil**. *Objection*: War is contrary to God's law because Jesus says 'Do not resist an evil person' (Matthew 5:39) and St Paul writes 'Do not take revenge my friends' (Romans 12:19). Therefore war is always sinful. *Reply*: In most cases we should intend to refrain from the personal use of resistance and self-defence but sometimes it is necessary to use resistance for the common good. We have a duty to punish people for their own good providing we intend that it is for their own good.
- **War is contrary to peace**. *Objection*: War is not good because it is contrary to peace. *Reply*: Those who fight war justly aim to achieve peace. Peace that is achieved through fear is not true peace. This is what Augustine means when he says: 'We do not seek peace in order to be at war, but we go to war that we may have peace.'

ii) Proportionate means

Natural law also supports two important parts of the JWA through the notion of proportion. The final stipulation of the **doctrine of double effect** states that foreseen but unwilled negative consequences of an action must be in proportion to the willed direct ends. **Proportionalism** has been developed by some modern natural law thinkers as a new form of natural law to ensure that it is more flexible. Proportionalism is well suited to discussions about war and peace because although peace must be the primary end of war, the means of achieving it requires taking into account the situation, not just applying a rigid law. For example:

- In the JWA both *ad bellum* and *ius in bello* stipulate that war must be justified rationally as a proportionate means for the good end (peace) both in calling for war and in the process of fighting war itself. Proportionalism ensures that damage to both sides is kept to a minimum.

THE HENLEY COLLEGE LIBRARY

- The double effect is also used to determine the problem of attacking legitimate targets and gauging damage to non–military targets and non–combatants.

Cross-reference

Read pages 133–34 above for a fuller discussion of non-combatant immunity.

Cross-reference

Read pages 8–13 on the sanctity of life argument.

e) Revealed ethics

Many of the religious ethical views of war have been covered in this chapter. Most are derived from the **sanctity of life** position that as human life is created in the image of God and belongs to Him it is not for humans to destroy it deliberately. A strong sanctity of life position would appear to rule out all forms of violence and especially lethal violence. This is the view of Christian **absolute pacifists** such as Tertullian, the Quakers, Martin Luther King and Charles Raven.

But for the Christian the essentially pacifist position is also modified by three factors: Bible inconsistencies that permit the use of war; the duty to protect the innocent; various views of eschatology. Christians therefore support a range of views (considered earlier): pacifism; militarism and holy war (Pope Urban II and Francis Bacon); war realism and just war (Augustine, Aquinas, Luther).

i) Bible inconsistencies

Early on Christian theologians struggled to reconcile the discrepancy between the Old Testament attitude to war and the New Testament's pacifism. The alternatives are either to reject the Old Testament (as the late first-century heretic Marcion did), to allegorise it, to be very selective or to see it as a stage *before* the revelation of the New Testament. The Old Testament permits **holy war**. In Joshua 6, Joshua leads the attack on Jericho as part of his invasion of Canaan. Another important passage referred to by early Christian writers is the killing of the Egyptian soldier by Moses (Exodus 2:11–15) as an act of revenge for abusing a Hebrew slave.

By contrast to the earlier texts which see war as part of Israel's fight for survival and existence, it seems that the prophets of pre- and post-exile (before and after 586BC) had grown war weary and whilst not condemning war in itself earnestly hoped that conflict would come to an end and the people would be able to enjoy the covenant with God to the full. Isaiah's words to the exiles promise peace now.

The situation of the New Testament is very different. Here a nation is neither carving out its existence nor suffering attack – although many passages reflect the situation where the Christian believer has to consider his beliefs under Roman rule. The outstanding passage is from Jesus' **Sermon on the Mount** (Matthew 5–7) where the exhortation to love one's enemies marks a decisive

Key quote

'Speak tenderly to Jerusalem, and cry to her that her warfare is ended, that her iniquity is pardoned, and she has received from the LORD's hand double for all her sins.'

ISAIAH 40:2

shift from the prevailing Graeco–Romano attitude of its day (which was to hate one's enemies):

> *You have heard that it was said, 'You shall love your neighbour and hate your enemy.' But I say to you, Love your enemies and pray for those who persecute you.*
>
> (Matthew 5:43)

> *... since there is nothing better or finer than when two people of one heart and mind keep house as man and wife, a grief to their enemies and a joy to their friends.*
>
> (Homer, *Odyssey*, Book 6:185)

Augustine interprets Jesus' teaching on 'turning the other cheek' in the Sermon on the Mount to refer to an inner attitude of peacemaking. He argues that although this is implicit in the Old Testament it takes the revelation of Jesus to make this promise of the Kingdom of God explicit.

Many argue that the Old and New Testaments are consistent but present the issues in a different way. For example the stories of Moses' killing of the Egyptian soldier and Peter's use of the sword at Gethsemane both illustrate their **desire for justice**, not revenge or lust for power. Furthermore, John the Baptist did not condemn the soldiers who came to see him because they were warriors, but warned them to act justly: 'Rob no one by violence or by false accusation, and be content with your wages' (Luke 3:14).

Finally, Augustine argued that Jesus did not teach explicitly for or against the use of war, so what he thought has to be inferred **from silence** on the issue. For instance, when he cures the centurion's servant (Matthew 8:8–10), the man is praised for his faith but not condemned for his job as a soldier.

ii) Protection of the innocent

Another major factor which has determined the interpretation of biblical texts has been the equally important notion of the Christian's allegiance to the state or ruler. The pacifist conscientious objector argues that a Christian's private morality supersedes his obligations to the state, but as Augustine argued, personal holiness is one matter, obligation to others is another. Jesus' command to love one's neighbour entails a responsibility to act on behalf of those who are weak and threatened by others. The use of lethal violence as a last resort (as the JWA argues) is necessary in protecting the innocent against the wicked.

For this reason Augustine (in his *Reply to Faustus the Manichaean* c.397) argued that Moses' action in killing the Egyptian soldier was justified (even though it was not legally sanctioned) because it was a preparation for Israel's later rebellion against the tyranny of Egypt.

Cross-reference

See pages 117–18 above for the views of the conscientious objector.

iii) Eschatology

Christian **eschatology** is an important element in the discussion about war and peace. The essential characteristic of the Kingdom of God is peace. It is the time looked forward to by many of the Old Testament prophets. Micah's vision of a time of justice, equality and peace is typical of many. For those Christians who imagine an imminent arrival of the Kingdom of God there is a moral urgency to maintain a standard of holiness which is greater than any ordinary expectation. The peace ideal must be kept at all times.

Others argue that the Kingdom is a process which is evolving and developing until the eschaton arrives (final judgement and the return of Christ) and the world achieves perfection. The end is peace, but this may only come through present struggle: it is an ideal to aim for. In an imperfect world coercive action may sometimes be necessary.

The earthly kingdom, though redeemed from the collective guilt of original sin, is tainted by the sinful will of individuals. In other words Christians may have a vision of what *could* be the case and strive towards it, but they live under secular authority and must learn to compromise. Early Christians had taken the texts in Mark 12:17 and Romans 13:1 to be minimal obligations to state and authority and had avoided military service.

The issue of loyalty to the state remains unresolved for Christians today. Whereas in many less crucial issues (arms trade, poll tax, animal testing, etc.) a democracy allows a Christian the means to protest without directly affecting whether people die, the refusal to participate in war inevitably means that others might die as a result. This potentially undermines the stability of the state (as Luther had feared).

Christian **war realists** accept that there will be an uneasy relationship between private and public morality. Public morality is almost by definition one of compromise. Some Christian theologians such as Reinhold Niebuhr argue that all political decisions are prone to sin. This view accepts the hazy relationship between public and private morality but does not reduce the moral duty to act and choose. In a tragic world such decisions become all the more important and recognise that humans cannot make perfect choices. He has little time for Christian absolute pacifists and their 'soft utopias'.

Key question

Does believing in the Kingdom of God as a future event encourage pacifism?

Key word

Eschatology means the study of the end of time and the arrival of the Kingdom of God.

Key quotes

'It shall come to pass in the latter days that the mountain of the house of the LORD shall be established as the highest of the mountains ... He shall judge between many peoples, and shall decide for strong nations afar off; and they shall beat their swords into ploughshares, and their spears into pruning hooks; nation shall not lift up sword against nation, neither shall they learn war any more.'

MICAH 4:1–4

'Render to Caesar the things which are Caesar's, and to God the things which are God's.'

JESUS, IN MARK 12:17

'Let every person be subject to the governing authorities. For there is no authority except from God.'

ST PAUL, *LETTER TO THE ROMANS* 13:1

Cross-reference

Read pages 118–19 above for more about Reinhold Niebuhr.

Summary diagram

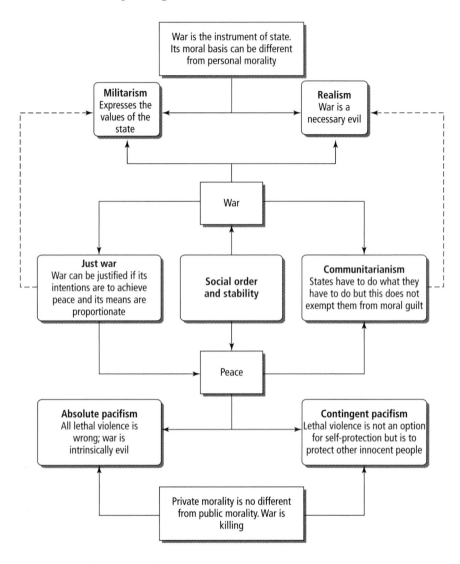

Study guide

By the end of this chapter you should have considered why some
people think that as human nature is aggressive war is often
inevitable and necessary but must be proportionate to certain ends.
You should be able to outline the just war argument and consider it
from a natural law as well as utilitarian viewpoint. You should also
be able to look at the reasons for war as an expression of society's
values and virtues and contrast this with the pacifist view that war is
a sign of human failure which can be overcome. You should be able
to compare and contrast the various normative ethical positions on
war and peace.

Revision checklist ✔

Can you define the following:

- Contingent pacifism
- UN Article 51
- Acts and omissions
- Eschatology
- Dirty hands argument.

Can you explain why:

- Some think pacifists cause and prolong wars
- Luther argued for obedience even to a tyrant
- Christians disagree on whether war is permissible
- Hobbes thinks war is inevitable.

Can you outline the views of the following on war and peace:

- Clausewitz
- Walzer
- Aquinas
- Kant
- King
- Tertullian
- Machiavelli.

Can you give arguments for and against:

- The use of the just war argument today
- The use of the double effect argument to justify deaths of non-combatants in war
- Absolute pacifism.

Essay question

1 a) Explain what is meant by absolute pacifism.

1 b) Assess the view that absolute pacifism is immoral.

The essay might begin by offering a simple definition of absolute pacifism; it is the view that it is immoral to use any kind of violent force against another human being. The essay then needs to develop the reasons why this view is held. Absolute pacifism is often based on the Christian view, as expressed by the Quakers, that according to the strong sanctity of life principle all human life is intrinsically worthwhile and that it is not ours to destroy but to protect (Job 1:21). Other elements of the sanctity of life argument might be developed to support this view. The essay might then deal specifically with the issue of war. The absolute pacifist considers that as there should be continuity between private and public values, then Jesus' teaching to love one's enemies and not to resist an evil person (Sermon on the Mount) rejects all forms of lethal force by the state. This view is supported by Tertullian and his 'disarming Peter' argument and Paul's comment in Romans 12 to 'repay no one evil for evil'. The essay might conclude with an explanation of how Martin Luther King's eschatological vision of the 'beloved community' persuaded him to reject violent struggle in favour of non-violent 'redemptive suffering'.

The second evaluative part of this essay might begin by considering some of the assumptions made by the absolute pacifist. Some of the counter-arguments could be taken from Aquinas' reading of the Sermon on the Mount and his view that Jesus' instructions were for personal moral conduct, not the conduct of the state. Aquinas' view that the innocent must be protected could be used to show how absolute pacifism would cause injustice. This view could be supported with reference to Anscombe's argument that absolute pacifism fails to distinguish between the innocent and non-innocent and allow bad people to do bad things – it appears to place principle before people. Finally the argument might consider Singer's rejection of the acts and omissions justification for absolute pacifism in that it diminishes responsibility. A defence for absolute pacifism might counter all of these views on the grounds that pacifism is not passive but an active involvement in doing good and its primary concern is to uphold human dignity, often at great cost to one's self.

Further essay questions

2a   Outline and explain the just war argument.
2b   'The just war argument is of no use today.' Discuss.

3   'True Christians must also be pacifists.' Discuss.

4   Can militarism be defended today?

Chapter checklist ✓

The possession of nuclear weapons poses a series of moral and practical paradoxes. It is because nuclear weapons are so powerful that used in war they could bring hostility quickly to an end but at the same time they have the potential to do so much damage that it is hard morally to justify their use. This chapter considers the morality of nuclear war by evaluating it against the just war argument and the morality of nuclear deterrence. Several normative ethical systems are considered.

1 The moral paradox of nuclear deterrence

Cross-reference

Paul Ramsey, *The Just War: Force and Political Responsibility* (1968), page 171.

Case study
Baby bumpers

The use of nuclear weapons poses an unusual moral dilemma in that it appears to sanction the use of highly dangerous and immoral means to justify extremely good moral ends. Paul Ramsey poses the following much discussed thought experiment:

> *Supposing on a national holiday, when increased car traffic often causes many fatal accidents, every car were to tie a baby onto its front bumper. Wouldn't this have the effect of ensuring that everyone drove very carefully in order not to kill babies and thereby eliminate car fatalities?*

Ramsey's point is that such a grossly immoral use of an innocent human being is morally unthinkable and yet the use of nuclear weapons, in effect, uses innocent citizens of the world as hostages to establish world peace. The difference is

that whereas the use of the baby bumpers is visible and obviously shocking, no citizen actually thinks of himself as a hostage whose bargaining power is being used to prevent catastrophe; yet the best moral justification for nuclear weapons as deterrence appears to rest on this paradox.

In January 2007, the Doomsday Clock (created in 1947) was moved by scientists to two minutes to midnight – midnight being the time of world annihilation of civilisation. The closest it reached to midnight was in 1953 when the USA's nuclear bomb 'Mike' destroyed the whole of the Pacific island test site. Yet many argue that as nuclear weapons have kept world peace for 60 years it is worth taking these risks.

a) Conventional war and nuclear war

The use of nuclear weapons in war raises a series of quite unique moral and ethical issues which are not necessarily posed in quite the same way by conventional war. Because nuclear weapons are so powerful the only way of ensuring that the enemy do not use their nuclear weaponry is to retaliate with the same means. Unlike conventional war, retaliation can be almost instantaneous; unlike conventional war, should two nations use their nuclear weapons there would be no winners.

The question is this: if the use of nuclear weapons cannot be justified using the usual arguments for conventional war, are there entirely new types of arguments which validate nuclear war? Steven P. Lee (*Morality, Prudence and Nuclear Weapons*, 1993, Chapter 1) raises the following dilemmas when a state attempts to justify the use of nuclear weaponry as a means of maintaining the social order:

Key people

Steven P. Lee is professor of philosophy at Hobart and Smith Colleges, USA. He has written mostly in the areas of ethics, nuclear weapons and just war theory.

i) National security

A state might argue that having an army and arsenal of conventional weaponry is justified to deter its enemies and defend itself from direct attack. Conventional weapons are justified **prudentially** on the grounds that a state can flourish economically and allow all its institutions to continue. The JWA has often provided a moral defence for the use of war but stops short at the excessive use of force. Therefore it is unclear whether the possession of nuclear weapons could have the same prudential justification as moral justification. It could be argued that if, as many think, a very large army is undesirable to maintain social order (too much force could reduce the sense of freedom that citizens enjoy) then nuclear weapons would be much more unacceptable prudentially and morally.

ii) Mutual vulnerability

Nuclear weapons have changed our view of armies and force in general. Modern conventional weapons have shifted our views of weapons: they can travel great distances and destroy targets with precision but nuclear weapons are unique in that they threaten to destroy civilised society on both sides. The acronym **MAD** or 'mutual assured destruction' describes the ability to annihilate the opposition and expect to be destroyed one's self when they retaliate. This makes the use of nuclear weapons very unusual. But as Lee argues, 'for mutual vulnerability to exist, each side's nuclear weapons must be largely *in*vulnerable ...'. This means that a nation state needs to possess more than one nuclear missile in order to retaliate. In reality, therefore, the situation is complex; not all nations are vulnerable and some are more vulnerable than others. It is almost inevitable that a nuclear attack will not be a one-way affair – it is almost certain that nuclear war will result in mass destruction of all social structures on both sides. Nuclear weapons are not survivable in the same way as the Black Death was survivable. Whereas the Black Death occurred slowly and allowed people to plan how to deal with the situation, a nuclear attack happens very quickly and causes almost instant meltdown of the social order.

iii) Unacceptable damage

Lee argues that mutual vulnerability alters the notion enshrined in JWA that there must be a reasonable chance of success. But in nuclear war success would have to be measured in different ways. Whereas there are losses in conventional war, in nuclear war losses would have to be separate from whichever side 'wins'. It is possible that success might be considered in ideological terms; some people say that they would **rather be dead than red**, in other words they would rather die for their beliefs than submit to an alien ideology.

Key word

Prudence means practical wisdom or reasoning. It is a matter of debate whether prudence is also a moral term. See the discussion on pages 163–65 below.

Key word

The term **MAD** or 'mutual assured destruction' was invented by Donald Brennan in 1967 as a criticism of the use of nuclear weaponry.

Key quote

'But for mutual vulnerability to exist, each side's nuclear weapons must be largely invulnerable ...'

STEVEN P. LEE, *MORALITY, PRUDENCE AND NUCLEAR WEAPONS*, PAGE 6

Key word

Rather dead than red means it would be better to die for one's own beliefs and way of life than be ruled over by a different ideology. 'Red' originally referred to USSR communism.

But it is dubious whether people would actually prefer to die rather than live under another nation's rule. This suggests that the use of nuclear weapons would *inevitably* bring about 'unacceptable damage'; whereas though conventional war might lead to the same conclusion, it need not do so necessarily because it can be controlled and contained more easily than nuclear war.

iv) Limited nuclear war

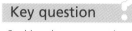
Key question

Could nuclear weapons be morally justified in a limited nuclear war?

Some have argued that if nuclear weapons are used in a 'limited nuclear war' then the problems of mutual vulnerability and the unacceptable damage to the social order might be avoided. This might be achieved by limiting the nuclear tonnage of the bomb and restricting damage only to military sites. The purpose of using a nuclear weapon rather than a conventional weapon would be to symbolise the power of the attacking nation.

On the other hand, once nuclear weapons have been used, the enemy might feel justified in using their own. The consequence of this is that while in conventional war both sides exercise restraint to some degree, nuclear weapons radically reduce the time usually available in war to plan and organise a response. The 'friction', as Clausewitz terms it, in war is now so intense (due to nuclear weapons) that the chain of command is unable to exercise its usual restraint.

But not everyone agrees with this conclusion; mutual restraint might be possible in limited nuclear war. For example A might only attack military sites to signal to B that if he wants A's restraint then he would have to limit his own attacks; the use of nuclear weapons would be necessary for striking a bargain of restraint. But in reality war is not so straightforward. Lee comments:

> *But due to the confusion of war, made worse by nuclear weapons, it would be overwhelmingly difficult for leaders successfully to send and receive such signals.*
>
> (Steven P. Lee, *Morality, Prudence and Nuclear Weapons*, page 15)

Finally, limited nuclear war would still cause huge devastation, so limiting the number of attacks and targets may not actually decrease the overall destruction to the social order. Some argue that risks are worthwhile – there is proportion between ends and means – but Lee considers that the likelihood of this happening is 'reasonably rare, at best'.

v) Moral justifiability

In most conventional war arguments the primary aim is to attack enemy combatants without destroying the nation as a whole. But as nuclear weapons cause considerable and indiscriminate damage both in the short and long term (through fallout and damage to the environment) it is dubious whether it could ever be morally justified. Lee concludes that, compared to the aims of conventional war, 'Nuclear war is a virtual moral impossibility' (page 20).

2 Why use nuclear weapons?

Key question

Why use nuclear rather than conventional weapons in war?

A single one megaton bomb, dropped by a single plane, could do the work of a million V-1 or V-2 bombs used in the Second World War and without the same risk of death to one's own troops and civilians. The cost and efficiency of nuclear weapons justify huge capital investment to offset what would be needed to support a conventional army with the same firepower capacity.

a) Conventional and nuclear missiles

Key thoughts

There are two kinds of nuclear bombs. In **fission** the nucleus of an atom is made to absorb a neutron, making it split into two nuclei, releasing at the same time a great deal of energy. **Fusion** (or thermonuclear reaction) is achieved by combining two nuclei to release energy.

Yield is the equivalent amount of explosion caused in a conventional bomb measured in terms of TNT. A one kiloton nuclear bomb therefore produces the same as 1000 tons of TNT.

There are two kinds of nuclear bombs, **fission** and **fusion**. Fission bombs are more common. Conventional and nuclear bombs both work by relying on the blast or shockwave caused by an explosion. But a nuclear bomb differs because:

- its explosion may be thousands or millions of times greater than a conventional bomb. Explosive energy of a nuclear bomb is measured as a **yield**.
- the temperatures caused by a nuclear bomb are much greater than a conventional bomb. Most of it is caused by **thermal energy**, i.e. intense light and heat (and can cause destruction at considerable distances).
- unlike conventional bombs nuclear bombs also produce radioactive **fallout**. Eighty-five per cent of a nuclear explosion is blast, shock and thermal energy, and 15 per cent is fallout, of which 5 per cent is the initial radiation (of gamma rays) produced within a minute of the explosion and 10 per cent is residual or delayed radiation.

Key quote

'Damage from the resulting firestorms could be far more devastating than the well-known blast effects.'

JOSEPH M. SIRACUSA, *NUCLEAR WEAPONS: A VERY SHORT INTRODUCTION*, PAGE 5

Key word

Fallout is the minute particles of radioactive materials caused by nuclear explosion and carried through the atmosphere by the wind. Radioactive decay can contaminate plants, animals and water. In humans fallout can cause leukaemia, bone cancer and damage to genes that can be passed on to future generations.

Conventional and nuclear bomb yields

- V-1 and V-2 bombs used by the Germans in the Second World War had yields of just under one ton of TNT.
- The nuclear bombs used at Hiroshima and Nagasaki in 1945 had yields of 12.5 and 22 kilotons (thousand tons of TNT).
- Nuclear bombs can now be of several megatons. The USSR tested a bomb in 1961 of 56 megatons (56 million tons of TNT).
- Some nuclear bombs for tactical purposes can have yields as little as 100 tons (0.1 kilotons).
- Modern weapons have MIRV capacity. That is, the ability to place on one missile many warheads which can be targeted to quite separate locations at great distances apart.

Key quote

'The hope of civilization lies in international arrangements looking, if possible, to the renunciation of the use and development of the atomic bomb.'

HARRY S. TRUMAN, PRESIDENT OF THE UNITED STATES, STATEMENT TO CONGRESS, 1945 (QUOTED IN JOSEPH M. SIRACUSA, *NUCLEAR WEAPONS*, PAGE 28)

Key question

How has the rise of international terrorism altered views about building up nuclear weapons?

Cross-reference

See Joseph M. Siracusa, *Nuclear Weapons*, Chapter 7, on non-proliferation in an age of terrorism.

i) Proliferation and non-proliferation

For many countries the lethal threat of possessing nuclear weapons has become a necessary means of protecting its interests. But the build-up of nuclear weapons has led to an **arms race** where each country develops a bigger and bigger arsenal of bombs. This is also referred to as **proliferation**. Proliferation of nuclear warheads is so that if the enemy should destroy one nuclear strategic arsenal then a country still has others at its disposal to retaliate or it might simply be to compensate for lack of conventional weapon fire-power. Right from the start in 1945 governments have developed **non-proliferation** strategies through treatises and agreements to reduce nuclear arsenals.

Since the attack on the World Trade Center building, New York (11 September 2001), the non-proliferation argument has become far more persuasive than the proliferation view. First, it appears to have made little difference to the terrorists that the USA has a large number of atomic bombs and, second, some have argued that proliferation of nuclear missiles may give terrorists greater reason and opportunity to use them. The threat of nuclear war is no longer between nation states but groups who operate outside conventional power structures and whose aims are not just political but ideological; some fundamentalist groups may actually wish to cause mass destruction.

ii) Symbolism of nuclear weapons

A nuclear explosion

Key thought

The **Cold War** was the period from 1953 to 1991 when the threat of invasion of the West from communist USSR led to a build-up of nuclear weapons. The historian John Lewis also described this period as the 'long peace'.

Key word

Hegemony means a monopoly or domination of one country's rule over all others.

Finally, nuclear weapons have come to be **symbolic** of a nation's independence and self-sufficiency. The period of the **Cold War** justified the increase and proliferation of nuclear missiles under a US **hegemony** to protect democracy against communism. Britain's nuclear capacity, for instance, was both a contribution to the USA's defence policy but equally a continuation of the idea that Britain was still a world power.

The **post-Cold War** era has posed a new set of problems for countries holding nuclear weapons. With the disintegration of the old USSR and the rise of nationalism, some have argued for a **new deterrence**, not only to limit the proliferation of nuclear weapons but the materials and technology needed to create weapons of mass destruction. But for some time the symbolism of having nuclear weapons has been to express the superiority of western democracy over other less well-developed states. During his presidency of the United States of America, Bill Clinton argued that MAD should be replaced by a policy of MAS – **mutual assured safety**. This subtle shift in the purpose of nuclear weapons prompted some reduction in nuclear weapon capacity, but even so a statement by Clinton in 1997 indicated that its primary purpose was deterrence and America's place in maintaining the world balance of power. The 1997 report to Congress stated:

> *The new directive provides a large measure of continuity with previous nuclear weapons employment guidance, including in particular the following three principles:*
>
> - *Deterrence is predicated on ensuring that potential adversaries accept that any use of nuclear weapons against the United States or its allies would not succeed.*
> - *A wide range of nuclear retaliatory options will continue to be planned to ensure the United States is not left with an all-or-nothing response.*
> - *The United States will not rely on a launch-on-warning nuclear retaliation strategy (although an adversary could never be sure the United States would not launch a counterattack before the adversary's nuclear weapons arrived).*
>
> *(Report to Congress on Arms Control, Nonproliferation and Disarmament Studies [1997], http://dosfan.lib.uic.edu/acda/reports/rptacnp.htm)*

b) Nuclear destruction

In 1945 two fission bombs were dropped on the Japanese cities of Hiroshima and Nagasaki. The Second World War was finally brought to an end and Europe then began the process of rebuilding its economy. The effects of the bombs were immediately obvious and terrifying in themselves. But it is only in the years following that we have been able to gauge the long-term consequences, because at the time, the effects of fallout had not been fully realised or anticipated. For instance, 140,000 people were killed in Hiroshima on 6 August 1945 but by 1978 another 2000 people had died from the radiation effects of the bomb. Hiroshima and Nagasaki are the *only* times, so far, when nuclear bombs have been used in warfare. Any predictions for the future for the way in which nuclear weapons will work can only be based on this event and on guess-work (through computer modelling, for instance).

A fission nuclear weapon exploding above ground at less than 10,000 feet:		
Explosion process	**Environmental effects**	**Time scale**
Blast and shock: 50%	Collapse of buildings, rupture of eardrums, haemorrhaging of lungs; earth tremors	First minute
Heat and light: 35%	Burns, fires caused; excessive heat of tens of millions of degrees centigrade	First few seconds
Initial radiation: 5%	1 megaton bomb causes radioactive cloud rising eleven miles	24 hours, cigar shaped, mainly down wind
Residual radiation and fallout: 10% (delayed)	Somatic (i.e. to body) harm to tissues, radiation sickness, cancer death, abortions; genetic (germ line) defects in subsequent children	After 24 hours, world wide and for 30–40 years subsequently
Electro-magnetic pulse	Blackout of communication through electro-magnetic interference	
For example, 1 megaton air burst over a city of 4 million people like Detroit: 470,000 people killed instantly, 630,000 injured. In addition the long-term effects of radiation fallout have to be taken into account and the likelihood of several targets being bombed at once. Casualties should be reckoned in tens of millions. (Based on *The Church and the Bomb*, Chapter 1)		

3 The morality of nuclear war

Many have concluded, along with Steven P. Lee (see page 151 above) 'Nuclear war is a virtual moral impossibility.' This is because set against the **just war argument** (JWA), which many use to determine whether a war is morally justifiable or not, the use of nuclear weapons fails to be morally justifiable at almost every stage. This is a very different argument as to whether nuclear weapons may be used as **deterrence**, which will be discussed in the next section.

The JWA propositions are:

Ius ad bellum principles:

1 There must be a just cause (those attacked must deserve it).
2 War must be sanctioned by a legitimate authority.
3 War must be fought with the right intentions (i.e. to achieve peace).
4 There must be a reasonable prospect of success.
5 War should be the last resort.
6 The damage done in war must be proportionate to the injustice which has provoked the war.

Ius in bello principles:

7 The actions taken in war must be proportional to their ends.
8 Non-combatants must be given immunity from attack.

Cross-reference

Read pages 128–34 for discussion on the JWA in conventional war.

The major issues which nuclear missiles pose are those of proportion, non-combatant immunity and success.

a) Limited nuclear war and the just war argument

Key word

Limited nuclear war is defined as limited nuclear tonnage of the bomb and restricting damage only to military sites. See page 150 above.

The first consideration is whether nuclear missiles could be proportionate *ius in bello* (justice within war). This could equally apply to other non-conventional methods, i.e. chemical and biological warfare. A **tactical warhead** used in the theatre of war might be used only against a military objective and not a city. Its tonnage could be calculated to inflict enough damage to reduce enemy morale sufficiently to bring about capitulation. This, it will be remembered, was the aim of Harris' controversial reasons for the conventional use of aerial bombing on Dresden and Hamburg. The purpose in using nuclear weapons in a limited nuclear war might be:

Cross-reference

Read page 134 above on the Hamburg bombing.

- cost and reduction of military personnel
- speed (i.e. reaction time to the threat)
- psychological effect caused by the horror of nuclear burns, etc.
- deterrent through a display and warning of military superiority.

On the other hand the use of nuclear weapons even in a limited nuclear war might be rejected because of the following:

- The major fear is that the enemy would retaliate with a larger bomb with less discrimination for non-combatant immunity. This might eventually **escalate** into a full-scale **nuclear war**.
- No use of nuclear (chemical or biological) weapons is sufficiently **discriminating** ever to be proportionate. The Chernobyl disaster

(in 1986) illustrates how even a small amount of radiation can affect animals and humans thousands of miles away and for some considerable time to come. The UN estimated that 50,000 babies have died prematurely between 1946 and 1976 because of the fallout and genetic damage caused from the *testing* of nuclear bombs. If a nuclear bomb is used in anger the results are simply too long term and horrendous to be considered even on a limited scale.

- Deterrence is an unstable factor, especially in war. There is no guarantee that the enemy will respond favourably. Deterrence worked in Hiroshima, but Japan had no nuclear means of its own with which to retaliate.

The counter-arguments for the limited nuclear war force us to consider whether nuclear missiles would always be disproportionate in nuclear war because of the psychological and symbolic effects on the enemy. Nuclear weapons change the mind-set of all those engaged in war. Whereas in conventional 'war' there is time to prepare (during which the propositions *ius ad bellum* can be weighed up) and a period in which the war is fought (allowing for tactical changes, reconsideration of enemy moves, deployment of troops), in nuclear war the two elements are merged into one – the time differential between firing a strategic missile and immediately being involved with the possible outcomes of engagement occur within moments of each other. Means and ends are inextricably fused into one. This is one reason why the JWA may not be entirely applicable in its traditional form.

Should this matter? A crucial aspect of the JWA derived from its natural law roots is that the intentional killing of the innocent is morally reprehensible (item 7). But even in limited nuclear war where the intention is to use sufficient force to bring about a conclusion there can be no guarantee that the enemy will not retaliate with its own nuclear missile, at which stage non-combatant immunity is severely compromised and the conflict becomes classified as a **total war**. JWA rejects total war.

Cross-reference

See page 123 above on total war.

b) Nuclear war and modified just war argument

Another way of judging the moral arguments for the use of nuclear weapons in war is to consider which elements of the JWA might be adapted. For example:

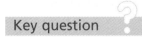

Key question

How could the just war argument be adapted to allow for the use of nuclear weapons?

- The JWA considers the *total* loss of life from all sides. Although there may be considerable loss of civilian life, even so this might be less than if conventional war was to be fought over a long period of time. One shouldn't also forget that psychological damage in conventional war/conflict can last for a very long time.

- It is reasonable to assume that all **cities** (i.e. areas occupied by civilians as well as combatants or 'soft targets') have to be treated as potentially hostile otherwise these might act as a human shield and give tactical advantage to the enemy.
- The alternatives might be hard to countenance. The prospect of an extremely murderous and anti-liberal regime could suggest that attack is the best form of defence. The use of considerable force might be the **best bet** to use as a **first strike** tactic.
- **Escalation** is not necessarily inevitable. Once the enemy sees the devastation of one nuclear bomb they might be forced to realise that there is nothing to gain by continuing the conflict.
- **Success** is not inevitably ruled out in nuclear war. Success does not need to be concerned with the enemy's social structures, only one's own.

However, many feel that altering the JWA to compromise protection of non-combatants, making attack defensible, use of disproportionate power and seeing success only in terms of the attackers produces an unacceptable version of the JWA. In addition they argue that nuclear war cannot be defended using any form of the JWA because of the following:

- It is likely there will be **no winners**. In the worse possible scenario any number of countries might be drawn into the conflict and use their nuclear missiles. The inevitability of escalation would result in mutual assured destruction. Even in a far less serious situation the effects of nuclear fallout, the severe effects on social structures and the devastation to the environment would still be sufficiently terrible always to be disproportionate.
- Some people have fondly believed in a 'big whoosh' notion that the scale of things will be so enormous that it will, in effect, mark the end of the world. They take some comfort in this fatalistic **Armageddon** view of the inevitable outcome of nuclear war because the kind of world left would be highly undesirable. Although this scenario is unlikely, it illustrates that the aims of just war to achieve peace or only to punish those who deserve to be attacked are impossible using nuclear weapons.
- Nuclear weapons are unacceptable because of **counter-value arguments**. Whereas some loss of civilian life is anticipated in conventional JWA (as an unfortunate side-effect) the scale of nuclear war suggests that there would be an actual **intention** to kill innocent lives. Even the **double effect argument**, which forms part of the JWA, is ineffective here because the number of *unintended* deaths of non-combatants has to be in proportion to the direct and willed intention to do good. The long-term and indiscriminate effects of nuclear fallout are not sustained by the JWA.

Key word

Counter-value arguments, as distinct from counter-power arguments, consider the moral effects of using nuclear weapons, not just their physical effects.

4 The morality of nuclear deterrence

Key quote

'The moral problem posed by nuclear weapons is special. The magnitude of the moral stakes involved in this dilemma represents a serious challenge to the coherence of our every day moral view.'

STEVEN P. LEE, *MORALITY, PRUDENCE AND NUCLEAR WEAPONS*, PAGE 59

Cross-reference

Read pages 147–51 above on nuclear deterrence.

Key quote

'I don't believe it's worked; I know it's worked. There has been no war for 40 years.'

LORD CARRINGTON, GENERAL SECRETARY OF NATO, IN 1985

Cross-reference

Read pages 115–16 on the problem of public and private in conventional war.

Key question

Is there any point in possessing nuclear weapons if one is never actually going to use them?

Although many argue that morally there is no defence for the use of nuclear weapons in war, they do not necessarily rule out the possession of nuclear missiles. Paradoxically it is because the results of nuclear weapons are so awful that the purchase, development and deployment of nuclear missiles is justified because they maintain peace without recourse to war. The MAD (mutual assured destruction) argument suggests that rational self-interest prohibits not only the use of nuclear weapons but also restrains nations from resorting to large-scale conventional war.

In other words nation states have, as we have seen, justified the **deterrent effect** of nuclear weapons to keep the peace. The argument is hardly new. Maintaining conventional armies is often justified because of their deterrent symbolism; also an argument has been presented above for the use of limited nuclear weapons in war as a threat or a deterrent. The argument here falls into two parts:

- **Prudential/political justification**: since the end of the Second World War, the nuclear deterrent has maintained peace or at least prevented wars from escalating. Even if there is no prudential evidence for nuclear deterrence, it is a matter of political reality that the political balance of power has come to rely on nuclear deterrent.
- **Moral justification**: it is morally justifiable to threaten violence or to hold innocent people as hostage if the greater good is achieved.

The tension between the two parts of the argument also illustrates the uneasy alliance between public and private morality.

a) Consequential defence for nuclear deterrence

It might be considered that the consequential argument is an essentially prudential or practical one. A narrowly prudential argument does not make moral judgements based on the greatest good of the greatest number, as effectively as the utilitarian consequentialist does. For nuclear deterrence to be morally acceptable, all effects on all people have to be considered.

i) Mutual vulnerability

Mutual vulnerability is a better description of MAD and is justified by the consequentialist because of the following:

- Mutual vulnerability threatens the opponent with necessarily unacceptable damage to ensure that he does not start a war. It creates stability not just for the nation but for all.
- **Unilateral disarmament** is not an option because it would create a political vacuum for others to exploit. The USA, for example,

Key word

Unilateral disarmament is when one country decides to disarm itself of all nuclear weapons regardless of whether other countries disarm or not.

Cross-reference

See page 152 above for the reasons for non-proliferation.

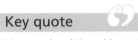

Key quote

'The atom bomb is nothing to be afraid of. China has many people. They cannot be bombed out of existence. If someone else can drop an atomic bomb, I can too. The deaths of ten or twenty million people is nothing to be afraid of.'

CHAIRMAN MAO (1957)

has justified nuclear deterrence as a 'nuclear umbrella' for an international balance of power.

On the other hand, the consequentialist also has to recognise that nuclear deterrence might cause conventional wars to proliferate, assuming that no nuclear weapons will be used. This in turn might cause super powers to increase nuclear fire-power and proliferate nuclear weapons arsenals even though non-proliferation is the safer option.

It is understandable that for prudential reasons state policy which has accepted nuclear deterrence has depended on a **trade-off defence**, which is prepared to cope with the inconsistencies of deterrence against the increased likelihood of war and political instability.

ii) Bluffs

Utilitarianism has no fundamental objections to the bluff argument. If, by pretending that nuclear weapons will be used in conflict when in fact there is no such intention, war is averted, so much the better. The utilitarian is not so much interested in intentions as outcome and so would support government practice of maintaining nuclear weapons as deterrence. The problem, though, is how far and to what extent the bluff can be maintained. The prudential challenge, as far as the public is concerned, is that the government would have to persuade them that it *would* fully intend to use the weapons as a last resort. Furthermore, all those who develop and maintain and all those who train to use nuclear weapons would have to do so fully believing that they might, one day, be used in anger. Clearly there would be no deterrent effect if a potential enemy thought the government was not utterly serious.

But can a government sustain a deception of this magnitude? How does it react to potential enemies with nuclear capability? The **Cuban missile crisis** of 1962 is often cited as the positive aspect of the deterrent defence. Undoubtedly the possession of nuclear weapons on both sides brought the American and the USSR presidents (Kennedy and Krushchev) to the negotiating table and secured a peaceful and non-violent agreement.

But, as some critics conclude, if the citizens of either country thought for one moment that bluff was anything other than a bluff they would not support the deterrence argument.

b) Deontological defence for nuclear deterrence

The argument here is based on the proposition that an action is morally right provided it is based on good intentions. The issue is whether a **counter-value** argument of deterrence can coherently support the intention of **threatening** to use nuclear weapons in

Key question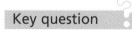

Is it always wrong to threaten someone with violence?

Key people

John Haldane is professor of philosophy and director of the Centre for Ethics, Philosophy and Public Affairs at St Andrew's University. As a Catholic he has developed a natural law approach to ethics and has written on Aquinas and the influence of scholasticism in metaphysics, philosophy of mind, and value theory.

Cross-reference

John Haldane in Bauckham and Elford, *The Nuclear Weapons Debate*, Chapter 9.

Key quote

'That would be no way to regulate traffic even if it succeeds *in regulating it perfectly, since such a system makes innocent human lives the* direct object of attack and uses them as a mere means for restraining the drivers of automobiles.'

PAUL RAMSEY, *THE JUST WAR: FORCE AND POLITICAL RESPONSIBILITY*, PAGE 171

order to dissuade potential aggressors. All traditions of natural law, Kantian ethics and most Christian traditions condemn the intentional killing of an innocent life – even if good should come of it. It is simply not possible to intend to deter if it means being prepared to use nuclear force as a very last resort unless there is some justification for an **evil will**.

i) Bluffs as threats

The bluff argument may be summarised as follows: as deterrence seems to work in maintaining peace then it is reasonable to threaten the use of nuclear weapons even though in reality they wouldn't actually be used.

However, the bluff appears to be morally contradictory. How is it possible to intend both to will to use (the threat) and not to use (the bluff) nuclear weapons at the same time? Some have argued for two kinds of intention: **unconditional intention** is the primary aim to deter from war; **conditional intention** is the secondary aim to wage war. This, it is claimed, makes it possible to will deterrence without the need to lie or bluff, because the secondary intention is dependent on the first. So, as my primary aim is to deter, I am not directly committed to intending nuclear war, unless circumstances change.

John Haldane argues that the *logic* of this kind of argument does not commit me to carrying out my intention when the situation arises. Supposing there was a significant change in circumstance, i.e. the aggressor *has* fired his first missile; there would be no reason why I should be held to my earlier intention which, when I made it, was not based on the possibility of an *actual* nuclear attack. I could, therefore, quite coherently justify a reassessment of my intentions. This conclusion, as it turns out, is not dissimilar to NATO's (1967) **flexible response** principle which encourages members to use mixed means (conventional and/or nuclear) as the situation develops.

ii) Deterrence as hostage taking

As we saw at the start of this chapter, Paul Ramsey offered his thought experiment of tying babies to bumpers to deter motorists from driving badly as an analogy of nuclear deterrence. The babies in the analogy, he suggested, was equivalent to citizens on both sides who are acting as unconscious hostages. But Paul Ramsey's complete rejection of the hostage taking (because it treats innocent people as a means to an end) is not shared by all deontologists. Some argue that the special nature of the nuclear weapon threat justifies the hostage-taking principle. As with the bluff argument, the primary aim is not to kill the civilians who are acting as part of the deterrent, but to assess the level of risk that the hostage-taking justification poses. As most of the time the actual risks and threats to life that possessing nuclear weapons pose to ordinary citizens are very few, the deontologist can therefore say that deterrence is good.

But the 'baby bumpers' hostage analogy is not entirely satisfactory:

- The risks for the babies are very clearly and directly life-threatening. But this is not the case for most citizens whose country has nuclear weapons. As citizens feel no direct threat to their lives they cannot act as a deterrent or be part of the negotiating process (which would be the case if it were an ordinary hostage case).
- It is assumed that as the citizens know the policy of their country they are not hostages as they have in effect volunteered to be used as part of the threat.
- Hostage keeping is not a good form of negotiation. Experience indicates that it is often unstable and causes people to do rash things in order to secure a rescue. As hostage taking is generally regarded to be a sign of a politically weak group, it sends out the wrong signal to those it is trying to deter.

Michael Walzer concludes on the poor use of the hostage analogy:

Key quote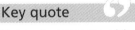

'That is why deterrence, while in principle so frightening, is so easy to live with. It cannot be condemned for anything it does to its hostages.'

MICHAEL WALZER, JUST AND UNJUST WARS, PAGE 271

> *That is why deterrence, while in principle so frightening, is so easy to live with. It cannot be condemned for anything it does to its hostages. It is so far from killing them that it does not even injure or confine them; it involves no direct or physical violation of their rights. Those critics of deterrence who are also committed consequentialists have had to imagine psychic injuries.*
>
> (Michael Walzer, *Just and Unjust Wars*, page 271)

5 Normative ethical responses to nuclear war and deterrence

a) Kantian ethics

i) Nuclear war

Cross-references

Read pages 8–10 for an outline of Kant's ethics. For a fuller discussion read Mel Thompson, *Ethical Theory*, Chapter 10.

For discussion on Kant's argument on war and peace in 'Toward Perpetual Peace' read pages 134–36 above.

We have seen in the previous chapter that Kant argues in his essay 'Toward Perpetual Peace' that there are some moral reasons for the use of conventional war. These include the following:

- Despite the human desire to act violently, humans also have an innate power to will each other good. The true human being struggles to overcome his lower animal self using reason.
- Peace has to be *established*; it does not occur naturally by itself. War is sometimes necessary providing it is fought in a controlled and reasoned way.
- War is not justified if it means interfering with the constitution or government of another state. The categorical imperative respects the autonomy of others to act as they wish.

- The categorical imperative ensures that no peace treaty can be established that does not rule out categorically recourse to war in the future.
- The practical imperative is one which gives dignity to every person as a rational and autonomous member of the human race; therefore killing in war can only be between combatants.

Cross-reference

Read page 150 on the arguments for and against limited nuclear war.

Kant's argument is therefore similar to the JWA. It is possible that the Kantian might support a limited nuclear war for the reasons already discussed but it is improbable that nuclear war would satisfy any of the conditions set out above. The aftermath of nuclear war is highly unlikely to have established sufficiently the civilised social conditions which justify the use of conventional war. Ultimately nuclear war must be intrinsically wrong because it relies on deliberately destroying cities and innocent citizens.

ii) Nuclear deterrence

The paradox of nuclear deterrence as expressed by Michael Walzer captures something of the Kantian position:

We threaten evil in order not to do it, and the doing of it would be so terrible that the threat seems in comparison to be morally defensible.
(Michael Walzer, *Just and Unjust Wars*, page 274)

As we have seen in Steven Lee's arguments, the present debates about nuclear deterrent have often divorced the prudential from the moral. This is equivalent to Kant's distinction between the hypothetical and the categorical imperative. In the kingdom of ends what we will is universal world peace and harmony. The hypothetical imperative might express it prudentially this way:

If we want world peace then the possession of nuclear weapons has proved itself to provide sufficient state of mutual vulnerability to do this.

But is this moral? The categorical imperative is presented with a dilemma as to which aspect of the hypothetical to universalise. On the one hand, the categorical imperative must reject the intended use of nuclear weapons as a means to an end because it would always be wrong to will our neighbour harm (through threats or 'hostage taking') if they have done no wrong. On the other hand, it might be argued that what is willed is not really evil because it does not actually intend to use nuclear weapons in anger but to rely on their deterrent effect. The good will *intends* universal peace.

Cross-reference

Read pages 159–61 on the deontological problems of bluffs, threats and hostage taking.

But the problem is how to resolve these two clashing duties. We have already considered the deontological arguments for and against bluffs, threats and hostage taking but the uneasy conclusion is that as long as the deterrence works as a threat using innocent people as part of the bluff, then nuclear deterrence cannot be a universal duty. The opening of 'Toward Perpetual Peace' suggests that if deterrence is seen in terms of a treaty to establish peace then it cannot also will to fight a future, especially one that involves mass destruction:

> *No peace settlement which secretly reserves issues for a future war shall be considered valid. For such a treaty would represent a mere cease-fire, a postponement of hostilities, and not peace.*
>
> (Immanuel Kant, *Toward Perpetual Peace* 8:343)

b) Virtue ethics

i) Nuclear war

Cross-reference

Read Mel Thompson, *Ethical Theory*, Chapter 16, for more discussion of virtue ethics.

Key quote

'A virtue is an acquired human quality the possession of and exercise of which tends to enable us to achieve those goods which are internal to practices and the lack of which effectively prevents us from achieving any such goods.'

ALASDAIR MACINTYRE,

AFTER VIRTUE, PAGE 178

The limitations of the consequential and deontological arguments for and against nuclear war is that the extraordinary nature of nuclear war makes the usual arguments for war and peace incapable of dealing with a situation which could quite radically and fundamentally alter human history. Lee argues that what is needed is an ethic which bridges the divide between the prudential (the practical considerations of using nuclear weapons) and the moral (the value judgements of consequential or deontological moral systems). Virtue ethics offers a possible bridge because whilst it takes existing moral values seriously, it also considers how they should actually be *practised*. Virtues are principle enabling.

- In its purist form (virtue orientated virtue ethics) virtue ethicists might argue that possession of nuclear weapons is a symbol of strength and a willingness to uphold the values of a nation and how it wishes to appear in terms of power or protection.
- The virtue ethicist (principle orientated virtue ethics) might counsel that the actual use of nuclear weapons requires considerable skill (*phronesis*) in judging its appropriateness, whether given the political situation it would be excessive (vice) or just (virtue). He might consider the motives which have caused the nation to take such excessive action – whether for instance the enemy have undermined basic values of human decency (for example mass exterminations or genocides) to place society or the world in jeopardy or whether, in fact, the motive is spite, greed or arrogance.

Nuclear war poses particular problems for the virtue ethicist. Iris Murdoch (1919–99), for example, argues (following Aristotle) that the virtues cannot simply be taught but must be acquired through a life-time of practice. Therefore when we come across a difficult situation we do not act entirely according to reason or emotion but from a virtuous character. However, whereas there have been many conventional wars in the past to practise and learn from, there have been no nuclear wars (with the exception of Hiroshima and Nagasaki but Japan had no nuclear missiles to retaliate or deter).

This makes the possibility of nuclear war practically and morally highly dangerous.

ii) Nuclear deterrence

Key question

How does a state justify the risks of having nuclear weapons as a deterrent?

Cross-reference

Read pages 136–38 on war and virtue ethics.

In the previous chapter we considered the story of Odysseus whose use of excessive force on his return home was commended by Homer to illustrate the value of the family as the essential building block of society. Odysseus' action was necessary as an example of the strong leader who reinforces the values of society by prudentially balancing the physical risks (the use of force) and moral values (attitudes to family/society). Modern virtue ethicists argue that this important relationship between making factual judgements *and* moral judgements is vital for statesmen when considering the risks of nuclear deterrence.

For modern writers such as Steven Lee and John Elford the nuclear deterrence debate has become confused, since Hume and Kant argued that prudence is only a form of rational calculation of risks and benefits and not, as in the Aristotelian tradition, a judgement of moral value. So, for example, to justify nuclear deterrence on the grounds that it has kept the peace for 60 years sounds prudentially neutral and sensible, except that it cannot be a neutral statement of fact (there may be many other good factual reasons for this state of peace) and there is an implied political value judgement that nuclear weapons are therefore good. This confusion is morally and politically dangerous and the modern virtue ethicist argues that he can offer some important insights.

Elford argues that Aristotle's and Aquinas' notion of prudence (*phronesis*) is the best way of considering the risks of nuclear deterrence because it combines and *balances* the intellectual virtues (rational calculation) and moral virtues. Elford argues:

> Rational calculation is, of course, a necessary condition of responsible risk management, but it is not a sufficient one.
>
> (R. John Elford, in *The Nuclear Weapons Debate: Theological and Ethical Issues*, page 160)

Aquinas comments on the relationship of rational/factual prudence (single matters) and moral prudence (universal principles):

Key quote

'Now actions are in singular matters: and so it is necessary for the prudent man to know both the universal principles of reason, and the singulars about which actions are concerned.'

THOMAS AQUINAS, *SUMMA THEOLOGICA* 2.2, Q. 47, ART. 3

> Prudence belongs not only to the consideration of the reason, but also the application to action, which is the end of the practical reason. But no man can conveniently apply one thing to another, unless he knows both the thing to be applied, and the thing to which it has to be applied. Now actions are in singular matters: and so it is necessary for the prudent man to know both the universal principles of reason, and the singulars about which actions are concerned.
>
> (Thomas Aquinas, *Summa Theologica* 2.2, Q. 47, Art. 3)

Elford argues that prudence works in three ways. First, it has rationally to assess the risks as facts; second, it has to consider the various moral assessments of risks; third, it has to combine and balance judgements between facts and values.

- **Intellectual prudence.** Any discussion about the risks of nuclear deterrence must have accurate information about the facts. Some argue that knowledge of nuclear technology is so biased by its supporters and critics alike that the public rarely receive a neutral view of its capabilities.
- **Practical prudence.** Discussion of nuclear deterrence has to consider the morality of bluffs, threats and hostage keeping by steering the middle path between those who advocate bluffs because they have been seen to work and those who absolutely reject deterrence because it treats ordinary people as a means to an end.

Elford concludes that the process of risk assessment (risk identification, risk evaluation, risk decisions, risk implementation and risk review) is not a static one. As Aristotle argued, the virtuous life is one of constant review and the nuclear deterrence argument has to be regularly reviewed factually and morally.

c) Utilitarianism

i) Nuclear war

Cross-references

Read pages 14–17 above on utilitarianism.

Read page 150 on limited nuclear war.

The utilitarian arguments for nuclear war are far more likely to support limited nuclear war if and only if the enemy's response did not escalate into full-blown nuclear war. The arguments for and against nuclear war have already been considered.

All forms of utilitarianism would probably find the justification **counter-force** arguments for full nuclear war unacceptable. It is dubious whether the situation after war would achieve the greatest happiness or social welfare; long-term damage in terms of fallout and damage to the environment would make any kind of civilised existence extremely unlikely. This might be the case for many generations to follow. Even if the **counter-value** argument was used (i.e. the 'I would rather be dead than red' view) to justify nuclear war, what minimum level of existence is needed to justify mass extermination? Ideal utilitarians (such as Mill and Moore) argue that humans need more than mere existence and we therefore have to consider the effects of nuclear war on irreplaceable aspects of human culture such as art, architecture and libraries.

ii) Nuclear deterrence

Cross-reference

Read pages 158–59 on utilitarian reasons for nuclear weapons as deterrence.

The arguments for utilitarian consequential nuclear deterrence have largely been discussed. The basic premise of all utilitarian deterrence arguments is prudential: if for the past 60 years the world has enjoyed unprecedented peace because of the notion of mutual vulnerability caused by the presence of nuclear weapons then according to the general utilitarian maxim of 'the greatest happiness for the greatest number', nuclear deterrence is justified.

- **Hedonic utilitarians** have no fundamental objections to the bluff deterrence argument if war is averted. Nor do they object to the threats as illustrated in the hostage-taking argument; if the majority of people are unaware that they are being used as a means to an end then they are not suffering any anxiety and can enjoy the pleasures that nuclear deterrence establishes. However, Bentham's **calculus** does pose some important practical considerations. For example, at what cost does nuclear armament and nuclear defence (such as the multi-billion dollar 'star wars' programme) come? Are there cheaper and less dangerous means of achieving the same ends? Finally, there is no certainty that the bluff might work, especially in an age of stateless powers – as various attacks by terrorists on major world cities has illustrated in recent years.

- **Rule utilitarians** share many of the concerns of the hedonic utilitarians but argue that past experience based on conventional wars must act as the basis for nuclear deterrence policy and rule making. One example might be based on the observation that in seeking to address the problem of proliferation (on the grounds of cost and potential danger) there should be a policy to work for **multilateral disarmament** on the grounds that unilateral disarmament would cause a major disruption in the world balance of power.

- **Preference satisfaction utilitarians** might argue that deterrence is based on lying to the people that their lives are being used as hostages, which for the deterrent effect to work would mean that in effect the state would be prepared to murder them in a nuclear war. Preference utilitarians might argue that whereas people might be prepared to be used *voluntarily* as part of the threat or bluff, the state's decision to deploy nuclear missiles as part of its defence strategy has the potential to affect too many people negatively to be justified.

- **Welfare utilitarians** argue that nuclear deterrence is justified if it enhances people's sense of security, produces a stable social system and enables there to be sufficient wealth to provide the basics of shelter and food. The welfare utilitarian is prepared to let the state make the decision of whether or not to treat the people as hostages, as part of the deterrent threat or bluff (based on factual evidence). However, even welfare utilitarians cannot ignore the fear, unease and mistrust of government caused by the deployment of nuclear weapons when it is seen to be causing actual social harm to the well-being of society.

Key thought

'Star wars' was the nickname given to President Reagan's Strategic Defense Initiative (SDI) in 1984 in which incoming enemy nuclear missiles would be intercepted and destroyed about 750 miles above earth before having a chance to hit their targets in the USA.

Key word

Multilateral disarmament aims to reduce the number of nuclear war heads or means for constructing nuclear weapons on both sides.

Cross-references

Read Mel Thompson, *Ethical Theory*, Chapter 7, for more discussion of natural law.

Read pages 154–57 on just war and nuclear war.

d) Natural law

i) Nuclear war

We have already considered the natural law arguments for and against nuclear war by evaluating it against the JWA, which is itself based on natural law reasoning. In summary the arguments are:

- **Proportionality** is central to the JWA. Some argue that in limited nuclear war, nuclear weapons might be justified against strategic military positions, especially as their symbolic power would quickly demoralise the enemy and hasten an early end to the war with less loss of life on both sides. On the other hand, using a nuclear missile, even in a limited nuclear war, could cause the enemy to retaliate with nuclear weapons, escalating to total war.
- **Ends and means.** In the conventional JWA the two processes of going to war (*ius ad bellum*) and the engagement of war (*ius in bello*) are sufficiently separate to make well-informed judgements. But nuclear war causes the two elements to be merged into one. For some this is not a problem: the reasons for going to nuclear war will inevitably have justified the use of this kind of force and the response of the enemy. But for others conventional war allows time to determine exactly how the war should be fought and by what means; the uncertainty and confusion caused by using nuclear weapons makes nuclear war unacceptable.
- Although the **intention** might be to use sufficient force to bring about a conclusion, there can be no guarantee that the enemy will not retaliate with its own nuclear missile, at which stage non-combatant immunity is severely compromised.
- **Success** is not inevitably ruled out in nuclear war. Some have argued that success does not need to be concerned with the enemy's social structures, only with one's own. Other natural law supporters find this unacceptable – the intention should be to protect all innocent life. It is likely there will be **no winners**.
- Even the **double effect argument** (which forms an important part of the JWA) is ineffective here because the *unintended* deaths of non-combatants have to be in proportion to the direct and willed intention to do good and there would be far too many deaths to regard them as an unfortunate side-effect of nuclear war.

Key quote

'Preserving the common good of society requires rendering the aggressor unable to inflict harm.'
CATECHISM OF THE CATHOLIC CHURCH, PAGE 488

Even though some natural law thinkers have argued that as nuclear war poses problems that are extraordinary it is reasonable to develop extraordinary means by adapting the JWA, the modern Catholic Church's natural law argument is that nuclear war is intrinsically wrong:

Cross-reference

Read pages 156–57 for a modified JWA.

Every act of war directed to the indiscriminate destruction of whole cities or vast areas with their inhabitants is a crime against God and man, which merits firm and unequivocal condemnation. A danger of modern warfare is that it provides the opportunity to those who possess modern scientific weapons – especially atomic, biological or chemical weapons – to commit such crimes.

(*Catechism of the Catholic Church*, page 497)

ii) Nuclear deterrence

Cross-reference

Read pages 159–61 on the deontological arguments for nuclear deterrence.

The natural law deontological reasons for the use of threats and bluffs have already been discussed.

Natural law condemns the intentional killing of innocent life – even if good should come of it. That position poses particular difficulty for the nuclear deterrent argument where the power of the deterrent is achieved by directly or indirectly threatening non-combatant civilians on both sides. To summarise some of the arguments already considered:

- Deterrence does not commit the state to having to carry out its threat if the situation arises. If for example the enemy were to fire his nuclear missile first, or attack using conventional methods, this new situation does not oblige one to stick to one's promise. The promise was first established when there was no actual nuclear attack.
- The special nature of the nuclear weapon threat makes hostage keeping good in itself. The aim is not to kill the civilians who are acting as part of the deterrent but to assess the level of risk which the hostage-taking justification poses. As most of the time the actual risks and threats to civilian life from possessing nuclear weapons are very few, deterrence is justified.

Key quote

'The accumulation of arms strikes many as a paradoxically suitable way of deterring potential adversaries from war. They see it as the most effective means of ensuring peace amongst nations. This method of deterrence gives rise to strong moral reservations. The arms race does not ensure peace. Far from eliminating the causes of war, it risks aggravating them.'

CATECHISM OF THE CATHOLIC CHURCH, PAGES 497–98

Nevertheless, some argue that the use of mutual vulnerability is never justified as grounds for nuclear deterrence because it fundamentally diminishes the respect for human life.

Therefore, given that the Catholic Church considers nuclear war to be intrinsically wrong, the deterrence argument fails primarily because the proliferation of nuclear weapons cannot ensure peace and is not *directly* aimed at peace. The conclusion of the Church is not to reject nuclear deterrence totally but to treat it with great caution and with 'strong moral reservations'.

e) Revealed ethics

i) Nuclear war

Cross-reference

Read Mel Thompson, *Ethical Theory*, Chapter 14, for more discussion of religious and revealed ethics.

Key question

What effect does Christian teaching on the end of the world have on the ethics of nuclear war?

Even those Christians who permit the use of conventional war draw the line at the use of nuclear weapons. Christian **nuclear pacifists** argue that the use of nuclear weapons, even in limited nuclear war, is nearly always disproportionate. Just as with conventional war arguments the Christian focus is on the establishment of God's Kingdom. But with its potentially universal effects, nuclear war

Cross-reference

Read pages 141–43 on Christian responses to conventional war and peace.

Key word

Apocalyptic means literally 'revelatory' and refers to biblical texts such as the Books of Daniel and Revelation, which reveal what will happen at the end of time.

Key quotes

'Jesus came into Galilee, preaching the gospel of God, and saying, "The time is fulfilled, and the Kingdom of God is at hand, repent and believe in the gospel."'

MARK 1:14–15

'In the world you have tribulation; but be of good cheer, I have overcome the world.'

JOHN 16:33

Key thought

Armageddon is the final catastrophic battle between the kings of the world as described in Revelation 16:16.

Key quote

'Until we take seriously the way in which early Christian writers came to a compromise between their eschatological convictions, realised and future, and their belief that their new lord did not mean separation from the world, we shall not understand a fundamental element of the dynamic of early Christian religion.'

CHRISTOPHER ROWLAND,
CHRISTIAN ORIGINS, PAGE 283

draws out a particular aspect of New Testament teaching on the Kingdom of God which emphasises its **apocalyptic** end time. Christian responses fall into two categories: active and passive. Active views consider humans as responsible for making the Kingdom of God a present reality; passive views consider that only God can bring about the Kingdom of God.

The **nuclear pacifist active view** of the end time argues the following:

- Jesus' teaching on the Kingdom suggested that it had already *begun* in his life-time (Mark 1:14–15).
- Jesus' own life-style and activity is not simply that of a prophet who warns about the coming catastrophe, but a man with a vision of God wanting to establish a new community and combat evil *now*. The Christian, therefore, is encouraged to build communities based on love (John 15:9, the image of the vine), co-operate with enemies (Matthew 5:43; Romans 12:14), struggle for peace and justice (Matthew 5:1–12, the Beatitudes) and, inspired by the renewed presence of the Holy Spirit, seek to avert catastrophe (2 Corinthians 5:17).
- New Testament scholars such as Christopher Rowland (*Christian Origins*, 1985) have argued that apocalyptic literature is not about finding a detailed plan of the end time but a hopeful vision of how things could be developing *now*. The metaphor of **Armageddon** is not just a prophecy of what *will* happen but a vision of the evil which the Christian must resist (Revelation 3:12) in the process of salvation already begun and continued in Christ.

In other words the active view of the end time leaves no place for complacency, fatalism or introverted morality. The Christian, if he understands the New Testament in this way, has a duty to resist any form of evil but not at the cost of world catastrophe.

On the other hand there are some who argue for a passive view of the end which permits the use of nuclear war. It is a controversial position. It argues that nuclear war and world catastrophe might be the means by which God would bring this age to an end and from which man's final redemption after judgement could take place. Such a view was surprisingly supported in 1958 by the Archbishop of Canterbury, **Dr Geoffrey Fisher**.

The **nuclear war passive view** of the end time argues the following:

- Although Jesus anticipated an imminent end of the present age, he was deliberately uncertain about when the apocalyptic moment would occur. He simply told them to be morally and spiritually prepared for the moment just as Jesus taught in his parable of the wise and foolish girls in Matthew 25:1–13.

Key quotes

'I am convinced that it is never right to settle any policy simply out of fear of the consequences ... For all I know it is within the providence of God that the human race should destroy itself in this manner [i.e. nuclear war].'
ARCHBISHOP GEOFFREY FISHER, REPORTED IN TIME MAGAZINE (28 JULY 1958)

'Watch therefore, for you do not know on what day your Lord is coming.'
MATTHEW 24:42

Key quotes

'Why not do evil that good may come?'
ST PAUL, LETTER TO THE ROMANS 3:8.

'Do not slay the innocent and righteous.'
EXODUS 23:7

Cross-reference

Read pages 147–48 for the example of the baby-bumpers thought experiment and discussion.

- The New Testament writers were clear that the world would come to a catastrophic end caused by human evil. The evil of nuclear war and its effects on the environment and social order are therefore necessary conditions for **final judgement** and the transformation of this world. Mark's Gospel, for example, gives a long description of the end, which closely resembles the effects of a nuclear war. He concludes, 'But in those days, after that tribulation, the sun will be darkened, and the moon will not give its light, and the stars will be falling from heaven, and the powers in the heavens will be shaken' (Mark 13:24–25).

- **Suffering** is part of the Christian life. Jesus' death did not rid the world of suffering, nor did he promise that his followers would not suffer. The effects of nuclear war on world suffering are therefore not a sufficient reason to reject its use; that is why Dr Fisher concluded, 'So I repeat, I cannot establish any policy merely on whether or not it will save the human race from a period of suffering or from extinction.'

ii) Nuclear deterrence

The dilemma posed for Christian theology as to whether nuclear deterrence is morally acceptable rests on two important biblical principles:

- It is intrinsically wrong to will evil means even if for its good consequences. St Paul argued that his critics had slanderously said that he had taught 'Why not do evil that good may come?' (Romans 3:8) in order to receive God's grace. But his answer is clear: 'Are we to continue in sin that grace may abound? By no means!' (Romans 6:1).
- It is intrinsically evil to deliberately kill an innocent person – as stated in the sixth of the Ten Commandments (Exodus 20:13).

Keeping these two notions in mind, the Protestant theologian **Paul Ramsey** has argued that there is a Christian argument for nuclear deterrence that does not involve immoral means (threats to kill innocent people). But in order to avoid the morally reprehensible baby-bumpers hostage example there has to be at least a *theoretical* reason to use nuclear weapons in war according to the just war principle of proportionality. Ramsey argues that having nuclear weapons would usually be sufficient to deter nuclear attack. However, in order for deterrence to be robust, we have to imagine a sliding scale of deterrence and its relationship with proportionality.

- An enemy might be deterred from nuclear attack because merely threatening his strategic sites would be enough (as in limited nuclear war). As this does not threaten cities, innocent civilians are not immorally threatened.

- If an enemy did attack, the response might legitimise nuclear attack on military targets even though this would cause civilian death. But as these deaths would only be an indirect consequence of the counter-force attack, it does not treat them as hostages who have been deliberately murdered. Their deaths are pointing out to the enemy the possible consequences of their action, should they attack. The use of the **double effect** therefore justifies **collateral damage**.

- Collateral damage may be disproportionate, but it doesn't make the threat immoral. Ramsey argues 'the threat of something disproportionate is not always a disproportionate threat'. That is because in just war *ius in bello* proportion considers tactical force within war against a particular target whereas the aim of deterrence is peace.

Key word

Collateral damage means unintended and secondary injury or damage to people or property.

However, many remain unconvinced by Ramsey's attempt to avoid the immorality of evil threats as deterrence. Making innocent people only an *indirect* threat does not validate the proportionate use of nuclear weapons. Michael Walzer comments:

> *He wants, like other deterrent theorists, to prevent nuclear attack by threatening to kill very large numbers of innocent civilians, but unlike other deterrent theorists, he expects to kill these people without aiming at them.*

(Michael Walzer, *Just and Unjust Wars*, page 280)

Cross-reference

Read pages 159–60 on threats and bluffs.

In addition to the problems of threats and bluffs the Church of England's report, *The Church and the Bomb* (1982), argues that human reason is not reliable enough in the heat of war to make deterrence a stable-enough position. It concludes:

> *For reasons which we have tried to spell out at various points we consider that the nuclear element in deterrence is no longer a reliable or morally acceptable approach to the future of the world. This judgement is reinforced by the fact that an integral part of deterrence in practice is crisis management, which may mean in effect going to the brink while relying on fallible human judgement, operating under tremendous stress, to see you through. Given all these considerations, we believe that a nuclear component in deterrence is not sufficiently compelling to outweigh the huge moral imperatives against using nuclear weapons at all.*

(*The Church and the Bomb*, page 154)

The report's conclusion marked a significant shift in current church thinking. The Methodist Conference in 1983 was more decisive and proposed unilateral disarmament.

Summary diagram

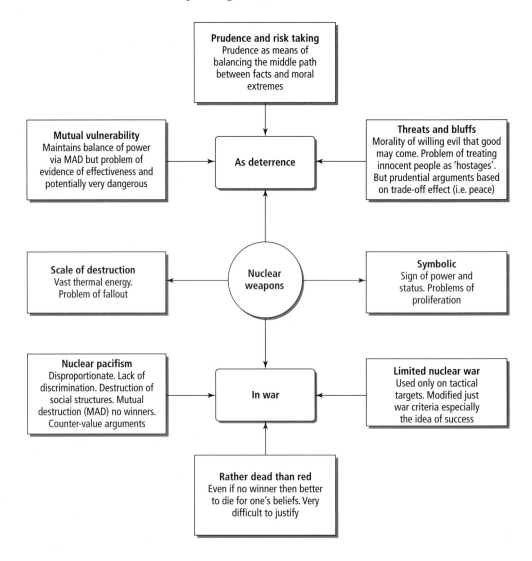

Study guide

By the end of this chapter you should have considered how the possession of nuclear weapons has fundamentally altered international politics and the use of war today. You should be able to explain the paradox of possessing nuclear weapons as a means of doing good but at potentially devastating cost. You should be able to discuss whether the just war argument can be modified to allow nuclear war or a limited nuclear war and whether the use of nuclear weapons is always disproportionate. You should also be able to discuss the nuclear deterrence argument and consider whether its use of bluffs and threats are morally and prudentially (practically) justifiable. All these ideas must be judged by various normative ethical systems.

Revision checklist ✔

Can you define:

- limited nuclear war
- proliferation and non-proliferation
- trade-off defence
- 'rather dead than red'
- mutual assured destruction
- counter-value
- prudential.

Can you explain the views of the following ethical approaches to nuclear deterrence:

- revealed or Christian ethics
- natural law ethics
- Kantian ethics
- utilitarian ethics
- virtue ethics.

Can you give arguments for and against:

- possessing nuclear weapons as bluff
- nuclear war as a just war
- possessing nuclear weapons as hostage taking
- unilateral and multilateral disarmament.

Essay question

1) 'Why not do evil that good may come?' Discuss the Christian arguments on nuclear deterrence.

The central theme of this essay is about intention as means and intention as ends. The paradox posed by nuclear weapons is based on the notion of mutual vulnerability or MAD, which from a prudential point of view appears to have kept world peace and the balance of power for 60 years. But Christian ethicists might argue that this is a consequencial argument that fails to take into account moral character.

Christian moral character might be discussed from two perspectives: first, from Jesus' teaching on purity of intention from the Sermon on the Mount ('let what you say be simply yes or no', Matthew 5:37) and the 'counsel of perfection' (Matthew 5:48) and from Paul's argument from Romans that no one may will evil to secure good (Romans 3:8); second, the Christian natural law tradition argues that the means must always be good and equivalent to what Aquinas calls 'interior acts'. In both cases, nuclear deterrence appears to rely on willing the deaths of innocent people (especially if nuclear war were to happen and escalate) and for that reason it must be rejected (Exodus 23:7).

Cross-reference

Read page 121 for the counsel of perfection.

The second part of the essay might wish then to consider the coherency of the bluffs and threats argument. John Haldane's argument of primary and secondary intentions of bluff might be considered along with the 'flexible response' view. Haldane's view might be rejected because of the evil which Paul Ramsey's 'hostage-taking' analogy highlights. A discussion of his analogy of the 'baby bumpers' could follow with Ramsey's own use of the double effect and collateral damage justification for deterrence.

The conclusion should consider the Christian teaching on the Kingdom of God and the implications of taking an active or passive view on the question of willing evil that good may come.

Further essay questions

2a   Explain the main ideas of natural law.
2b   'Natural law cannot justify nuclear deterrence.' Discuss.

3a   Explain the purpose and aims of the just war argument.
3b   Assess the view that the just war argument is of no use in an age of nuclear weapons.

4   'Virtue ethics is the only morally effective means of evaluating nuclear war.' Discuss.

GLOSSARY

abolitionist refers to countries that have abolished the death penalty.

abrogation means to defy a rule, duty or law and therefore to abolish.

a fortiori means literally in Latin 'from the stronger'. An *a fortiori* argument suggests that if x is wrong/right then y is even more so.

agape is the Greek word sometimes used in the New Testament to mean generous, sacrificial love.

annul means to cancel out.

antinomianism means no laws or rules.

apocalyptic means literally 'revelatory' and refers to biblical texts such as the Books of Daniel and Revelation, which reveal what will happen at the end of time.

begging the question is when the conclusion is implied in one of the premises of the question. Often an argument which begs the question has failed to give a convincing case for the conclusion.

biconditional if and only if... statements are the usual way of expressing necessary and sufficient conditions.

Cartesian is the adjective describing those who follow Descartes' philosophy.

categorical imperative is Kant's notion that morality is based on universal, rational, absolute and consistent duties, which treat all people in a dignified manner. The categorical imperative is to: 'Act as if the maxim of your action were to become through your will a universal law of nature' (*Grounding for the Metaphysics of Morals*, paragraph 421).

collateral damage means unintended and secondary injury or damage to people or property.

conscientious objector is a person who refuses, for moral reasons, to fight in a war when called by the state to do so.

counter-value arguments consider the moral effects of using nuclear weapons, not just their physical effects.

dialectic comes from the Greek meaning 'to discuss' (as in question and answer). There are many different uses of the term dialectic. In contemporary philosophy it often refers to the way in which opposites can be combined.

empirical means gaining knowledge through observation and experience rather than logic or theory.

epistemology means the study of knowledge.

eschatology means the study of the end of time and the arrival of the Kingdom of God.

eugenics means literally 'the production of good off-spring'.

fallout is the minute particles of radioactive materials caused by nuclear explosion and carried through the atmosphere by the wind. Radioactive decay can contaminate plants, animals and water. In humans fallout can cause leukaemia, bone cancer and damage to genes that can be passed on to future generations.

hegemony means a monopoly or domination of one country's rule over all others.

holiness means 'set apart' or sanctified. It is this word which gives rise to the phrase 'sanctity of life'.

incarnation is the Christian notion that God became human in the form of Jesus Christ.

instrumentalism considers that judgements are good only if they are effective in achieving their ends.

ius post bellum means justice after war and includes reinstating the rights of those attacked, restoring law and order and punishing war criminals.

just deserts implies that there is a law of nature which demands punishment which is equal to the crime committed.

lex talionis is Latin, meaning 'law of retaliation' or, as it is expressed in the Old Testament, 'an eye for an eye'.

limited nuclear war is defined as limited nuclear tonnage of the bomb and restricting damage only to military sites.

MAD or 'mutual assured destruction' was invented by Donald Brennan in 1967 as a criticism of the use of nuclear weaponry.

maxim is defined by Kant as a 'subjective principle of acting' that is a general rule or principle governing the action of all rational people.

mens rea is the Latin phrase meaning a 'guilty mind' and used to refer to the criminal whose act is the result of an evil intention.

mind–body dualists believe that souls and bodies are made of quite different substances.

mitigation means alleviation and in law is used to refer to factors which can be used to justify a lesser punishment.

mortal sin is a deliberate and conscious rejection of God's grace and results in eternal damnation.

multilateral disarmament aims to reduce the number of nuclear war heads or means for constructing nuclear weapons on both sides.

palliative care is the use of drugs and medicine to relieve pain but without directly causing the death of patients.

paternalism means literally to 'act in a fatherly way' and justifies overriding a person's autonomy if it is for their own good.

phronesis is the Greek word used by Aristotle to mean practical wisdom. By this he meant the skill of living the golden mean between the vices of excess and deficiency.

post hoc justification means finding evidence to match an existing belief.

pre-emptive strike means to make the first tactical move in war before the enemy.

prima facie duties were developed as an idea by W.D. Ross (1877–1971) to mean that some duties can be overridden by a stronger moral duty according to situation. *Prima facie* means literally 'on first appearance'.

prudence means practical wisdom or reasoning. It is a matter of debate whether prudence is also a moral term.

rather dead than red means it would be better to die for one's own beliefs and way of life than be ruled over by a different ideology. 'Red' originally referred to USSR communism.

retentionist refers to countries that have kept or reintroduced the death penalty.

sentience means being able to have sense perceptions.

speciesism means to discriminate against animals in favour of human beings.

star wars was the nickname given to President Regan's Strategic Defense Initiative (SDI) in 1984 in which incoming enemy nuclear missiles would be intercepted and destroyed about 750 miles above earth before having a chance to hit their targets in the USA.

teleological comes from the Greek *telos* meaning a final state.

telos is used in natural law to denote that everything has its purpose. Aquinas suggested that humans have five related primary ends. The spiritual *telos* is the worship of God.

total war is often used to refer to the lack of discrimination between enemy military and civilian targets.

unilateral disarmament is when one country decides to disarm itself of all nuclear weapons regardless of whether other countries disarm or not.

vindication is proof that the law has been applied through punishment and justice achieved.

vitalism is the view that for the human body to be alive it must also possess a soul.

weak sanctity of life supports the case that human life should not always be preserved at all costs.

FURTHER READING

Alvarez, A. 1974, *The Savage God: A Study of Suicide.* Penguin.

Amnesty International 1989, *When the State Kills: The Death Penalty v. Human Rights.* Amnesty International Publications.

Augustine 1972, *City of God* (Translator: David Knowles). Penguin.

Bauckham, Richard and Elford, John R. (editors) 1989, *The Nuclear Weapons Debate: Theological and Ethical Issues.* SCM.

Beauchamp, Tom and Childress, James 1994, *Principles of Biomedical Ethics.* Oxford University Press, 4th edition.

Bentham, Jeremy 2007, *An Introduction to the Principles of Morals and Legislation* (1789). Dover Publications.

Biggar, Nigel 2004, *Aiming to Kill.* Darton, Longman and Todd.

Bonhoeffer, Dietrich 1955, *Ethics.* SCM.

Brown, David 1983, *Choices: Ethics and the Christian.* Blackwell.

Camus, Albert 1975, *The Myth of Sisyphus* (Translator: Justin O'Brien). Penguin.

Catholic Church 1994, *Catechism of the Catholic Church* (English translation). Chapman.

Charlesworth, Max 1993, *Bioethics in a Liberal Society.* Cambridge University Press.

Church of England 1993, *Abortion and the Church: What are the Issues?* Church House Publishing.

Clausewitz, Karl von 1976, *On War* (Editors: Peter Paret and Michael Howard). Princeton University Press.

Coates, A.J. 1997, *The Ethics of War.* Manchester University Press.

Cohen, Marshal (editor) 1974, *War and Moral Responsibility.* Princeton University Press.

Dworkin, Ronald 1993, *Life's Dominion.* HarperCollins.

Fletcher, Joseph 1966, *Situation Ethics.* Westminster John Knox Press.

Fletcher, Joseph 1993, *Joseph Fletcher: Memoir of an Ex-Radical* (editor: Kenneth Vaux). Westminster John Knox Press.

Frankena, William 1973, *Ethics.* Prentice Hall, 2nd edition.

Gide, André 1989, *The Vatican Cellars* (Translator: D. Bussy). Penguin.

Gill, Robin 1995, *A Textbook of Christian Ethics.* T&T Clark, 2nd edition.

Glover, Jonathan 1977, *Causing Death and Saving Lives.* Penguin.

Graham, Gordon 1997, *Ethics and International Relations.* Blackwell.

Guthrie, Charles and Quinlan, Michael 2007, *Just War. The Just War Tradition: Ethics in Modern Warfare.* Bloomsbury.

Harries, Richard 1986, *Christianity and War in a Nuclear Age.* Mowbray.

Harris, John 1985, *The Value of Life: An Introduction to Medical Ethics.* Routledge.

Honderich, Ted 1989, *Punishment: The Supposed Justifications.* Polity Press.

Hume, David 1986, 'Of Suicide' (in Peter Singer, editor, *Applied Ethics*). Oxford University Press.

Jones, David Albert 2004, *The Soul of the Embryo.* Continuum.

Kant, Immanuel 1981, *The Grounding for the Metaphysics of Morals* (Translator: James W. Elington). Hackett.

Kant, Immanuel 2006, 'Toward Perpetual Peace' and Other Writings on Politics, Peace, and History (Editor: Pauline Kleingeld. Translator: David L. Colclasure). Yale University Press.

Kilner, John F., Cameron, Nigel M. de S. and Scheidermayer, David L. 1995, *Bioethics and the Future of Medicine: A Christian Appraisal.* Eerdmans.

Kim, Sebastian C.H. and Draper, Jonathan (editors) 2008, *Liberating Texts?* SPCK.

King, Martin Luther 1981, *The Strength to Love* (1963). Fortress Press.

Lee, Steven P. 1993, *Morality, Prudence and Nuclear Weapons.* Cambridge University Press.

MacIntyre, Alasdair 1985, *After Virtue.* Duckworth, 2nd edition.

MacIntyre, Alasdair 2002, *A Short History of Ethics: A History of Moral Philosophy from the Homeric Age to the Twentieth Century.* Routledge, revised edition.

Messer, Neil 2006, *Christian Ethics.* SCM.

Mill, John Stuart 2006, *On Liberty* and *The Subjection of Women* (Editor: Alan Ryan). Penguin.

Palmer, Michael 2005, *Moral Problems.* Lutterworth, 2nd revised edition.

Pence, Gregory 1995, 2008, *Classic Cases in Medical Ethics.* McGraw-Hill, 2nd and 5th editions.

Plato 2003, *Phaedo* in *The Last Days of Socrates* (Translators: Hugh Treddenick and Harold Tarrant). Penguin, revised edition.

Pojman, Louis 2005, *Ethics: Discovering Right and Wrong.* Wadsworth Publishing Co. Inc, 5th revised edition.

Pojman, Louis and Reiman, J. 1998, *The Death Penalty: For and Against.* Rowman & Littlefield.

Potter, Harry 1993, *Hanging in Judgement.* SCM.

Ramsey, Paul 1968, *The Just War: Force and Political Responsibility.* Scribner.

Singer, Peter 1979, *Practical Ethics.* Cambridge University Press.

Singer, Peter (editor) 1986, *Applied Ethics.* Oxford University Press.

Singer, Peter (editor) 1993, *Companion to Ethics.* Blackwell.

Singer, Peter 1995, *Rethinking Life and Death.* Oxford University Press.

Siracusa, Joseph, M. 2008, *Nuclear Weapons: A Very Short Introduction.* Oxford University Press.

Smart, J.C.C. and Williams, Bernard 1973, *Utilitarianism: For and Against.* Cambridge University Press.

Society for the Protection of Unborn Children 1994, *Love Your Unborn Neighbour.* SPUC.

Thompson, Mel 2008, *Ethical Theory.* Hodder, 3rd edition.

Vardy, Peter and Grosch, Paul 1999, *The Puzzle of Ethics.* Fount, 2nd revised edition.

Walzer, Michael 2006, *Just and Unjust Wars.* Basic Books, 4th edition.

Warburton, Nigel (editor) 1999, *Philosophy: Basic Readings.* Routledge.

Watt, Helen 2000, *Life and Death in Healthcare Ethics.* Routledge.

Wilcockson, Michael 2008, *Medical Ethics.* Hodder.

On-line resources for this book and others in the series

New books and websites are appearing all the time.
Keep up-to-date and share your own suggestions with other students and teachers.

For suggestions for further reading, comments from the authors of the *Access to Religion and Philosophy* series and further advice for students and teachers, **log on to the** *Access to Religion and Philosophy* **website at**:

www.philosophyandethics.com

INDEX

abortion 41–64
  on demand 52
  and four principles of medical
    ethics 56, 59
  and handicap 52–54, 58
  and the law 48–50
  normative ethical responses to
    56–62
  Old Testament treatment of 60
  preferences of the foetus vs.
    preferences of the mother 55,
    56
  the problem of personhood 45–48
  and rape 50–52, 57, 58, 60, 61
  rights of the foetus vs. rights of the
    mother 43–44, 49, 51–52, 52
  RU-486 abortion pill 45
  statistics 42, 50
  therapeutic 48
  threats to the mother's life 54–56,
    58, 60
  upper limit for legal 48
  women's autonomy and rights
    41–45, 61
Abortion Act 1967 48, 49, 51, 55, 58
Abortion and Infanticide 48
Abortion and the Church 55, 60
abrogation 28
acts and omissions doctrine 97–98,
  119–120
actual and potential persons 7–8
After Virtue 163
agape 35, 60, 118
Alvarez, A 27
Americans with Disabilities Act (USA
  1992) 53
Amnesty International 85, 96, 97
amniocentesis 52
An Advertisement Touching a Holy War
  127
anger and retribution 91–92
annul 89
Anscombe, G.E.M. 119, 139
antinomianism 60
apocalypse 169–170

Aquinas, Thomas 7–8, 11, 57
  on capital punishment 106–107
  on just war 128, 131, 140
  on natural law 10, 139
  notion of prudence 164
  on the soul 7, 47
  on suicide 32
Aristotle 10, 105, 164, 165
  on personhood 4
  on the soul 6, 7, 47
  on suicide 32, 34
  telos 10, 57, 106
  on virtue and militarism 126
Armageddon 157, 169
Art of War, The 137
Assisted Dying for the Terminally Ill Bill
  68
Augustine of Hippo 29
  on pacifism 121
  on suicide 35
  on war 54, 128, 129, 130, 131,
    140, 142
authority
  to carry out God's judgement
    109–110
  legitimate 130–131, 137, 140, 143
autonomy 56, 61, 136
  as the basis for the quality of life
    17–18
  suicide as exercise of 33–35, 36
  women's rights and 41–45, 61

Baby Bumpers, analogy of 147–148,
  160, 161, 170
Baby Charlotte 68
Baby Doe 14
Bacon, Francis 127
Bauckham, Richard 160
Beauchamp, Tom 56, 59
Beccaria, Cesare 94
begging the question 45, 46
beneficence 56, 76–77
Bentham, Jeremy 14, 17, 93–94, 166
Bentley, Derek 85, 91
best bet argument 95–96, 97, 157

Biathanatos 33
Bible
  Acts of the Apostles 108
  Amos 60
  Cain and Abel story 103, 110
  Corinthians 12, 28, 79, 169
  Deuteronomy 12, 79, 108
  Exodus 12, 29, 59, 79, 108, 109,
    141, 170
  Genesis 11, 12, 59, 79, 89, 103,
    108, 109–110
  Hebrews 35, 79
  Jeremiah 28, 46
  Job 12, 59, 79
  John 11, 12, 35, 59, 60, 61, 109,
    121, 122, 169
  Joshua 141
  Judges 35
  Kings 60
  Leviticus 108
  Luke 12, 60, 108, 142
  Mark 143, 170
  Matthew 29, 79, 109, 117, 121,
    140, 141, 142, 169
  Micah 143
  Numbers 108
  Peter 122
  Psalms 46, 47, 60
  Revelation 169
  Romans 13, 79, 89, 108, 110, 117,
    122, 127, 140, 143, 169, 170
  Samson story 35
  Samuel 28, 79
  Sermon on the Mount 109, 117,
    121, 141–142
  teachings on war 122, 126, 140,
    141–142
Bland, Tony 73
blasphemy, suicide as 29–30, 79
blood-guilt psychology 103, 104
bluffs 159, 160, 165
Boethius 5
Bonhoeffer, Dietrich 130
Bourne, Dr Aleck 50
boxing 36–37

brain activity 47
brain death 73–74
British Medical Association (BMA) 36, 37, 73, 74, 77
British Pregnancy Advisory Service 42
Burke, Edmund 126

Calvin, John 57
Camus, Albert 30
capital punishment 83–86
    current situation 85–86
    Derek Bentley 85, 91
    as deterrence 94–100, 104
    extracting confessions of guilt 103
    and forgiveness 100–101
    history of legal reforms 85
    as inhumane 92–93
    Jesus' teachings on 108, 109, 140
    murder rates and death penalty rates 86, 95, 96, 96–97
    normative ethical responses to 102–110
    Patrick Sonnier 83–84, 92–93
    as a public example 95, 99
    and reform 100–102
    as retribution 87, 89–93, 103–104, 106–107
Capital Punishments 94
Carrington, Lord 158
Cartesian dualism 6
casuistry 11
Catechism of the Catholic Church 30, 46, 71, 78, 107–108, 168
categorical imperative 9, 31, 61, 102, 103, 135–136, 162
Causing Death and Saving Lives 19, 98
Centre for Bioethics 68
Chernobyl 155–156
Cheshire, Leonard 116, 121
Chicago Economic Club 131
Childress, James 56, 59
Church and the Bomb, The 154, 171
Church of England
    position on abortion 51, 55, 60
    position on capital punishment 89, 101
    position on nuclear deterrence 171
Cicero 10
City of God, The 29, 35
civil war 125
Clausewitz, Karl von 122–124, 139
cleft palate deformity 53

Clinton, President Bill 153
Clough, Arthur 76, 77
Coates, A.J. 132, 133
Cohen, M. 124
Cold War 153
collateral damage 171
communism 116
communitarian view of war 124–125, 138
companions in guilt move 37
conscientious objectors 117–118, 120, 140
consciousness
    as the basis for quality of life 19–20
    and personhood 5, 6, 47
consequentialists 71
    debate with deontologists on euthanasia 72–73, 75, 77–78
    defence for nuclear deterrence 158–159
    view of war 122–124, 139
contract retributivism 88, 89–90, 91, 92
counsel of perfection 121
counter-value arguments 157, 159, 165
Crusades 126–127
Cuban missile crisis 159

Darrow, Clarence 91
De Re Publica 10
de Vitoria, Francisco 10, 128, 132
dead donor rule 74
Dead Man Walking 84, 93
death, definitions of 73–74
death penalty. *see* capital punishment
Death Penalty Information Center 95, 96
Death Penalty, The 99, 101
Declaration on Euthanasia 78
Defence of Abortion, A 43–44, 51
defensive war 129
delayed ensoulment 7, 47, 56–57, 60
deontologists 71
    debate with consequentialists on euthanasia 71–73, 75, 77–78
    defence for nuclear deterrence 159–161
Department of Health 50
Descartes, René 5, 6
deterrence. *see also* nuclear deterrence
    and act utilitarianism 104–105

capital punishment as 94–100, 104
    punishment as 87, 93–94
dialectic 122, 123
Dickens, Charles 99
diminished responsibilities 91
dirty hands argument 124
doctor–patient relationship 59, 76–77
    doctrine of double effect 11
    and abortion 54, 55–56, 57
    and euthanasia 71–73
    and war 134, 140, 141, 157, 167, 171
Donne, John 33
Donum Vitae 7, 56
Durkheim, Emile 98–99
Dworkin, Ronald 4

ectopic pregnancy 11, 54
Elford, R. John 160, 164, 165
end time, the 169–170
ends and means 71, 123, 139, 150, 167
enduring self 6, 45–46
Engels, Frederick 116
ensoulment 7, 8, 46
epistemology 6
eschatology 143
Essay Concerning Human Understanding, An 5
eugenics 68–69
European Court of Human Rights 67
euthanasia 65–82
    allowing to die and cutting short a life 70–73
    and the law outside the UK 69–70
    non-voluntary 66, 68–69, 73–74, 75, 78
    normative ethical responses to 74–79
    passive 66, 77, 78
    problem of definition 65–66
    and UK law 66–69
    voluntary 66, 69, 76, 77
Evangelium Vitae 12, 78, 107
execution, an 92–93
existentialism 30

Falklands War 131, 132–133
fallout, nuclear 151, 154
Fisher, Dr Geoffrey 169, 170
fission bombs 151, 153, 154
Fletcher, Joseph 7, 41, 60
    four working principles 60–61

foetus
    feeling pain 58
    personhood of the 45–48
    preferences vs. preferences of the
        mother 55, 56
    rights vs. mother's rights 43–44,
        49, 51–52, 52
    stages of development 46
forgiveness 100–101
Fox, George 117
Frankena, William 59, 137
Freedom to Box, The 36, 37
Freud, Sigmund 27–28
Furedi, Ann 42
fusion bombs 151

Gandhi, Mahatma 118
Gide, André 1, 2
Glover, Jonathan 19, 98
Golden Rule 89
good will 8–9, 135
Goodin, Robert 15
Gospel of Life, The 107
Graham, Gordon 120, 129, 130–131
Grosch, Paul 140
Grotius, Hugo 128
Grounding for the Metaphysics of Morals,
    The 8, 9, 31, 99
Gulf War 124, 125, 132
Guthrie, Charles 128

Haldane, John 68, 160
handicap and abortion 52–54, 58
Harris, Air Marshall 121, 155
Harris, John 20
Hauerwas, Stanley 13
hedonic utilitarians
    on abortion 57–58
    on euthanasia 75
    on nuclear deterrence 166
    on the quality of life 14
    on suicide 33
hegemony 153
Hippocratic Oath 54, 70
Hiroshima 153–154, 156
Hobbes, Thomas 18, 135
holiness 12
holy war 126–128, 141
Homer 138, 142, 164
Honderich, Ted 87, 91
hospice movement 77
hostage taking 147, 160–161, 166
human beings and human persons
    4–5. *see also* personhood

Human Fertilisation and Embryology
    Act 1990 49, 53
human rights 19
Humanitarian Theory of Punishment, The
    101
Hume, David
    on prudence 164
    on suicide 18–19, 27, 33–35

ideal utilitarians
    on abortion 58
    on capital punishment 104
    on euthanasia 75–76
    on nuclear war and deterrence
        165, 166
    on punishment as a deterrence 98
    on quality of life 15
incarnation 12
infanticide 7, 48, 60
innocent lives 10–11
    duty to protect 32, 46, 78, 79, 142
    failure to protect 119
instrumentalism 13, 19, 122, 123
insurrection 130–131
International Bill of Human Rights
    93
Introduction to the Principles of Morals
    and Legislation, An 94
Iraq War 124, 129, 131, 132

Jepson, Joanna 42, 53
Jesus
    disarming Peter 117
    Sermon on the Mount 109, 117,
        121, 141–142
    teaching on altruistic suicide 35
    teaching on killing 108, 140
    teachings on the apocalyptic time
        169
    teachings on war 122, 140, 142,
        143
Jim and the Indians 16–17
John Paul II, Pope 12, 107
Johnson, Daniel 76
Johnson, Dr Samuel 83
Joseph Fletcher: Memoir of an Ex-Radical
    61
Just and Unjust Wars 124, 161, 162, 171
just cause 129
just deserts 88, 103, 105
just war argument (JWA) 115, 116,
    124, 128–134
    Aquinas' argument 128, 131, 140

basis in natural law 128, 129, 131,
    139–141, 167
discrimination and non-combatant
    immunity 133–134, 138, 156,
    157, 167
ius ad bellum 128, 132, 155
ius in bello 128, 132, 155
ius post bellum 131
and nuclear war 133, 154–157
proportionality 131, 132–133, 167
and utilitarianism 138
and virtue ethics 137
justice, principle of 56

Kant, Immanuel
    on capital punishment 102–103
    categorical imperative 9, 31, 61,
        102, 103, 135–136, 162
    critique of utilitarianism 15
    ethical response to abortion
        61–62, 64
    on euthanasia 74
    good will 8–9, 135
    kingdom of ends 9, 136, 162
    practical imperative 9, 31, 61, 99,
        135
    on retribution 89, 90, 92
    sanctity of life argument 8–10, 54
    on suicide 30–31, 74
    on war 134–136, 161–163
Khomeini, Ayatollah 116
King, Martin Luther 118
Kolbe, Maximilian 24, 25, 35
Kosovo 131
Kuhse, Helga 68–69, 75

leadership and virtues 137–138
League of Nations 136
Lee, Steven P. 148, 150, 158, 163, 164
lesser of two evils argument 55
Leviathan 18
Lewis, C.S. 101, 102
lex talionis 88, 89, 92, 95
liberalism 17
Liddell, George 70–71
life as valuable 1–3
Life's Dominion 4
Locke, John
    critique of his notion of
        personhood 7–8
    on human rights 19
    on personhood 5, 6, 47
Lund, Frank 65
Luther, Martin 122, 130

Machiavelli, Niccolo 137
MacIntyre, Alasdair 68, 98, 163
MAD or 'mutual assured destruction'
    149, 153, 158. *see also* mutual
    vulnerability
Mao, Chairman 159
Marx, Karl 116
MAS or 'mutual assured safety' 153
maxim 9
medical ethics 54, 56, 59, 70
mens rea 90
Metaphysics of Morals, The 102
Methodist Church 60, 171
militarism 115, 116, 125–128
Mill, John Stuart 17–18, 104, 124
    on suicide 17, 33
mind-body dualists 6
mitigation 90
Moltke, Helmuth von 126
monozygotic twins 8, 47
Moor, Dr David 70–71
Moore, G.E. 15
moral law 8–9
    suicide as defiance against 30–31
moral paradox of nuclear deterrence
    147–151
moral punishment 87
moral utopians 125
morality
    dialectic of moral and physical
        factors in war 122–123
    of nuclear deterrence 158–161
    of nuclear war 150–151, 154–157
    public and private 116, 121, 124,
        142, 143, 158
    and the social contract 34
Morality, Prudence and Nuclear Weapons
    148, 150, 158
mortal sin 29, 33
multilateral disarmament 166
murder rates and death penalty rates
    95, 96, 96–97
Murdoch, Iris 163
mutual vulnerability 149, 150,
    158–159, 162, 166
Myth of Sisyphus, The 30

Nagasaki 153–154
NATO 160
natural law
    argument against suicide 32, 34
    basis for JWA 128, 129, 131,
        139–141, 167

response to abortion 56–57, 62
response to capital punishment
    106–108
response to euthanasia 77–78
response to nuclear war and
    deterrence 167–168
sanctity of life arguments 8, 10–11
natural rights 19
naturalistic fallacy 11
necessary and sufficient conditions 5
Niebuhr, Reinhold 118–119, 130, 143
non-combatant immunity 133–134,
    138, 156, 157, 167
non-maleficence 56
non-proliferation 152
non-violence 118, 119
nuclear deterrence
    consequential defence for 158–159
    deontological defence for 159–161
    at Hiroshima 156
    hostage taking 147, 160–161, 166
    Kantian ethical response to
        162–163
    moral paradox of 147–151
    morality of 158–161
    natural law response to 168
    prudential argument for 149, 158,
        159, 162, 163, 165–166
    revealed ethics response to
        170–171
    utilitarian response to 165–166
    virtue ethics response to 164–165
nuclear war
    Kantian ethical response to
        161–162
    limited 150, 155–156
    and modified JWA 156–157
    morality of 150–151, 154–157
    and mutual vulnerability 149, 150,
        158–159, 162, 166
    natural law response to 167–168
    revealed ethics response to
        168–170
    utilitarian response to 165
    virtue ethics response to 163–164
nuclear weapons
    conventional and nuclear 151–153
    destruction in Japan 153–154
    fission bombs 151, 153, 154
    fusion bombs 151
    limited use of 150, 155–156
    reasons to use 151–154
    symbolism of 152–153
    tactical warheads 155

Nuclear Weapons: A Catholic Response
    119

Odyssey 138, 142, 164
Of Crimes and Punishment 94
Of Suicide 33, 34, 35
Office of Public Sector Information
    26
On Idolatry 117
On Liberty 17, 18
On War 122
Orwell, George 99
Overall, Christine 61

pacifism 116–121
    absolute 116, 117–120, 137, 139,
        141, 145–146
    biblical inconsistencies over
        141–142
    contingent 117, 120–121
    nuclear 121, 168–169
    personal 121
    virtue ethics support for 136–137
    war realist criticisms of 125
pacifist utopians 125
palliative care 66, 77
Palmer, Michael 119
*Parliamentary Debate on Capital
    Punishment Within Prisons Bill* 104
paternalism 18, 36–37
persistent vegetative state (PVS) 74
personalism 61
personhood 4–8
    of the foetus 45–48
    'gradient view of' 49
Phaedo 29, 31
phronesis 126, 137, 163
physician aid in dying 66, 68–69
physician-aided suicide 66
Planned Parenthood v. Casey (1992) 49
Plato 6, 29
    on suicide 31–32, 34, 35
Pojman, Louis 92, 97
positivism 61
post hoc justification 95
potential persons 7–8
practical imperative 9, 31, 61, 99, 135
pragmatism 60
pre-embryo 47
preference satisfaction utilitarians
    on abortion 53, 55, 56, 58
    on capital punishment 103–104
    on euthanasia 76
    on nuclear deterrence 166

quality of life arguments and 15, 56
    on suicide 33
Prejean, Sister Helen 83–84, 93
Pretty, Diane 67
prima facie duty 44
primitive streak 47
Principia Ethica 15
Principles of Biomedical Ethics 56
privacy, a woman's right to 44–45
pro-life groups 8, 11, 47, 50
proliferation 152
proportionalism 140
proportionality, principle of 10, 131, 132–133, 167, 170–171
Protocol to the American Convention on Human Rights to Abolish the Death Penalty 86
prudence 149, 164–165
punishment
    aims and justification of 86–87
    backward looking view of 87, 93, 107
    as deterrence 87, 93–94
    forward looking view of 87, 93, 100, 107
    legal and moral 87
    normative ethical responses to killing as 102–110
    as reform 87, 100
    as retribution 87, 88–89
Punishment: The Supposed Justifications 87
PVS (persistent vegetative state) 74

QALYS (quality adjusted life years) 73, 75
Quakers 117
quality of life arguments and 13–20
    and abortion 48, 50, 53, 56
    autonomy as the basis of 17–18
    consciousness as the basis for 19–20
    rights as the basis for 18–19
    vs. sanctity of life debate 3
    and utilitarianism 14–17, 56
Quinlan, Michael 128

Ramsey, Paul 147, 160, 170, 171
rape 50–52, 57, 58, 60, 61
'rather be red than dead' 149
rationality 7–8
Raven, Charles 117, 118

Rawls, John 92
Reagan, Ronald President 3, 166
reform
    capital punishment and 100–102
    punishment as 87, 100
Reiman, Jeffrey 92, 97
relativism 60–61
Reply to Faustus the Manichaean 142
Report to Congress on Arms Control, Nonproliferation and Disarmament Studies 153
restorative retributivism 88–89, 90, 91
Rethinking Life and Death 3, 13–14, 53
retribution
    capital punishment as 87, 89–93, 103–104, 106–107
    punishment as 87, 88–89
    and unfair advantage argument 95
    and utilitarianism 103–104
revealed ethics
    anti-capital punishment 109
    pro-capital punishment 108
    problem of authority and judgement 109–110
    response to abortion 59–61, 62
    response to euthanasia 79
    response to nuclear deterrence 170–171
    response to nuclear war 168–170
    response to war 141–143
    sanctity of life arguments 11–12, 141
revealed law 8, 12, 34
revenge 87
right intention 131
right to life, minimal 99
rights retributivism 88, 89, 104, 106–107
Roe v. Wade (1973) 49, 51, 55
Roman Catholic Church
    ensoulment 7, 46
    position on abortion 46, 56–57
    position on capital punishment 107–108
    position on euthanasia 78
    position on nuclear deterrence 168
    position on nuclear war 167–168
    position on sanctity of life 12
    position on suicide 29–30
Ross, W.D. 10, 44
Rowland, Christopher 169
RU-486 abortion pill 45
rule utilitarianism 75–76, 98, 104, 166

Sanchez, Thomas 54
sanctity of life arguments 8–13
    and forgiveness of the sinner 100–101
    and issues of paternalism 36
    position on abortion 50, 51, 52, 53, 54, 55–56, 59–60
    position on violence 141
    vs. quality of life debate 3
    reinforced in the 1961 Suicide Act 26
    rejection of euthanasia 79
    undermined in 1967 Abortion Act 48
Sartre, Jean-Paul 124
Savage God, The 27
Second Optional Protocol to the International Covenant on Civil and Political Rights 86
Second World War 132, 134, 153
self-defence, right to 44, 51, 52
self-determination, right to 67–68
Seneca 34
sentience 20
September 11, 2001 152
Singer, Peter 3, 7, 13–14, 15, 34, 44, 48, 53, 56, 68, 69, 75, 104, 120
Siracusa, Joseph M. 151, 152
Situation Ethics 41, 60, 61
situationism 60
Six Day War 129
slippery slope 15, 52, 55, 58, 68, 92
Smart, J.C.C. 17
social contract 18–19, 34, 89
society
    impact of abortion on 59
    impact of suicide on 24–26, 31–32
Society for the Protection of Unborn Children (SPUC) 47, 52, 55, 60
Socrates 35
Sonnier, Patrick 83–84, 92–93
soul, the 6–7, 35–36
    delayed ensoulment 7, 47, 56–57, 60
    ensoulment 7, 8, 46
speciesism 53
'Star Wars' 166
state, duty to the 122, 140, 142, 143
Stephen, James Fitzjames 94
Strength to Love, The 118
strong sanctity of life view 8, 11–12
    on abortion 52, 53, 55, 59–60
    on euthanasia 79

suicide 24–40
  as an abrogation of duty to God
    28–30, 79
  altruistic 26, 35
  arguments against 28–32
  arguments for 32–35
  assisted 25, 26, 66
  as avoidance of unnecessary pain
    33
  as blasphemy 29–30, 79
  changing attitudes to 25
  as defiance against moral law
    30–31
  egoistical 26, 28, 34, 35
  as exercise of autonomy 33–35
  Hume on 18–19, 27, 33–35
  impact on society 24–26, 31–32
  is not a sin 33
  and the law 25–26
  and paternalism 36–37
  physician-aided 66
  psychology of 26–28, 30
  as a sign of human failure 30
  as violation of the principle to
    protect innocent life 32
Suicide Act 1961 25–26, 66–67
Summa Theologica 7, 10, 32, 107, 140,
  164

tactical warheads 155
targets in war 134
telos 10, 57, 106
Temple, William 99, 101
termination of pregnancy 55, 57
Tertullian 117
theatre of war 134
Theory of Justice, A 92
therapeutic abortions 48
Theseus, ship of 4
Thompson, Judith Jarvis 43–44, 51
Thompson, Mel 10, 14, 91, 92, 94,
  134, 135, 136, 139, 161, 163
threats to the mother's life 54–56, 58,
  60
Tooley, Michael 48
total war 123, 130, 131, 156
Toward Perpetual Peace 134, 135, 136,
  161, 162–163
treaties 86
Truman, President Harry S. 152
Two Laws of Penal Evolution 99

UN Declaration of Human Rights 84
unfair advantage argument 94–95
unilateral disarmament 158, 159, 166,
  171
United Nations 129, 136
  Article 51 129
United States of America
  abortion laws 49
  euthanasia law 69
  murder rates and death penalty
    rates 86, 95, 96
unsound mind, suicide due to 26–27
Urban II, Pope 127
utilitarianism
  as the basis for quality of life
    14–17, 56
  punishment as deterrence
    argument 93–94
  response to abortion 51, 53, 55,
    56, 57–58, 62
  response to absolute pacifism 139
  response to capital punishment 94,
    98, 103–105
  response to euthanasia 75–76
  response to nuclear war and
    deterrence 165–166
  response to suicide 33
  response to war 138–139
Utilitarianism: For and Against 16–17
utopianism 118, 125

Vardy, Peter 140
Vatican Cellars, The 1, 2
viability and birth 48, 49
victimisation 98, 101–102
vindication 88
violence, use of 115–116, 131, 138,
  141, 142
virtue ethics
  arguments for and against capital
    punishment 105–106
  response to abortion 58–59, 62
  response to euthanasia 76–77
  response to nuclear war and
    deterrence 163–165
  response to suicide 31
  response to war and pacifism
    136–138
virtues, war as expression of 126
vitalism 6, 8, 11, 60
volition 26
voluntarism 33

Waltham Black Act 1723 91
Walzer, Michael 124, 138, 161, 162,
  171
war. *see also* just war argument (JWA);
    nuclear deterrence; nuclear war;
    nuclear weapons
  Biblical teachings on 122, 126,
    140, 141–142, 143
  conventional and nuclear 148–151
  militarism 115, 116, 125–128
  normative ethical responses to
    134–143
  realism 115, 116, 121–125, 137,
    143
  reasons for 114–115
  and the use of violence 115–116
war on terror 124, 152
Warburton, Nigel 36, 37
Watt, Helen 55
weak sanctity of life view 8, 12–13
  on abortion 51, 60
  on euthanasia 79
weapons of mass destruction 133
welfare utilitarians
  on abortion 58
  on euthanasia 76
  on nuclear deterrence 166
  on pacifism 139
  on quality of life argument 15
  on suicide 33
When the State Kills 97
Whether Soldiers, Too, Can be Saved 122
Wilcockson, Michael 59, 74
Williams, Bernard 15, 16, 138
Williams, Shirley 131
Willis, Ellen 42
Wink, Michael 116
women's rights 41–45, 61
  to privacy 44–45
  vs. rights of the foetus 43–44, 49,
    51–52, 52